MARY MAGDALENE

Mary Magdalene is a key figure in the history of Christianity. After Mary, the mother of Jesus, she remains the most important female saint in her guise both as primary witness to the resurrection and as 'apostle of the apostles'. This volume, the first major work on the Magdalene in more than thirty years, focuses on her 'lives' as these have been imagined and reimagined within Christian tradition. Philip C. Almond expertly disentangles the numerous narratives that have shaped the story of Mary over the past two millennia. Exploring the 'idea' of the Magdalene – her cult, her relics, her legacy – the author deftly peels back complex layers of history and myth to reveal many different Marys, including penitent prostitute; demoniac; miracle worker; wife and lover of Jesus; symbol of the erotic; and New Age goddess. By challenging uniform or homogenized readings of the Magdalene, this absorbing new book brings fascinating insights to its subject.

PHILIP C. ALMOND is Professor Emeritus in the History of Religious Thought at the University of Queensland and a fellow of the Australian Academy of the Humanities. His recent books include *The Antichrist: A New Biography* (Cambridge University Press, 2020), *God: A New Biography* (Bloomsbury Publishing, 2018), and *Afterlife: A History of Life after Death* (Cornell University Press, 2016).

'If, as the author notes, there is a Magdalene for all seasons, this just might be the Magdalene for ours.'

'Timely, engaging and full of fascinating detail on the history of the Mary Magdalene cult.'

MARY MAGDALENE

A CULTURAL HISTORY

PHILIP C. ALMOND
The University of Queensland

CAMBRIDGE
UNIVERSITY PRESS

CAMBRIDGE
UNIVERSITY PRESS

Shaftesbury Road, Cambridge CB2 8EA, United Kingdom

One Liberty Plaza, 20th Floor, New York, NY 10006, USA

477 Williamstown Road, Port Melbourne, VIC 3207, Australia

314–321, 3rd Floor, Plot 3, Splendor Forum, Jasola District Centre,
New Delhi – 110025, India

103 Penang Road, #05–06/07, Visioncrest Commercial, Singapore 238467

Cambridge University Press is part of Cambridge University Press & Assessment,
a department of the University of Cambridge.

We share the University's mission to contribute to society through the pursuit of
education, learning and research at the highest international levels of excellence.

www.cambridge.org
Information on this title: www.cambridge.org/9781009221696

DOI: 10.1017/9781009221702

First published 2023

Printed in the United Kingdom by TJ Books Limited, Padstow Cornwall

A catalogue record for this publication is available from the British Library.

ISBN 978-1-009-22169-6 Hardback

Cambridge University Press & Assessment has no responsibility for the persistence
or accuracy of URLs for external or third-party internet websites referred to in this
publication and does not guarantee that any content on such websites is, or will
remain, accurate or appropriate.

For George Clayton Agostini

CONTENTS

vii

Contents

The colour plate section can be found between xvi and 1.

PLATES

ACKNOWLEDGEMENTS

This book was written in the Institute for Advanced Studies in the Humanities at the University of Queensland in Australia. For the past fifteen years, this institute and its predecessor, the Centre for the History of European Discourses, have provided a congenial, stimulating, and, more often than one can hope to expect, exciting context in which to work. For me, this has been and remains the collegium of scholars at its best. I am indebted in particular to my friends and colleagues, Professor Peter Harrison, the director of the Institute, Associate Professor Anna Johnston, Emeritus Professor Peter Cryle, and Emeritus Professor Ian Hunter. They have all have given of their time to talk with me on various occasions. I am especially grateful to Emeritus Professor Fred D'Agostino. He has read this work section by section as it progressed and provided many valuable comments. I am grateful also to the many postdoctoral fellows and other research fellows of the Institute, all whose dedication to their work has provided so much encouragement to my own.

A wide-ranging book such as this is inevitably indebted to those scholars who have previously done the hard yards in this intellectual domain. As a result, this is a genuinely collegiate and collaborative work. Without their often groundbreaking research, this book would not have been possible. There are too many to mention here, although

I have expressed my debt to many of them in the course of this study.

I am, however, especially indebted to Susan Haskins and her seminal book *Mary Magdalen*. I need also to mention the invaluable studies of the medieval Magdalene, *The Making of the Magdalen* by Katherine Ludwig Jansen, and the early modern Magdalene, *The Magdalene in the Reformation* by Margaret Arnold. Various essays in Edmondo F. Lupieri's edited collection *Mary Magdalene from the New Testament to the New Age and Beyond* have been enormously helpful.

I am indebted also to Ariel Sabar for several helpful communications. Finally, I want especially to thank David Foley for his masterly translations, particularly of the first biography of Mary Magdalene by pseudo-Odo. I have far more confidence in his translations than in any of my own.

I take the opportunity once again to thank Alex Wright and Beatrice Rehl, my editors at Cambridge University Press, for their support and encouragement of this work, their task undoubtedly made more difficult by our very own 'years of the plague'. I am grateful to my partner, Patricia Lee. She has listened yet again day by day to this text as it progressed and has offered much helpful advice. This book is dedicated to my first grandson, George Clayton Agostini.

Plate 1 Mary Magdalene at the Crucifixion of Jesus.

Plate 2 Mary Magdalene, the first witness of the resurrection of Jesus.

Plate 3 Mary of Egypt covering her nakedness.

Plate 4 Mary kissing the feet of Jesus.

Plate 5 Christ in Bethany at the house of Mary and her sister Martha.

Plate 6 Martha driving the dragon out of the wilderness of Tarascon.

Plate 7 The marriage feast at Cana in Galilee.

Plate 8 Mary anointing the feet of Jesus.

Plate 9 The resurrection of Lazarus from the dead.

Plate 10 Mary boarding a ship for France.

Plate 11 Mary listening to the sermon of Christ.

Plate 12 Mary raises the wife of the governor of Marseilles.

Plate 13 Mary carried aloft by angels.

Plate 14 The seven sleepers of Ephesus sealed in a cave.

Plate 15 Mary's nakedness covered by her long hair.

Plate 16 Titians's penitent Mary of the Italian Renaissance.

Plate 17 An eroticized Mary.

Plate 18 Mary, the penitent coquette.

Plate 19 The noble and courtly Mary.

Plate 20 Mary with the alabaster jar in a northern landscape.

Plate 21 The erotic and ascetic Mary in a wilderness setting.

Plate 22 Mary redeemed through her self-sacrificing love.

Plate 23 The pre-Raphaelite Mary at the door of Simon the Pharisee.

Plate 24 Mary, more *femme fatale* than fallen woman.

Plate 25 An eroticised Mary reading.

Plate 26 The actress Sarah Bernhardt as Mary Magdalene.

Plate 27 Mary, erotic and ascetic, in her cave.

Plate 28 Leonardo Da Vinci's 'The Last Supper'.

Plate 29 The fragment of 'The Gospel of Jesus's Wife'.

PROLOGUE

∼

She came to the sepulchre, laden with perfumes and aromatic herbs to
embalm a dead man; but, finding him alive, she received a very
different office from that which she had thought to discharge –
messenger of the living Saviour, sent to bear the true balm of life
to the apostles.

Pseudo-Rabanus, *The Life of Saint Mary Magdalene*

Within Eastern and Western Christianity, Mary
Magdalene is one of the most important saints. After
Mary, the mother of Jesus, she is by far the most important female saint. This was because she was the archetype
of the penitent sinner. It was she who most demonstrated
to everyone that no one was beyond redemption.

This book tells the story of Mary Magdalene from its
beginnings in the New Testament up to the present time.
It focuses on the history of the 'lives' of Mary Magdalene
as they were imagined within the Christian tradition and
within the modern secular West. It aims to undermine the
simple reading of Mary Magdalene in popular literature,
both theological and secular, by demonstrating the complexity of her history. But it also hopes to bring greater
clarity to the very complicated mix of traditions that have
made up the history of Mary Magdalene over the past two
millennia. Thus, this book is a history of the 'idea' of
Mary Magdalene. It is a history of how and why
Christianity, with the minimal historical data at its dis-
posal, created its ideal Christian saint. It reveals how she
represented the sinner we should aspire not to be and the
saint we should desire to become.

At the centre of the story of Mary Magdalene there lies a paradox. We know virtually nothing of her. The Gospels in the New Testament tell us little. According to them, she had once been possessed by demons, but they had gone from her. She may have come from Magdala. She was probably a wealthy woman who provided for Jesus and his disciples. She was present at the crucifixion and, we are told, she was the first witness to the resurrection. It was she, we read, who informed the disciples of Jesus that he had risen from the dead.

Yet, this very paucity of information made possible and necessary the construction within Christianity of an array of 'lives' of Mary Magdalene over the next 2,000 years. She would become a woman for all seasons – available for all times, adaptable to all occasions, and accessible to all people, both men and women. This was because, as we will see, there were many different Mary Magdalenes. She was the penitent prostitute and the woman possessed by seven demons. She was the first witness to the resurrection and the first to inform the disciples of it. She was the wife and lover of Jesus and the bride at the wedding at Cana in Galilee. She was the model for the contemplative monastic life and the solitary desert dweller whose nakedness was covered by her hair. She was a symbol of the ascetic and the erotic. She was the female leader of the early church, the wealthy heiress, and the party girl from Magdala. Symbolically, she was the second Eve and the 'bride' of Christ.

That there are many different Mary Magdalenes was also the result of her being identified with other female characters within the New Testament. Within the Eastern Church, she remained the single Mary whose appearances in the New Testament we outlined above. But within the Western Church, from the beginning of the seventh century, she became a composite figure. For it was in the year 591 that Pope Gregory the Great identified her with two other women within the New Testament. On the one hand, she was identified as Mary of Bethany, the sister of Martha and Lazarus. As Mary of Bethany, she had anointed Jesus's feet with a costly perfume of pure nard and wiped them with her hair in the Gospel of John. On the other hand, Mary Magdalene was also identified as the sinful woman of the gospel of Luke. She too had anointed Jesus's feet with ointment from an alabaster jar, had bathed them with her tears, and dried them with her hair. This book adopts the interplay, often tension and sometimes conflict, between the 'idea' of the simple and the composite Mary as the key to untangling her history.

The 'idea' of Mary Magdalene over the past two millennia has been a fluid and unstable one, not least because of her many 'personae' and her dual identity. However, we can identify six key moments in her history that are elaborated on and illuminated in the chapters that follow. First, there was the creation of the composite Mary Magdalene by Gregory the Great at the end of the sixth century. Gregory's construction brought to a conclusion some five and a half centuries of discussion and debate about the identity, role, and significance of Mary Magdalene.

Second, this enabled the composition of the first coherent life of Mary Magdalene. Entitled 'A Sermon in Veneration of Saint Mary Magdalene', it was attributed traditionally to Odo, the Benedictine Abbot of Cluny

(879–942). This sermon provided the template for all subsequent accounts of the life of Mary Magdalene up to the time of Christ's ascension. In the early ninth century, we find the development of the earliest life of Mary Magdalene – the *vita eremitica*. In the eleventh century, a more extensive account of her life after Christ's ascension developed. The *vita apostolica* included her exile from Palestine, her arrival in France, and her role in the conversion of the French. Then, in the late twelfth century, a detailed account of Mary's pre-ascension life along with all the features of the post-ascension *vita apostolica* emerged. Finally, there was the *vita apostolica-eremitica* that combined the apostolic and the eremitic lives, exemplified in *The Golden Legend* of the Dominican Jacobus de Voragine (c. 1230–c. 1298).

Third, from the tenth to the end of the fifteenth centuries, the cult of Mary Magdalene developed around her earthly remains. There was an intricate weaving of her lives with the 'afterlives' of her remains within the broader development of the Christian tradition of relics and the cult of the saints. Five narrative traditions grew up around her remains – the Palestine, the Ephesus, the Constantinople, the Vézelay, and the Saint-Maximin traditions.

Fourth, at the beginning of the sixteenth century, the debate about the single versus the composite Mary broke out in earnest between Renaissance Humanists, Catholic theologians, and eventually Protestant Reformers and Protestant radicals. This was a debate that threatened the viability of the cult of Mary Magdalene and the veracity of her relics. From this time on, the separation of the penitent prostitute from Mary Magdalene undermined the central narrative within the West of Mary Magdalene as the repentant sinner.

Fifth, the rise of the Protestant traditions aligned with an incipient Western secularization generated a new proliferation of Marys. Now viewed as either the single or the composite Mary, her identity became yet more malleable and indeterminate. Separated from harlotry, she became a model of sanctity. Separated from sanctity, she became profane, sensual, and erotic.

Sixth, and finally, she emerged as the most important modern saint of the last seventy years within the secular West. She became Jesus's wife and lover within a new array of contemporary lives of Mary that began with Nikos Kazantzakis's book entitled *The Last Temptation of Christ* and ended with the apparent discovery of an ancient papyrus in which Jesus called Mary, 'My wife'.

The imaginings of Mary Magdalene detailed in this book have played a decisive role in the shaping of Western and Eastern religious belief and piety. Her history is a history of how her devotees perceived the relationship between the sacred and the profane, how they negotiated the connection between the spiritual and the material realms, how they experienced the transcendent in the everyday, how they thought about the natures of men and women, and how they were inspired by her life to fashion themselves in her image.

Thus, the importance of Mary Magdalene ultimately lies in what she tells us about the religious life of humankind over the past two millennia. Her lives mattered because they were believed by her devotees to capture the truth of the person depicted. And the 'true' events in the life of Mary Magdalene were endowed with transcendental meaning. Thereby, they created deep meaning in the lives of those living religiously through them. The lives of Mary Magdalene manifested truth. Through her lives, as Paul Ricoeur would put it, 'new possibilities of being-in-the-world are opened up within everyday reality ... . And in this way everyday reality is metamorphosed by means of what we would call the imaginative variations that literature works on the real'.[1]

[1] Paul Ricoeur, *Figuring the Sacred: Religion, Narrative, and Imagination* (Minneapolis, MN: Fortress Press, 1995), p. 43.

I

Who Was Mary Magdalene?

≈

Now after he arose early on the first day of the week, he appeared first
to Mary Magdalene, from whom he had cast out seven demons.

Mark 16.9.

Three Marys in One Person

Rome, in the year 590, was beset by the plague.[1] On 25
April, Pope Gregory the Great (c. 540–604) called for a
procession to take place at dawn. The faithful gathered in
groups around the city, and, singing and praying, walked
through the streets towards the church of Santa Maria
Maggiore, one of the first churches built in Rome in
honour of the mother of Christ. Eighty people died from
the effects of the plague as they walked towards the
church. Pope Gregory met them upon their arrival, and
the procession continued on its way, preceded by a picture
of the mother of Christ said to have been painted by Saint
Luke. In the version of this legend in *The Golden Legend* of
Jacobus de Voragine, we are told that 'voices of angels
were heard around the picture, singing'.[2] The sacred
image cleansed the air of infection, 'as if the pestilence

---

[1] Unless otherwise indicated, all dates are in CE; that is, Common Era.
On occasion when necessary for clarity, the periods BCE and CE
are indicated.
[2] Granger Ryan and Helmut Ripperger (trans.), *The Golden Legend of
Jacobus de Voragine* (New York: Arno Press, 1969), p. 180.

could not withstand its presence'.[3] As the procession neared the fortress that was to become known afterwards as Castel Sant'Angelo, Saint Michael the archangel appeared sheathing his bloody sword. From this, Gregory understood 'that the plague was at an end, as indeed it was'.[4]

It was Gregory's conviction that prayer and repentance would bring an end to the plague. The procession was to be a witness to this, he declared in a sermon, 'so that when the strict Judge sees that we punish our faults ourselves, He may refrain from passing the sentence of condemnation, now ready to be passed upon us'.[5] In the following year, on 14 September 591, Gregory preached another sermon on repentance in the Basilica of San Clemente in which he took as his exemplar of repentance the sinful woman in the gospel of Luke (Luke 7.36–50).

According to the gospel of Luke, Jesus was invited by a Pharisee named Simon to eat at his house. An unexpected guest arrived. A woman in the city who was a sinner, having learned that Jesus was there, brought an alabaster jar of ointment to the house. Weeping, she began to bathe the feet of Jesus with her tears and to dry them with her hair. Then she continued to kiss his feet and anoint them with the ointment. The Pharisee said to himself, 'if this man were a prophet, he would have known who and what kind of woman this is who is touching him – that she is a sinner' (Luke 7.39).[6] Jesus, divining this, then told the

---

[3] *Ibid.*   [4] *Ibid.*

[5] Quoted by F. Homes Dudden, *Gregory the Great: His Place in History and Thought* (London: Longmans, Green, & Co., 1905), p. 218.

[6] Unless otherwise indicated, all biblical quotations are from the *New Revised Standard Version.*

Pharisee of a creditor to whom was owed 500 denarii by one man and 50 by another. When neither could pay, he cancelled their debts. In answer to Jesus's question, 'which of them will love him more?' (Luke 7.42), Simon suggested that it was the one with the greater debt. Jesus pointed out to Simon that, unlike the sinful woman, he had not given water for his feet, nor dried them with his hair; he had given Jesus no kiss, nor anointed his head with oil. Therefore, declared Jesus, 'her sins, which were many, have been forgiven; hence she has shown great love. But the one to whom little is forgiven, loves little' (Luke 7.47). Jesus then forgave her sins and said, 'Your faith has saved you; go in peace' (Luke 7.50); in short, honour for the sinful woman, shame for the haughty Pharisee.

There is no suggestion in Luke of the nature of the sins of this woman. But the probability is that she was known around town as a 'loose woman' or a prostitute. Moreover, as Kathleen E. Corley reminds us, given the setting, the description of the woman, and her anointing of his feet, 'the erotic overtones of the story are obvious. Only slaves or prostitutes would perform such a function in the context of a meal'.[7]

In the course of this sermon, Gregory the Great tells us who this woman is: 'She whom Luke calls the sinful woman, whom John calls Mary, we believe to be the Mary from whom seven devils were ejected according to

---

[7] Kathleen E. Corley, *Private Women, Public Meals: Social Conflict in the Synoptic Tradition* (Peabody, MA: Hendrickson Publishers, 1993), p. 125.

Mark.'[8] First, Gregory identified the sinful woman with Mary of Bethany, the sister of Martha and Lazarus whom Jesus raised from the dead. According to the Gospel of John (12.1–8), shortly before his arrest, Jesus had come to Bethany. There, Mary, Martha, and Lazarus gave a dinner for Jesus. Martha served and Lazarus sat at the table with Jesus. During the course of the meal, Mary took a pound of costly perfume made of pure nard or spikenard, anointed Jesus's feet, and wiped them with her hair. Judas Iscariot questioned the virtue of her act in anointing Jesus with perfume that could have been sold for 300 denarii and the money given to the poor. Jesus rebuked him: 'Leave her alone. She bought it so that she might keep it for the day of my burial. You always have the poor with you, but you do not always have me' (John 12.8).

Gregory also identified the sinful woman of Luke with her out of whom Jesus had driven seven devils. This woman was Mary Magdalene, one of the women who accompanied Jesus during the time of the ministry. 'The twelve were with him', reads the gospel of Luke, 'as well as some women who had been cured of evil spirits and infirmities: Mary, called Magdalene, from whom seven demons had gone out, and Joanna, the wife of Herod's steward Chuza, and Suzanna and many others' (Luke 8.1–3).

---

[8] Quoted by Susan Haskins, *Mary Magdalen: Myth and Metaphor* (London: Harper Collins, 1994), p. 96. This remains the seminal work on Mary Magdalene. I am indebted to it. For the Latin original of this passage, see H. Hurter S. J., *Sanctorum Patrum Opuscula Selecta* (Oeniponte: Libraria Academica Wagneriana, 1892), pp. 6, 264–265.

Gregory identified the seven devils that had been driven out of Mary Magdalene with all the vices. For he had established the definitive list of the seven deadly or cardinal sins: pride, greed, lust, envy, gluttony, anger, and sloth. Thus,

[a]nd what did these seven devils signify, if not all the vices . . . It is clear, brothers, that the woman previously used the unguent to perfume her flesh in forbidden acts. What she therefore displayed more scandalously, she was now offering to God in a more praiseworthy manner. She had coveted with earthly eyes, but now through penitence these are consumed with tears. She displayed her hair to set off her face, but now her hair dries her tears. She had spoken proud things with her mouth, but in kissing the Lord's feet, she now planted her mouth on the Redeemer's feet. For every delight, therefore, she had in herself, she now immolated herself. She turned the mass of her crimes to virtues, in order to serve God entirely in penance, for as much as she had wrongly held God in contempt.[9]

On the face of it, Gregory was strongly suggesting that, on the matter of sins, the sinful woman was no stranger to all of them. Yet his listeners, and later his readers, would have detected that he believed her greatest sin to be lust and her profession that of a prostitute. She perfumed 'her flesh in forbidden acts', he declared. It was the overuse of perfume that was often described in ancient literature as the hallmark of the prostitute. She 'displayed her hair to set off her face', he preached, thus offending the Christian tradition that women's heads should be covered and their faces veiled. As the Latin theologian

---

[9] Haskins, *Mary Magdalene*, p. 96.

Tertullian (c. 155–240) put it, 'be you mother, or sister, or *virgin* daughter … veil your head: if a mother, for your sons' sakes; if a sister, for your brethren's sakes; if a daughter, for your fathers' sakes. All ages [of men] are periled in your person'.[10] As a result of his declaration of the sinful woman as a prostitute, she, along with Mary Magdalene and Mary of Bethany, became the penitent whore and the harlot saint. Gregory the Great had thereby created the composite Mary Magdalene.

Within the Eastern church, the single Mary Magdalene remained distinct from both the fallen woman of Luke and Mary of Bethany. But the identification of Mary Magdalene with both the fallen woman of the gospel of Luke and Mary of Bethany was at the heart of the biography of Mary Magdalene in the West from this time on. Gregory's composite Mary Magdalene remained the Mary Magdalene of the Western Church until the second half of the twentieth century. His construction of the composite Mary Magdalene brought to an end within the Western Church 500 years of uncertainty and confusion about who Mary Magdalene was and about her role within the life of Jesus.

A Follower of Jesus

From its beginnings, the religious movement inspired by Jesus included both men and women. The names of Jesus's male disciples in the gospels of Mark, Matthew, and Luke are well known. The lists of his twelve disciples always have Simon (whom Jesus called Peter) and Judas

---

[10] S. Thelwall (trans.), *On the Veiling of Virgins*, 16, in *ANF*, 4, 37.

Iscariot (who betrayed Jesus). All three lists include James and his brother John; the sons of Zebedee, Andrew, Philip, and Bartholomew; Matthew; Thomas; James, son of Alphaeus; and Judas Iscariot. Mark and Matthew include a Thaddaeus, while Luke replaces Thaddaeus with Judas, son of James. All the lists begin with Simon and end with Judas Iscariot (Mark 3.16–19, Matthew 10.2–4, Luke 6.14–16).

But Jesus also had many female disciples. Along with Mary Magdalene, the gospel of Mark speaks of Mary, the mother of James the younger, and of Joses, and of Salome (Mark 15.40). The gospel of Matthew does not mention Salome, but along with Mary Magdalene, it includes Mary the mother of James and (now) Joseph, and the mother of the sons of Zebedee (Matthew 27.56). In one list, the gospel of Luke has Mary Magdalene, Joanna, Mary the mother of James, and 'the other women with them' (Luke 24.10). In another, Luke names Mary 'called Magdalene' along with Joanna the wife of Herod's steward Chuza, Susanna, and 'many others' (Luke 8.2–3).

It is clear that Mary Magdalene was a key figure amongst those who surrounded Jesus. She appears in all the lists of Jesus's female followers and is always mentioned first.[11] As we will see, she was not only present during his ministry but was there at his crucifixion and at his tomb. She is clearly a more important figure during the ministry of Jesus than his mother. Outside the stories of the birth of Jesus in the gospels of Matthew and Luke that tell of Mary the mother of Jesus, Jesus's mother is

---

[11] John 19.25, where she follows several other Marys, is an exception (although this may not be a list of Jesus's followers).

mentioned by name only once in the gospels. When Jesus is teaching in a synagogue in Nazareth, some wondered where he had gotten all his wisdom. 'Is not this the carpenter, the son of Mary and brother of James and Joses and Judas and Simon, and are not his sisters here with us?' (Mark 6.3).

The mother of Jesus is mentioned, but not by name, at only three other places in the four gospels. While Jesus is teaching, Mark has his mother and brothers asking for him. But Jesus rebuffs them saying that his true family – 'brother and sister and mother' – are those who do the will of God (Mark 3.35).[12] John's gospel has her present at Jesus's first miracle of turning water into wine at the wedding at Cana. When the wine ran out, it was Jesus's mother that alerted him to this (John 2.3). John has her appear again at the crucifixion of Jesus, along with her sister, Mary of Clopas, and Mary Magdalene (John 19.25) (see Plate 1).

In contrast to the minor role of Mary the mother of Jesus during the ministry of Jesus, Mary Magdalene was a key player. She is mentioned thirteen times in the gospels. Luke has her with Jesus from early on in his ministry. She was one of the female followers of Jesus 'who had been cured of evil spirits and infirmities' (Luke 8.2). More specifically, she was identified by Luke as the

---

[12] I omit here the complicated scholarly discussion of whether the Mary described as the mother of James the younger and of Joses present at the crucifixion of Jesus, or the Mary described as the mother of James and Joses who went to the tomb of Jesus, was the mother of Jesus (Mark 15.40, 47; 16.1). The weight of scholarly opinion is against this identification. For a brief discussion, see Susan Miller, *Women in Mark's Gospel* (London: T & T Clark, 2004), pp. 154–157.

Mary 'called Magdalene, from whom seven demons had gone out' (Luke 8.2). Mary Magdalene is the only major character in the New Testament out of whom, it was said, demons had been exorcized. That said, this is the only mention of Mary Magdalene in the gospels prior to the crucifixion of Jesus. So, prior to that event, we hear no more of her. We do not know, for example, if, like some of the other disciples, she was called by Jesus to follow him. There is no teaching by Jesus during his ministry that involves or invokes her. All we can say is that she, along with other female followers of Jesus, provided for Jesus and the twelve disciples 'out of their resources' (Luke 8.23).

Three of the gospels – Mark, Matthew, and John – named her as present at the crucifixion. Mark named her as one of the 'women looking on from a distance' (Mark 15.40). Similarly, Matthew named her as one of the many women looking on from a distance who 'had followed Jesus from Galilee and had provided for him' (Matthew 27.56). John had Mary Magdalene 'standing near the foot of the cross' (John 19.25) with the (unnamed) mother of Jesus and the (unnamed) 'disciple whom Jesus loved' (John 19.26). Their proximity to the cross made it possible for Jesus to say to his mother, 'Woman, here is your son' and to the beloved disciple, 'Here is your mother' (John 19.26–27). The gospels of Mark and Matthew also mentioned her, along with Mary the mother of Joses, as being present at the burial of Jesus (Mark 15.47, Matthew 27.61).

The significance of Mary Magdalene within the history of Christianity lies in her role in the story of Jesus after his resurrection, for she was the key witness to it.

According to the gospel of Mark, after Jesus had died, Joseph of Arimathea laid his body in a tomb carved out of the rock and rolled a stone against its door. Mary Magdalene and Mary the mother of Joses, having seen where Jesus had been laid, returned on the third day after his death so that they might anoint his body. When they arrived, they saw that the stone had been rolled back. As they entered the tomb, a young man in a white robe told them that Jesus had been raised and that they should 'tell Peter and his disciples that he is going ahead of you to Galilee' where they would see him (Mark 16.7). Terrified, they fled from the tomb 'and said nothing to anyone' (Mark 16.8).

This failure of Mary to say anything despite the young angelic figure's direction was corrected within later manuscript traditions of the gospel of Mark. Two alternative endings were subsequently produced. In the shorter version, the two Marys do report that they told all that had been commanded to those around Peter. The longer version, probably added early in the second century, heightened the role of Mary Magdalene. For, in this version, the young man in the white robe is absent, and Jesus himself appeared to Mary Magdalene – 'from whom he had cast out seven demons' (Mark 16.9) – alone. Mary then went and told those who had been with him that she had seen Jesus, but 'when they heard that he was alive and had been seen by her, they would not believe it' (Mark 16.11).

The Gospel of Matthew, by contrast, offers an even more highly elaborated account of the encounter of two Marys with both the 'young man in a white robe' and the resurrected Jesus. According to this, Mary Magdalene and 'the other Mary' went to see the tomb. Suddenly, we read, there was a great earthquake, and an angel of the Lord, descending from Heaven, rolled back the stone and sat on it. His appearance was 'like lightning, and his clothing white as snow' (Matthew 28.3). The angel told the women not to be afraid and that Jesus had been raised from the dead. He told them to let the disciples know that he was going ahead to Galilee and that they would see him there. They left the tomb quickly and ran to tell his disciples. Matthew's Gospel was the first to say that Mary Magdalene saw the resurrected Christ. For suddenly, we are told, the two Marys encountered Jesus who greeted them. They went to him, took hold of his feet, and worshipped him. Jesus said to them, 'Do not be afraid; go and tell my brothers to go to Galilee; there they will see me' (Matthew 28.10).

A slightly different account again was given in the Gospel of Luke. According to this, it was Mary Magdalene, Joanna, Mary the mother of James, and a number of other women who went to the tomb, taking the spices they had prepared. They found the stone rolled back and the tomb empty. Suddenly, two men in dazzling clothes stood beside them. The women were terrified and bowed their faces to the ground. The two men told them that Jesus had risen from the dead as he had predicted he would. They were not commissioned to tell the disciples. But, returning from the tomb, they nevertheless told all this to his remaining eleven disciples who thought it an idle tale and refused to believe them.

Finally, in the Gospel of John, it was Mary Magdalene alone who was the first to the tomb and the first to encounter the risen Jesus. It was early on the first day of the week that Mary went to the tomb and saw that the stone had been removed. She ran and told Simon Peter and the rest of the disciples that Jesus had been taken from the tomb. When Peter arrived, he entered the tomb and saw that it was empty, although the linen in which Jesus had been wrapped was there, along with the cloth that had been on his head. Then another disciple who had arrived at the tomb before Peter also entered it. This mysterious disciple was noted in the Gospel of John as the first to believe. The disciples, not yet understanding the scriptures 'that he must rise from the dead' (John 20.9), returned to their homes.

After Mary Magdalene had reported to the disciples that the tomb was empty, she had returned to the tomb with them and stayed weeping outside the tomb. As she wept, she looked into the tomb and saw two angels in white, sitting where Jesus had been lying. They asked her why she was weeping. 'They have taken away my Lord,' she replied, 'and I do not know where they have laid him' (John 20.13). Then she turned around and Jesus was standing there, although she failed to recognize him. Jesus asked her why she was weeping and whom she was seeking. Mary, assuming that he was the gardener, asked him if he had carried the body of Jesus away and where he had laid him, so that she might take him away. Jesus said to her, 'Mary!' She turned and said to him, 'Rabbouni!' Jesus said to her, 'Touch me not ["Μή μου ἅπτου" in the Greek New Testament, "noli me tangere" in the Latin Vulgate]; for I am not yet ascended to my Father: but go to my brethren, and say unto them, I ascend unto my Father, and your Father; and to my God, and your God' (John 20.17 KJV) (see Plate 2). Mary went and told the disciples that she had seen the Lord and that he had said these things to her.

It is impossible to determine historically which of the various accounts of Mary Magdalene and her role in the story of Jesus after his death has the best claim to historical accuracy. The gospels were not eyewitness accounts. Rather they were written sometime between thirty-five years after the death of Jesus (in c. 33) in the case of Mark, sixty years in the case of Luke and Matthew, and some seventy years after his death in the case of John. Moreover, Mary Magdalene was never mentioned in any of the remaining books that make up the New Testament. Granting the centrality of Mary to the resurrection accounts in the Gospels, we might have expected her to be named as one of the witnesses to the resurrection who were listed by Paul in his first letter to the Corinthians (15.5–8) written around twenty years after the death of Jesus. There Paul named Cephas (Peter), the twelve, 500 brothers some of whom he said were still alive, James, all the apostles, and finally himself. Among these, no woman received a mention, much less Mary Magdalene.[13]

However, we can conclude from the gospel accounts that, among the female followers of Jesus, she was by far the most notable. Clearly, there was an early and widespread tradition that she was present at the crucifixion. More importantly, we can say there was an early and widespread tradition, incorporated into all of the Gospels, that she was among those who were the first to

[13] The new RSV has 'five hundred brothers and sisters'. The Greek text mentions only 'brothers' (ἀδελφοῖ).

see the risen Jesus and was among those who first announced his resurrection to his other followers.

On the evidence that we have available within the New Testament, Mary Magdalene became an increasingly important figure over the first century. She is absent in Paul. She is a 'failure' when she doesn't say anything to anyone about what was told her by the young man dressed in white at the tomb in the original version of Mark. But her role is increasingly significant in the three later Gospels. In the Gospel of Matthew, Mary Magdalene and 'the other Mary' encounter the risen Jesus and receive a commission from him to tell his disciples. In Luke, she along with a number of others reported to the disciples that Jesus had risen from the dead. In John, she alone is the first to speak with the risen Jesus and to act as the mediator between Jesus and his male disciples. She has become the first to announce to the apostles what they will announce to the world. As a result, she was to become commonly known in the twelfth century as 'apostolorum apostola' – 'the apostle of the apostles'.

The Magdalene

Within the New Testament, twenty-six women were mentioned by name. Of these, seven were called Mary. Of these seven, two appeared outside of the Gospels – Mary the mother of John Mark (Acts 12.12) and a Mary in Rome to whom Paul sent greetings (Romans 16.6). Of the eleven women named in the Gospels of Matthew, Mark, Luke, and John, five were called Mary. As we have seen, Mary Magdalene was one of these. Ambiguities within and discrepancies between the texts make identification of the remaining four difficult. But we are pretty secure in singling out, along with Mary Magdalene, Mary the mother of Jesus, Mary of Bethany the sister of Lazarus and Martha, Mary of Clopas, and Mary the mother of James the younger and Joses (Joseph). The identity of 'the other Mary' who accompanies Mary Magdalene to the tomb in the gospel of Matthew (27.61, 28.1–4) remains uncertain, but she was probably Mary the mother of James the younger and Joses whom the gospel of Mark tells us accompanied Mary Magdalene. That said, and as we will see in more detail later, in the history of interpreting the identity of these many Marys, there was a complete muddle.

The prevalence of the name Mary (Μαριαμ or Μαρια in Greek) in the New Testament is not all that surprising. Over the period from 330 BCE to 200, in Palestine, roughly a quarter of all women bore the name Mary in its Hebrew form (Mariam, מִרְיָם), while another quarter were called Salome. Thus, remarkably, half of all the women were called one of these two names.[14] Perhaps even more remarkably, five out of eleven or almost one in every two women in the gospels was called Mary. Thus, it was necessary, unlike in the cases of Anna, Elizabeth, Joanna, Salome, and Susanna (of whom there is only one woman of each name in the Gospels) to distinguish the Marys from each other. Our Mary (if we may call her that) was distinguished from the others, not by her relation to her children, nor by her husband,

---

[14] Tal Ilan, 'Notes on the Distribution of Jewish Women's Names in Palestine in the Second Temple and Mishnaic Periods,' *Journal of Jewish Studies* 40 (1989), pp. 186–200.

but by a title. She was 'Mary, the Magdalene (Μαρία ἡ Μαγδαληνὴ), or 'the Magdalene, Mary (ἡ Μαγδαληνὴ Μαρία), or 'Mary, called the Magdalene' (Μαρία ἡ καλουμένη Μαγδαληνή). Thus, she was defined as a woman independent of a man. But whether she was unmarried, divorced, or widowed, we cannot tell. Moreover, she along with other women provided for Jesus and his twelve disciples 'out of their resources' (Luke 8.3). So she was not only an independent Jewish woman, but one of independent means with control over her finances.

Traditionally, the name 'Magdalene' has been taken as referring to Mary's place of origin. She was Mary *Magdalene* because she came from somewhere called Magdala (although whether this was her home or her birthplace is unclear). For the better part of the last 1,500 years, this has been identified as a town on the shores of the Sea of Galilee about three miles north of Tiberias. It is now known as Migdal in Hebrew (*Magdal* in Aramaic and *al-Majdal* in Arabic). In the late twentieth century, it bore the signs of centuries of desolation and neglect.[15] In 1922, it had a population of fifty-one – forty-two Jews and nine Muslims. In 1876, Baedeker's guide to Palestine and Syria spoke of the 'miserable village of *Mejdal* situated here ... identical with *Magdala*, the birthplace of Mary Magdalene.'[16] A decade earlier, Mark Twain was less than impressed. It was not a beautiful

---

[15] See Jane Schaberg, *The Resurrection of Mary Magdalene: Legends, Apocrypha, and the Christian Testament* (New York: Continuum, 2002), pp. 47–64.

[16] K. Baedeker (ed.), *Palestine and Syria: Handbook for Travellers* (Leipsic: Karl Baedeker, 1876), p. 371.

place, he wrote, 'thoroughly ugly, and cramped, squalid, uncomfortable and filthy.'[17] Twain and his companions rode through the town until they 'came to a bramble-infested inclosure and a Roman looking dwelling of St. Mary Magdalen, the friend and follower of Jesus. The guide believed it and so did I'.[18]

Theodosius in his *The Topography of the Holy Land* was the first to identify Magdala as the place of origin of Mary Magdalene in the early sixth-century. It was two miles from Tiberias to Magdala, he wrote, 'where my Lady Mary was born'.[19] The mid-late eighth century guidebook by the monk Epiphanius wrote of 'a church containing the house of the Magdalene at the place called Magdala'. It was there, he went on to say, that 'the Lord healed her'.[20] That Migdal was the site of Mary's origins was reinforced by the belief that the church at the site had been built, along with many others in the Holy Land, by Helena (c. 250–330), the mother of the Emperor Constantine, who had visited the Holy Land in 326–328. Thus, in an anonymous *Life of Constantine* (c. 715–1009), we read that, after leaving Tiberias, she 'went on her way in gladness and joy for a further two miles, where she found the *House of Mary Magdalene*, and there she too erected a church'.[21] By the turn of the first

[17] Mark Twain, *The Innocents Abroad or, The New Pilgrims' Progress* (Leipzig: Bernard Tauchnitz, 1879), p. 178.
[18] *Ibid.*, p. 179.
[19] John Wilkinson, *Jerusalem Pilgrims before the Crusades* (Warminster: Aris & Phillips, 1977), p. 63.
[20] *Ibid.*, p. 120. [21] Wilkinson, *Jerusalem Pilgrims*, p. 203.

millennium, as the town of Mary Magdalene, Magdala had become a standard part of the pilgrims' itinerary.[22]

Unfortunately for this identification, in the writings of the first to the fourth centuries, a town or city called 'Magdala' was never mentioned. Moreover, the name 'Magdala' would not have clearly identified any particular town since *'Magdal'* in Aramaic or *'Migdal'* in Hebrew simply meant 'tower'. When it appeared in place names, it did so as part of the name of a specific place – Migdal Nuniya, Migdal Senna, Migdal Eder – the Tower of Nuniya, Senna, Eder, and so on. Of these various sites, the most likely candidate for Mary's place of origin is Migdal Nuniya (Tower of Fish) on the Sea of Galilee. Mary was, after all, one of those women who provided for Jesus 'when he was in Galilee' (Mark 15.41). It was a mile or so north of Tiberias and several miles south of the traditional site of Magdala.

How then did a town several miles to the north of Migdal Nuniya (Tower of Fish) become identified as Magdala?[23] To answer that, we need to turn to the Gospel of Matthew 15.39. In the oldest manuscripts of the gospel, we read that, after the feeding of 4,000 men with seven loaves of bread and a few fish, Jesus got into a boat and went 'to the region of Magadan' (εἰς τὰ ὅρια Μαγαδάν).[24] Later, fifth-sixth century manuscripts altered

---

[22] See Denys Pringle, *Pilgrimage to Jerusalem and the Holy Land, 1187–1291* (London: Routledge, 2012).

[23] The town of Migdal Nuniya was probably named after a lookout tower for shoals of fish in the Sea of Galilee.

[24] 'Magadan' is found in codex Sinaiticus (fourth century), codex Vaticanus (fourth century), and codex Bezae (fifth century), and in Jerome's Latin version of the Bible, the Vulgate (late fourth century).

'Magadan' to 'Magdalan', an alteration that would become standard for later manuscripts.[25] All this suggests that, as pilgrims reached Magadan in the fifth to sixth centuries, they believed they had reached Magdala, the home of Mary Magdalene. Mary Magdalene has now become Mary from Magdala (Magadan).[26]

All that said, however, even as an identifier of her place of origin, it was anything but specific. As we noted above, it could refer to any number of places where a tower was the distinguishing feature. Thus, it is likely that the term 'Magdalene' is doing more work than merely specifying a place of origin. There is a hint in this direction in the Gospel of Luke (8.2). Here, she is designated 'Mary, called the Magdalene' (Μαρία ἡ καλουμένη Μαγδαληνή). This looks like a title or a nickname, perhaps one given to her by Jesus. Other disciples of Jesus had similar nicknames bestowed upon them. Simon was called 'Kepha' meaning 'rock' (Πέτρος – Petros, hence Peter) to distinguish him from another Simon nicknamed 'Zelotes' – 'the zealous one' (Ζηλωτὴς). John and James were called 'Boanerges' – 'noisy ones' (Βοανηργές). Judas who would betray Jesus was named 'the Iscariot' – 'the choked up one' (ὁ Ἰσκαριώτης). On this reading, 'the Magdalene' simply meant 'the Tower-woman'. This was a metaphor

---

[25] 'Magdalan' is found is found in codex Ephraemi (fifth century), Purpureus Petropolitanus (sixth century), and codex Washingtonensis (late fourth-fifth century). The King James version reads 'Magdala'.

[26] The issue of the place of origin of Mary Magdalene is immensely complicated and much contested. In the above, I have attempted to simplify the most recent, complex, and erudite discussion of the issue. See Joan E. Taylor, 'Missing Magdala and the Name of Mary "Magdalene",' *Palestine Exploration Quarterly* 146 (2014), pp. 205–233. I am indebted to Taylor for this discussion of 'the Magdalene'.

suggestive of care, oversight, and protection. Her nickname reflected her key role among Jesus's disciples. She was, as the book of Micah put it, 'the tower of the flock' (Micah 4.8); in the words of the Psalms, 'you are my refuge, a strong tower against the enemy' (Psalm 61.3).

We noted earlier that, prior to the crucifixion, there was only one mention of Mary Magdalene in the Gospels. The Gospel of Luke tells us that she was one of the female followers of Jesus 'who had been cured of evil spirits and infirmities' (Luke 8.2). More specifically, she was the Mary 'called Magdalene, from whom seven demons (δαιμόνια ἑπτὰ) had gone out' (Luke 8.2). The text suggests that Mary and others among the women had been possessed by and cured of evil spirits before they began to follow Jesus. But Mary's case might have been particularly severe for, we are told, seven demons had gone out of her. It is possible that, as a demoniac, Mary was alienated from her family and marginalized within society more generally. Perhaps, it was this alienation from family and society that gave her the freedom to join a new family – the new community around Jesus.

Although we can read it as implied, there is no suggestion in the text from Luke that it was actually Jesus who cured Mary and the other women from their evil spirits and illnesses. This was clarified in the only other reference to Mary's demonic possession. This occurs in the longer ending of the Gospel of Mark. There we read that Jesus had appeared first to Mary Magdalene 'from whom *he had cast out* seven demons (ἑπτὰ δαιμόνια)' (Mark 16.9).

Actually, this later Markan version better fits the overall profile of Jesus. His ability to cast out demons, along with his capacity as a healer, was at the core of his ministry. For him, it was by the spirit of God that he did so and it was a sign that the Kingdom of God was at hand. When people murmured that it was by Beelzebul, 'the ruler of the demons', that Jesus was casting out evil spirits, he responded 'Now if I cast out the demons by Beelzebul, by whom do your exorcists casts them out? . . . But if it is by the finger of God that I cast out the demons, then the Kingdom of God has come to you' (Luke 11.19–20).

Within the gospels, we find four accounts of Jesus's activity as an exorcist.[27] In the first of these, Jesus encountered a man with an unclean spirit whom Jesus ordered to come out of the man (Mark 1.21–28). In the second, Jesus exorcized the so-called Gerasene demoniac from the 'legion' of unclean spirits within him and sent them into a herd of swine (Mark 5.1–20). In the third, Jesus exorcized a mute and deaf boy from the spirit that was keeping him from speaking and hearing, while in the fourth, he exorcized a demon at a distance from the daughter of a Syro-Phoenician woman.[28] Thus, it is more than likely that it was Jesus who cast out the seven demons within Mary Magdalene. That he had done so would explain her apparent devotion to him and perhaps that of the other women whose demons he had expelled or whose illnesses he had cured.

---

[27] All four are in Mark, but only three in Matthew and Luke. Matthew omits the exorcism in the synagogue and Luke that of the daughter of the Syro-Phoenician woman. There are no exorcisms in the Gospel of John.

[28] 'Unclean spirit', 'demon', 'evil demon', 'evil spirit', and 'unclean demon' are variously used within the Gospels to describe the spirits exorcized by Jesus. On Jesus and exorcism, see Amanda Witmer, *Jesus the Galilean Exorcist: His Exorcisms in Social and Political Context* (London: T & T Clark International, 2012).

A Mingling of Marys

Within the early church, from the second century onwards, the centrality of the figure of Mary Magdalene in the crucifixion and resurrection narratives, the paucity of information about her earlier life, and the multitude of Marys within the gospel accounts had a number of effects. On the one hand, it led to a mingling of Marys and the emphasis upon one to the detriment of the others. On the other hand, it led to an embellishment and an elaboration of her life, both prior to and after the crucifixion and resurrection of Jesus, particularly in that group of texts now known as the New Testament Apocrypha. These are early Christian texts outside of the New Testament that might give us new information, both about the early church and about the lives of Jesus, his family, and his followers. They were texts considered within the early church as informative if not divinely inspired.

The *Twentieth Discourse of Cyril of Jerusalem*, for example, was a Coptic text perhaps written around the early fifth century and traditionally attributed to Cyril of Jerusalem (c. 315–86). Its overall purpose was to extol Mary, the mother of Jesus, as a fully human being who was also the God-bearer (*Theotokos*). It undoubtedly reflects a time when the importance of Mary is surging within the community from which the text came. During the course of the discourse, Mary tells Cyril her family lineage:

My parents who produced me were of the tribe of Judah and of the House of David. My father was Joakim, which is, being interpreted, 'Kleopa'. My mother was Anna, who brought me forth, and who was usually called 'Mariham'. I am Mary

Magdalene, because the name of the village wherein I was born was 'Magdalia'. My name is 'Mary who belongeth to Iakkobos [James], the son of Joseph the carpenter, into whose charge they committed me'.[29]

In this text, Mary, the mother of Jesus, has identified herself, not only with Mary Magdalene, but also with Mary of Clopas, and Mary of James. It would seem that the author is identifying as one person the three women present at the crucifixion in the Gospel of John (19.25), namely, Mary the mother of Jesus, Mary of Clopas, and Mary Magdalene. But he is also identifying Mary the mother of Jesus with the 'Mary of James' (Μαρία ἡ Ἰακώβου) who was with Mary Magdalene when the 'two men in dazzling clothes' told the women of the risen Jesus in the Gospel of Luke (24.10). Messily, Mary the mother of Jesus seems both to be with and to replace Mary Magdalene. But in either case, the author intends to place Mary the mother of Jesus (whether as Mary Magdalene or Mary of James or both) as one of the witnesses (or the key witness) to the resurrection, thus exalting her status. Mary Magdalene is here being absorbed into the mother of Jesus.

The matter was, however, further confused later in the text when Mary the mother of Jesus and Mary Magdalene were clearly distinguished. After the resurrection of Jesus, Mary the mother of Jesus lived with 'the beloved disciple' (John). She gathered about her a large number of virgins to show them by her example the blessings of a life

---

[29] E. A. Wallis Budge, *Miscellaneous Coptic Texts in the Dialect of Upper Egypt* (London: Longmans & Co., et alia, 1915), pp. 629–630.

dedicated to God. Ten years later, having been told by her son in a vision that she had only three days to live, Mary had the apostles summon the virgins to her. When they came, we read, she took the hand of one of them, now exceedingly old – 'Mary Magdalene, out of whom the Christ had cast seven devils', and she told the virgins 'Behold your mother from this time forward'.[30] Female monasticism was being established around the time this text was written. The commissioning of Mary Magdalene as a female leader over a community of virgins by the mother of Jesus in this text was probably endorsing leadership of women *by women* in the developing tradition of female monasticism in Coptic Egypt.

Mary Magdalene also appeared with Mary the mother of Jesus in other narratives of the death of the latter that reflect her increasing importance. In a later Coptic fragment (fourth-sixth century), when the disciples were gathered around the tomb of Mary the mother of Jesus after her death, Jesus appeared in a chariot of fire. He called into the tomb, 'Mary, my mother, arise!' Jesus took her into the chariot and they ascended together into heaven. It was a miracle, the narrator declared, 'even greater than that of the resurrection of Jesus, which no one saw except Mary and Mary Magdalene'.[31]

If Mary the mother of Jesus was here appearing alongside Mary Magdalene, elsewhere she appears to have taken her name and assumed her role. Thus, for example, in the Coptic *The Book of the Resurrection of Christ by*

---

[30] *Ibid.*, p. 646.
[31] J. K. Elliott, *The Apocryphal New Testament* (Oxford: Clarendon, 1993), p. 700. This text is known as *Sahidic Fragment* (Revillout no. 16).

Bartholomew the Apostle, there was a much increased number of women at the tomb of Jesus on the third day. Mary Magdalene headed the list, followed by Mary the mother of James. There then followed a number of women: Salome, Mary of Bethany and her sister Martha, Joanna, Bernice, Leah the widow, and 'the sinful woman'.[32] It is reasonably clear that, by the name 'Mary Magdalene' at the top of this list of women at the tomb, Mary the mother of Jesus was intended. For the Mary Magdalene with whom Jesus spoke in the Gospel of John was now called in this text, 'thou holy Virgin, the mother of the Christ'. The risen Jesus hailed 'My mother, My house, My place of abode. Hail, My mother, My city, My place of refuge'.[33] At the conclusion of the dialogue between Jesus and Mary, the narrator declared, 'These were the things which the Saviour spake unto Mary His mother'.[34]

Again, in the Greek *Acts of the Holy Apostle Thaddeus* (seventh century at the earliest), Mary Magdalene has disappeared altogether from the narrative and has been replaced by Mary the mother of Jesus. 'And on the third day before dawn', we read, 'He rose leaving His burial-clothes in the tomb. And He was seen first by His mother and other women, and by Peter and John first of my fellow

---

[32] E. A. Wallis Budge, *Coptic Apocrypha in the Dialect of Upper Egypt* (London: Longmans & Co. et alia, 1913), p. 219. Salome is described as 'the one who had tempted him'. Salome appears at the crucifixion in Mark but the meaning of her as a temptress is unclear. Bernice is described as the woman 'whom he had healed of a flow of blood in Capernaum' (Mark 5.25–34). Leah is the widow of Nain 'whose son the Saviour raised from the dead' (Luke 7.11–17). The names Bernice and Leah do not appear in the gospels.

[33] *Ibid.*, p. 190.   [34] *Ibid.*, p. 192.

31

disciples, and thereafter to us the twelve, who ate and drank with Him after His resurrection for many days'.[35]

In the New Testament narratives of the resurrection, Jesus's mother was absent. But within the New Testament Apocrypha, she came to occupy an increasingly important role – from being with Mary Magdalene at the tomb of Jesus, to taking her name and assuming her role, right through to replacing her altogether within the resurrection story. In short, there was a mingling of Marys that diminished Mary Magdalene in favour of the mother of Jesus.[36] This is probably the consequence of a developing cult of the mother of Jesus at the expense of Mary Magdalene.

By contrast, as a result of Mary Magdalene's central role in the resurrection narratives, there was an exaltation of her post-resurrection role within the Gnostic texts of the second-fourth centuries. These were discovered in 1945 near the Egyptian town of Nag Hammadi. Unlike the New Testament Apocrypha, these gnostic texts were not endorsed by the early church and were thought of as 'antilegomena' – texts whose authenticity or value was disputed. The Gnostic traditions within early Christianity from which these texts arose privileged knowledge (gnosis) rather than faith as the key to

---

[35] Alexander Walker (trans.), *Acts of the Holy Apostle Thaddaeus*, in *ANF* 8.559.

[36] On Mary Magdalene in the New Testament Apocrypha, see Trent A. Rogers, 'The Apocryphal Magdalene: Expanding and Limiting Her Importance,' in Edmondo F. Lupieri, *Mary Magdalene from the New Testament to the New Age and Beyond* (Leiden: Brill, 2020), pp. 26–49. This is a 'state of the art' collection of studies on the figure of Mary Magdalene. I am significantly indebted to it.

salvation. Rather than a saviour, Jesus was a teacher of this knowledge. His own liberation from the body symbolized the journey of each soul freed from its corporeal prison and returning to the heaven whence it originally came.[37]

The Gnostic Mary

In these Gnostic texts, Mary was variously a key partner in dialogue with Jesus, a recipient of revelation, a revealer herself, and Jesus's spiritual partner.[38] In the Coptic *Sophia of Jesus the Christ* (early second century), for example, Mary Magdalene was one of seven women (along with twelve men) who gathered together on a mountain in Galilee after the resurrection. They were said to be 'perplexed about the underlying reality of the universe and the plan, and the holy providence, and the power of the authorities, and about everything the Savior is doing with them in the secret of the holy plan'.[39] The Saviour then appeared to them, 'not in his previous form, but in the invisible spirit' resembling 'a great angel of

---

[37] See Elaine Pagels, *The Gnostic Gospels* (London: Phoenix, 2006).

[38] There is a large discussion on the meaning of 'Gnostic' within contemporary scholarship and, as a result, on the identification of Gnostic texts. In the discussion to follow, I examine a number of texts generally recognized as Gnostic in which Mary Magdalene plays a key role. I have followed Antti Marjanen, *The Woman Jesus Loved: Mary Magdalene in the Nag Hammadi Library and Related Documents* (Leiden: Brill, 1996) in his determining of the borders of 'Gnostic texts'. At times, within the Gnostic texts, there are difficulties in distinguishing the Marys. I have utilized passages in the following where it is clear that Mary Magdalene was intended.

[39] Douglas M. Parrott (trans.), *The Sophia of Jesus Christ*, in James M. Robinson (ed.), *The Nag Hammadi Library*, p. 138. Available at http://khazarzar.skeptik.net/books/nhl.pdf.

light', and a dialogue between Jesus and his followers began.[40] Mary Magdalene, along with Philip, Matthew, Thomas, and Bartholomew, are the only persons named to put questions to the Saviour, the answers to which were intended to demonstrate the truth of Gnostic Christianity. While Mary was the only one of the seven women to ask questions, hers have no more significance than any of the questions asked by others.

At best, while the text demonstrates the importance of Mary Magdalene within the Gnostic community out of which the text came, she has no *particular* significance. Indeed, although she is viewed positively, the text (like many Gnostic texts) generally has a negative view of women. The Gnostic community was referred to as the 'masculine multitude' and salvation was dependent on knowing 'the words of the masculine light'. Nevertheless, at the end of the text, all the disciples including the women, we can assume, accepted the new Gnostic version of Christianity delivered to them by Jesus, and began to 'preach the Gospel of God, the eternal, imperishable Spirit'.[41] At the least then, the inclusion of Mary, along with six other unnamed women, was intended to emphasize that Gnostic Christianity was also for them in spite of their gender.

In the Coptic *Pistis Sophia* in the third century, the role of Mary Magdalene was further magnified. She now featured as the chief interlocutor of Jesus along with a number of the apostles, Martha, Salome, and Mary the mother of Jesus. She was the most important of those who conversed with Jesus. 'Mariam, thou blessed one', Jesus

[40] *Ibid.*, p. 138.   [41] *Ibid.*, p. 142.

said, 'whom I will complete in all the mysteries of the height, speak openly, thou art she whose heart is more directed to the Kingdom of Heaven than all thy brothers'.[42] She it was who, Jesus added, would be 'the *pleroma* [*fullness*] of all *pleromas* and the completion of all completions'.[43] After a more than obscure discourse by Mary as to who would be first and who last in the Kingdom of the Light, the Saviour 'marvelled greatly at the *answers* to the words which she gave, because she had completely become *pure Spirit*. Jesus answered and said to her: "*Excellent*", thou *pure spiritual* one, Maria. This is the interpretation of the discourse'.[44] Elsewhere, Jesus spoke of all his disciples being Kings in his coming Kingdom. 'But Mary Magdalene and John the Virgin', he went on, 'will be superior to all my disciples'.[45]

However that may be, although Mary was from a quite early time extolled as the key interpreter of the words of the Saviour, she seems to have been allowed no role in teaching or ritual activities. In some texts at least, Mary seems to accept that it was her 'brothers' who would initiate others into the 'mysteries'.[46] In several places within *Pistis Sophia*, there was also the strong suggestion of a rivalry between Peter and Mary Magdalene that may well reflect tensions within or between Gnostic communities over the role of women. Thus, on one occasion, Peter complained to Jesus that Mary was hogging the interpretative limelight: 'My Lord, we are not able to suffer this woman who takes the opportunity to speak

---

[42] Carl Schmidt (ed.) and Violet MacDermot (trans.), *Pistis Sophia* (Leiden: Brill, 1978), 1.16, p. 26.

[43] *Ibid.* 1.19, p. 28.   [44] *Ibid.*, 2.88, p. 200.

[45] *Ibid.*, 2.96, p. 232–33.   [46] See *ibid.* 3.123, p. 311; 3.123, p. 312.

from us, and does not allow anyone of us to speak, but she speaks many times'.[47] Mary, for her part, saw Peter as a hostile enemy and a woman-hater: '*but* I am afraid of Peter, for he *threatens* me and he hates our *race* [sex]'.[48] For Jesus, and we can say, for the author of the text, gender was no barrier to spiritual understanding nor to true discipleship. Everyone who is 'filled with the *Spirit* of light [may] come forward to give the interpretation of those things which I say, him no one will be able to *prevent*'.[49]

There is no doubt that Mary Magdalene was an important figure within Gnostic circles, sufficiently so for a Gospel to be written in her name. In the Coptic *Gospel of Mary* (mid-second century), she became the revealer of previously unknown Gnostic truth told to her by the risen Lord. The Gospel of Mary consists of two discourses, one spoken by Jesus (most of which is missing) and another spoken by Mary (several pages of which are missing). At the end of the first discourse, Jesus commissioned the disciples to 'Go then and preach the gospel of the Kingdom'.[50] Jesus then departed, leaving the disciples in despair as to what to do. It was Mary who courageously stood up and encouraged them: 'Do not weep and do not grieve nor be irresolute, for His grace will be entirely with you and will protect you'.[51] At Mary's words, the disciples turned their hearts to the Gnosis and began to reflect on the words of Jesus in this discourse.

---

[47] *Ibid.*, 1.36, p. 58.   [48] *Ibid.*, 2.72, p. 162.   [49] *Ibid.*, 2.72, p. 162.
[50] Douglas M. Parrott (ed.), George W. MacRae and R. McL. Wilson (trans.), *The Gospel of Mary (BG 8502, 1)*, in James M. Robinson (ed.), *The Nag Hammadi Library in English* (Leiden: Brill, 1977), p. 472.
[51] *Ibid.*, p. 472.

It was clear to Peter that Jesus loved Mary more than all other women and thought her the bearer of secret knowledge. So he asked Mary to 'tell us the words of the Saviour which you remember which you know, but we do not, nor have we heard them'.[52] Mary then told the disciples the new knowledge that had been hidden from them but revealed to her that day in a vision by the Lord. She then told the disciples of the ascent of the soul and of its encounter with the seven powers of wrath (darkness, desire, ignorance, the excitement of death, the kingdom of the flesh, the foolish wisdom of flesh, and the wrathful wisdom) that attempted to stop the soul from its ascent. Mary then recited the phrases that enabled the soul to attain to its eternal rest: 'What binds me has been slain, and what turns me about has been overcome, and my desire has been ended, and ignorance has died'.[53] Mary then fell silent, 'since it was to this point that the Savior had spoken with her'.[54]

Andrew expressed his doubt that Jesus had said this 'for certainly these teachings are strange ideas'.[55] While Andrew disagreed with the content of Mary's vision, Peter questioned its mode of delivery: 'Did He really speak privately with a woman and not openly to us? ... Did He prefer her to us?'[56] For Peter, Mary was no longer merely Jesus's favourite woman, but now his favourite disciple. His initial encouragement of Mary had disappeared in resentment at Jesus having so privileged her. For her part, Mary was bewildered by the response of Peter. 'Do you think,' she asked him, 'that I have thought this up myself in my heart, or that I am lying about the Savior?'[57] Levi

---

[52] *Ibid.*, p. 472.   [53] *Ibid.*, p. 473.   [54] *Ibid.*   [55] *Ibid.*   [56] *Ibid.*
[57] *Ibid.*

(Matthew) sprang to her defence, accusing Peter of being hot tempered and of being in alliance with those powers of wrath that attempt to entrap the soul. For Levi, Mary *was chosen* to reveal truth because Jesus did love her more than them. Thus, in the *Gospel of Mary*, Mary Magdalene has become the mediator between the risen Jesus and his disciples of a new saving knowledge. It is hard to resist the feminist reading of the ending of this Gospel that the author's intention was to endorse the equal authority of women to men in matters spiritual in spite of the resistance of some powerful men.[58]

In the Coptic *The Gospel of Philip*, Mary's status was further increased – from the most favoured of the disciples to the 'companion' of Jesus.[59] Thus, we read, 'There were three who always walked with the Lord: Mary his mother, and her sister and Magdalene, the one who was called his companion. His sister and his mother and his companion were each a Mary'.[60] This was a text that recalls the three Marys present at the foot of the cross in the gospel of John (19.25). But the key to the relationship between Jesus and Mary Magdalene in *The Gospel of Philip* turns on the meaning of 'companion' (ⲕⲟⲓⲛⲱⲛⲟⲥ in Coptic, κοινωνός in Greek). On the one hand, it may mean that, in *The Gospel of Philip*, Mary Magdalene was

---

[58] See, for example, Karen L. King, 'The Gospel of Mary', in E. Schüssler Fiorenza, *Searching the Scriptures. Volume Two: A Feminist Commentary* (London: SCM Press, 1997), pp. 623–624.

[59] *The Gospel of Philip* was originally in Greek. The only extant copy is in Coptic.

[60] Wesley W. Isenberg, *The Gospel of Philip*, in Robinson (ed.), *The Nag Hammadi Library in English*, pp. 135–136. There is a slip in this text from 'her sister' to 'his sister'. It is probably the result of a scribal slip of the reed pen.

the marital partner of Jesus. If this were its intended meaning, this would be the earliest reference to the long tradition that viewed Mary as the wife of Jesus.[61] On the other hand, and far more likely, 'companion' may only be intended to denote the special *spiritual* relationship that Mary had with Jesus. In either case, we should ask whether her role as a companion involved a sexual dimension.

In part, this is a question, the answer to which goes to the role of sexuality within Gnosticism more generally. Did Gnostic Christians live together in sexual or non-sexual unions? The evidence cuts equally both ways. But that said, there is one text within the Gospel of Philip that is suggestive of, at the least, an eroticized relationship between Jesus and Mary Magdalene: 'As for the Wisdom who is called "the barren", she is the mother [of the] angels. And the companion of the [Savior is] Mary Magdalene. [But Christ loved her] more than [all] the disciples, [and used to] kiss her [often] on her [mouth]'.[62] The text being silent on this point, the word 'mouth' is here only assumed. Even so, it is unlikely that the kissing of Mary by Jesus is to be read sexually. Rather, the kiss symbolizes Mary's spiritual superiority over the rest of the disciples, albeit one that might imply a special relationship. When the disciples immediately went on to ask Jesus why he loved Mary more than them, he replied 'Why do I not love you like her? When a blind man and one who

---

[61] This was especially popularized in recent times by Dan Brown's *The Da Vinci Code*. See Chapter 6.

[62] Isenberg, *The Gospel of Philip*, in Robinson (ed.), *The Nag Hammadi Library in English*, p. 138.

sees are both together in darkness, they are no different from one another. When the light comes, then he who sees will see the light, and he who is blind will remain in darkness'.[63] In sum, in the *Gospel of Philip*, as the companion of Jesus, at the most, we might say that Mary Magdalene and Jesus were spiritual partners and Mary perhaps his spiritual spouse.

All that granted, the figure of Mary within the *Gospel of Philip* might have a yet deeper meaning. She is, in fact, a complex composite figure. The sentence that we noted above – 'His sister and his mother and his companion were each a Mary' – suggests that there were three Marys of which Mary Magdalene was one. But the passage can be alternatively translated as 'Mary is his sister (and she is) his mother, and (she is) his companion'.[64] This translation would suggest that there was one cosmic 'spiritual' Mary who has manifested herself in the three women accompanying Jesus – a *metaphysical* mingling of Marys, we might say. This transcendent Mary was the divine in feminine form, both Holy Spirit and divine Wisdom (Sophia), present in the life of Jesus as his mother, his sister, and his spiritual spouse. She is a kind of incarnate Trinity – one divine Mary in three human persons.

The relationship between Jesus and Mary Magdalene in *The Gospel of Philip* may then be one of participants in a spiritual but not a physical marriage. There is one Gnostic text, however, that unambiguously attributed sexual behaviour to Jesus, if not with Mary Magdalene. We should perhaps take this with a pinch of salt. For we know of this third century text – the *Great Questions of*

---

[63] *Ibid.*, p. 138.   [64] See Marjanen, *The Woman Jesus Loved*, pp. 160–62.

Mary – only from the writings of an opponent, Epiphanius of Salamis (c. 310/20–403) in his *Panarion*. Among the eighty heretical sects of which Epiphanius gave an account were the Gnostics or Borborites. In discussing the Gnostic *Great Questions of Mary*, Epiphanius tells us that Mary Magdalene was a witness to Jesus creating a new Eve from his side, having sex with her, and then eating his semen:

For in the so-called 'Greater Questions of Mary'– there are also 'Lesser' ones forged by them – they claim that he [Jesus Christ] reveals it to her [Mary Magdalene] after taking her aside on the mountain, praying, producing a woman [Eve] from his side, beginning to have sex with her, and then partaking of his emission, if you please, to show that 'Thus we must do, that we may live.' (3) And when Mary was alarmed and fell to the ground, he raised her up and said to her, 'O thou of little faith, wherefore didst thou doubt?'[65]

This story was intended to give a mythical justification for the Gnostic ritual of semen and menstrual blood consumption. Elsewhere in the *Panarion*, Epiphanius wrote of a ritual in which a husband told his wife to make love with a fellow Gnostic. The woman and the man receive the male emission in their own hands and offer it up to God with the words, 'We offer thee this gift, the body of Christ'.[66] Then they eat it saying, 'This is the body of Christ'.[67] Similarly, Epiphanius informs us, when the woman is menstruating, they eat the menstrual blood

---

[65] Frank Williams (trans.), *The Panarion of Epiphanius of Salamis*, 26.8,2–3 (Leiden: Brill, 2009), p. 96.
[66] *Ibid.*, 26.4,6, p. 94.   [67] *Ibid.*, 26.4,7.

saying, 'This … is the blood of Christ'.[68] Through such practices, the Gnostic man and woman were enabled through the power of semen and menses to be saved from the material world. 'The idea,' wrote Epiphanius, 'is that they [can] obtain freedom of access to God by a practice of this kind'.[69] Elsewhere, he remarked, 'the power in the menses and semen is soul, they say, "which we gather and eat. And whatever we eat – meat, vegetables, bread or anything else – we are doing creatures a favour by gathering the soul from them all and taking it to the heavens with us"'.[70]

In the book of Genesis, the Eve, the first woman, was created by God from a rib taken from Adam (Genesis 2.21–24). This act eventually brought the procreation of the human race in the material world and, after the Fall, subjection to death. In the *Great Questions of Mary*, this process was reversed. By the act of Jesus in eating seminal emissions, and the Gnostic ritual repetition of it, death was abolished and souls were liberated from their bodily prisons. In the story, and perhaps not surprisingly, Mary was alarmed and fell to the ground. Jesus criticized her for her lack of faith. That said, as the witness to this practice after the resurrection of Christ, we can assume that it was Mary whom Jesus was trusting to pass this revelation on to others. In sum, she was the key authority for a Gnostic group seeking to liberate the soul from its material imprisonment by rescuing it through the ritual act of gathering and eating bodily emissions.

[68] *Ibid.*, 26.4,8, p. 94.   [69] *Ibid.*, 26.5,7.   [70] *Ibid.*, 29.9,4, p. 97.

A Catena of Confusions

Within the early 'orthodox' Church, Mary Magdalene was often viewed positively as the first witness of the resurrection. That said, it was a recognition that was often incidental to discussion of the nature of the resurrected Christ – that it was a bodily resurrection, that it demonstrated his divine status, that it showed that the Son of God was distinct from his heavenly Father, or that the redemption was not yet complete.

Even so, her status was often ambiguous. Ambrose of Milan (339–397), for example, saw Mary Magdalene as the new Eve. Yet, he also criticized her. Thus, he saw Jesus's refusal to allow Mary to touch him as a warning to others not to seek Jesus amongst earthly things. 'But if thou shouldst seek Him amongst earthly beings', declared Ambrose, 'even as Mary of Magdala sought Him, take heed lest He say to thee, as unto her: "Touch Me not, for I am not yet ascended unto My Father"'.[71]

Jerome (c. 342–420) was similarly ambiguous. His translation of the Bible into Latin would become the standard edition throughout the Middle Ages. He knew his Hebrew well and he recognized the meaning of the term 'Magdalene'. She was 'called the tower', he wrote in a letter to Principia, 'from the earnestness and glow of her faith'.[72] Yet, in a letter to Paula to console her for the death of her daughter, he chided her for behaving like Mary Magdalene:

---

[71] H. de Romestin (trans.), *St. Ambrose's Exposition of the Christian Faith*, 4.2.25, in *NPNF (Second Series)*, vol. 10, p. 265.

[72] W. H. Fremantle et al. (trans.), *Letter 127*, 5, in *NPNF (Second Series)*, vol. 6, p. 255.

If you prostrate yourself in grief at your daughter's tomb you too will hear the chiding of the angel, 'Why seek ye the living among the dead?' It was because Mary Magdalene had done just this that, when she recognized the Lord's voice calling her and fell at His feet, He said to her: 'Touch me not, for I am not yet ascended to my Father;' that is to say, you are not worthy to touch, as risen, one whom you suppose still in the tomb.[73]

Overall, confusions and complications dominated the early Church.[74] Thus, for example, the Archbishop of Ravenna, Peter Chrysologus (d. c. 450), appears to have taken a leaf out of the *Gospel of Philip* in a sermon on the resurrection account in the gospel of Matthew (28.1). Here, the two Marys – Mary Magdalene and 'the other Mary' – were the same, or perhaps better, the one who came to the tomb changed into the one who went back to tell the disciples of the risen Lord.

In the evening, which was dawning on the first day of the week, Mary Magdalene and the other Mary came (v.1). Mary: she came in name only one, she who the reading now says is 'the other', in terms of being a different person. *Mary and the other Mary came*, whereby both the unity of name would represent one in two, and the difference of persons would reveal that the woman had been changed. For *she came* [*venit*], not 'they came' ['venerunt']; and when it says *the other*, it designates with mystic

---

[73] W. H. Fremantle et al. (trans.), *Letter 39*, 6, in *NPNF (Second Series)*, vol. 6, p. 53.

[74] On Mary Magdalene and the early church, see Amanda Kunder, 'The Patristic Magdalene: Symbol for the Church and Witness to the Resurrection,' in Lupieri, *Mary Magdalene from the New Testament to the New Age and Beyond*, pp. 105–127.

language that the same person is in both, in order to show that one came before faith and another would return after faith. The woman came, but Mary returns; there came the one who brought death, there returns the one who gave birth to life; there came the one who led Adam down to the underworld, there returns the one who received Christ from the underworld.[75]

It is not clear which Mary was coming and which was going. But what is clear is that Mary Magdalene was the new Eve. As the old Eve was the bearer of death, so the new Eve brought news of resurrected life. As Chrysologus declared, she came to see the place of death to remind herself of her original wicked deed – 'the fatal business she transacted with the Devil' – so that she might recover her faith.[76]

The notion that Mary Magdalene was the new Eve was not exclusive to Peter Chrysologus. Although Ambrose Bishop of Milan (c. 340–397) was inclined to subordinate Mary to the rest of the disciples (and women, ever weaker vessels, to men more generally), she represented both men *and* women in freeing them from the bondage in which Eve had placed them. 'For Mary worshipped Christ,' declared Ambrose, 'loosening the hereditary bond, and the huge offence of womankind . . . . And rightly is a woman appointed [as messenger] to men; that she who first had brought the message of sin to man

---

[75] William B. Palardy (trans.), *St. Peter Chrysologus: Selected Sermons Volume 3* (Washington, DC: The Catholic University Press of America, 2005), Sermon 77.4, p. 27. Receiving Christ from the underworld refers to the doctrine of the harrowing of hell – that between his death and resurrection, Christ descended into hell to preach to those there imprisoned.

[76] *Ibid.*, Sermon 77.5, p. 27.

should first bring the message of the grace of the Lord'.[77] Similarly, Gregory of Nyssa (c. 330–c. 395) held that a woman should have been the first to receive the news of the resurrection 'that she might retrieve by her faith in the resurrection the overthrow caused by her disobedience, and that . . . she might become to men the guide to faith, whereby with good reason the first proclamation of death is annulled'.[78]

There was, of course, another candidate for the new Eve, namely, Mary the mother of Jesus.[79] As Bishop Irenaeus of Lyon (c. 130–c. 200) put it, 'And thus, as the human race fell into bondage to death by means of a virgin [Eve], so is it rescued by a virgin [Mary]; virginal disobedience having been balanced in the opposite scale by virginal obedience'.[80] So it is not surprising that there was a desire to have Mary the mother of Jesus as a witness to the resurrection.

One way to do this was to make the mother of Jesus 'the other Mary' of Matthew 28.1. Thus, for example, Severus of Antioch (c. 465–538) argued that 'the other Mary' was the God-bearer ($\Theta\varepsilon o\tau \acute{o}\kappa o\varsigma$), the mother of God.[81] The alternative was *completely to replace* the figure of Mary Magdalene with Mary the mother of Jesus, symbolizing the Church, as the key witness to the

---

[77] H. de Romestin (trans.), *Three Books of St. Ambrose, Bishop of Milan, On the Holy Spirit*, 3.11.74, in *NPNF (Second Series)*, vol. 10, p. 145.

[78] H. C. Ogle (trans.), *Against Eunomius*, 12.1, in *NPNF (Second Series)*, vol. 5, p. 242.

[79] On Mary, the mother of Jesus, as the second Eve, see Marina Warner, *Alone of All Her Sex: The Myth and Cult of the Virgin Mary* (London: Quartet, 1978), ch. 4.

[80] Anon. (trans), *Irenaeus Against Heresies*, 5.19.1, in *ANF*, vol. 1, p. 547.

[81] *PG*, vol. 46, p. 633. In *PG*, this homily is wrongly ascribed to Gregory of Nyssa.

resurrection. Thus, Ephrem the Syrian (c. 306–373), in a poetic sermon for Holy Week wrote,

He drew Mary Magdalen / to come and see his resurrection. / And why was it first to a woman / that he showed his resurrection, and not to men? / Here he showed us a mystery concerning his Church and his mother. / At the beginning of his coming to earth / a virgin was first to receive him, / and at his raising up from the grave / to a woman he showed his resurrection. / In his beginning and in his fulfilment / the name of his mother cries out and is present. / Mary received him by conception / and saw an angel before her; / and Mary received him in life and saw angels at his grave. / Again, Mary is like the Church, the Virgin, who has borne the first-fruits by the Gospel. / In the place of the Church, Mary saw him.[82]

If for Ephrem, Mary the mother of Jesus symbolized the Church, for Pope Leo the Great (d. 461), it was undoubtedly Mary Magdalene who represented a Church that would only be more perfect after Christ's ascension. Here, Christ's 'Touch me not' was understood by Leo to mean 'when I have ascended to My Father, then thou shalt handle Me more perfectly and truly, for thou shalt grasp what thou canst not touch and believe what thou canst not see'.[83] Augustine (354–430) struck a similar note. Literally, 'Touch me not' meant that Mary represented the Gentiles who would only believe in Jesus after his ascension. Spiritually, it meant the recognition that Jesus and the Father were one:

---

[82] Quoted by Robert Murray, *Symbols of Church and Kingdom: A Study in Early Syriac Tradition* (London: T & T Clark, 2006), p. 147.
[83] Charles Lett (trans.), *Sermon 74*, 4, in *NPNF (Second Series)*, vol. 12, p. 189.

Either, therefore, 'Do not touch me; I have not yet ascended to my Father' was said in such a way that in that woman was represented the Church of the Gentiles, which did not believe in Christ except when he had ascended to the Father, or Jesus wanted it believed in him on these terms, that is, that he be touched spiritually . . . that he and the Father are one thing. For indeed he has in a certain way ascended to the Father in the innermost perceptions of him who has recognized him as equal with the Father . . . . There you will touch me when you have believed that I am God not unequal with the Father.[84]

It was to the mysterious theologian Hippolytus (c. 170–c. 236) and his equally mysterious commentary on the Old Testament book *The Song of Songs* or *The Song of Solomon* that the later medieval church owed the designation of Mary Magdalene as 'the apostle of the apostles'.[85] 'And after this with a cry,' we read,

The synagogue expresses a good testimony for us through the women, those whom were made *apostles to the apostles*, having been sent by Christ: those to whom the angels said, 'Go and announce to the disciples, 'He has gone before you into Galilee. There you shall see him' (Mark 16.7). But in order that the apostles might not doubt [that they were sent] from the angels, Christ himself met with the apostles, in order that the women

[84] John W. Rettig, *Tractates on the Gospel of John 112–24; Tractates on the First Epistle of John*, 121.3 (Washington, DC, The Catholic University Press of America, 1995), p. 59

[85] See J. A. Cerrato, *Hippolytus between East and West: The Commentaries and the Provenance of the Corpus* (Oxford: Oxford University Press, 2002). See also, Brendan McConvery, 'Hippolytus' *Commentary on the Song of Songs* and John 20: Intertextual Reading in Early Christianity,' *Irish Theological Quarterly* 71 (2006), pp. 211–222.

might become apostles of Christ and might complete through obedience the failure of old Eve.[86]

Who were these women according to Hippolytus? First, they were the new Eve, now remarkably an apostle: 'O new consolations! Eve is being called an apostle! Behold from now on the fraud of the serpent is understood and [Eve] no longer goes astray'.[87] Second, they were identified as the bride of the *Song of Songs* who will not let the bridegroom Christ go: 'However he called to them saying: "Mary and Martha!" But they held on to his feet. And he says to them: "Do not hold on to me, I am not yet ascended to my father." But they held him firmly while they said: "I will not let you until I lead you into my heart," not wanting to be separated from their "Beloved" Christ'.[88] Thus, in Hippolytus' commentary on *The Song of Songs* lie many of the key themes in the history of Mary Magdalene – the new Eve, the Bride of Christ, and the apostle to the apostles.

Third, and surprisingly, they were named as Mary and Martha: '"By night I sought him, whom my soul dearly loves" [Song of Solomon 3.1]. See this is fulfilled in Martha and Mary, who themselves sought the dead Christ, not believing he was alive'.[89] Martha, we recall, was never named in the New Testament as having been a witness to the resurrection of Christ, although there is a widespread tradition to this effect that goes back to the early second century, at the end of the New Testament period. Martha, we recall,

---

[86] Yancy Smith (trans.), *Commentary on the Song of Songs*, 25.6, in Yancy Smith, *The Mystery of Anointing: Hippolytus' Commentary on the Song of Songs in Social and Critical Contexts* (Piscataway, NJ: Gorgias Press, 2015), p. 540 (my italics).

[87] *Ibid.*, 25.7, p. 542.   [88] *Ibid.*, 25.2, p. 533–534.

[89] *Ibid.*, 24.2, p. 526–527.

waited on the table while her sister Mary anointed Jesus's feet with expensive perfume (John 12.1–8). But in Hippolytus, it was Martha who anointed Jesus, and it was Martha who seems to play the key role in the resurrection scene.[90]

That said, the presence of Martha at the resurrection scene would suggest that her sister, Mary of Bethany, was intended by Hippolytus as present with Mary when they encountered the risen Christ. Certainly, Hippolytus gave no indication that by 'Mary' he meant Mary Magdalene, the title 'Magdalene' never receiving a mention. The conclusion to be drawn from this is that, rather than Mary Magdalene being named by Hippolytus as 'apostle to the apostles', it was Mary of Bethany and her sister Martha who were so called. In this case, the figure of Mary Magdalene has been absorbed into that of Mary of Bethany, rather than the reverse. This was the earliest conflation of the figures of Mary Magdalene and Mary of Bethany. It was a conflation that was never going to prevail. The predominance of Mary Magdalene in the gospel accounts of the resurrection would ensure that, if there were to be absorption, it would be of Mary of Bethany into Mary Magdalene. All of which takes us back to the conflation of Marys by Pope Gregory the Great in the year 591 with which this chapter began – that of Mary Magdalene with both Mary of Bethany and the sinful woman and the absorption of these latter two into Mary Magdalene.

In the first 600 years of Christianity, we can distinguish five different positions within the early Church on the

---

[90] *Ibid.*, 2.29; 25, p. 458; 25, p. 532–545. Susan Haskins sees Mary and Martha in Hippolytus as a joint figure Mary/Martha. See Haskins, *Mary Magdalene*, pp. 63–66.

relation of Mary Magdalene to Mary of Bethany and the sinful woman, each of which had its supporters. The first possibility was that Mary Magdalene was identical with Mary of Bethany but distinct from the sinful woman; second, that Mary of Bethany and the sinful woman were one, but different from Mary Magdalene; and third, that Mary Magdalene and the sinful woman were one and the same, but different from Mary of Bethany.[91]

The fourth position was that they were three distinct persons; the fifth, that the three women were one and the same person. As we noted above, Hippolytus conflated Mary Magdalene and Mary of Bethany, but he did not include the sinful woman in this. More common was a tendency to conflate Mary of Bethany and the sinful woman. After all, both had anointed Jesus. Augustine certainly hinted along these lines:

Look, the very sister of Lazarus (if, perhaps, she is the same one who anointed the feet of the Lord with perfume and wiped with her hair what she has washed with her tears) was better raised up than her brother; she was freed from a huge mass of bad habit. For she was an infamous sinner [famosa peccatrix], and about her it was said, 'Many sins are forgiven her, because she has loved much'.[92]

The Greek theologian Origen (c. 185–c. 254) was strongly opposed to this: 'For neither is it credible,' he

---

[91] See Urban Holzmeister, 'Die Magdalenfrage in der kirchlichen Überlieferung,' *Zeitschrift für katholische Theologie* 46 (1922), pp. 402–406. Holzmeister here identifies five different positions taken up by modern scholarship. He finds no evidence in the early Church of the identification of Mary Magdalene and the sinful woman.

[92] John W. Rettig, *Tractates on the Gospel of John 28–54* (Washington, DC: Catholic University Press of America, 2010) 49.4, p. 241.

declared, 'that Mary, the sister of Martha whom Jesus loved, who chose the better part, was the woman in the city who was called a sinner'.[93]

On balance, the early Church followed Origen and kept Mary of Bethany and the sinful woman as discrete persons. Jerome, for example, clearly distinguished the woman who anointed Jesus's head from the woman who anointed his feet: 'Let no one think that she who poured ointment on his head and she who poured it on his feet are the same woman. For the latter also washes them with her tears and wipes them with her hair and is openly called a prostitute. But no such thing is written about this woman. For a prostitute could not at once become worthy of the Lord's head'.[94]

Nor was Mary Magdalene ever identified with the sinful woman by the early Church. Ironically, the only identification of Mary Magdalene with the woman who was a sinner was made (possibly) by the neo-Platonist philosopher Porphyry (c. 234–c. 305). He had wondered why Christ had not appeared to Herod, the High Priest, or Roman senators but instead 'to Mary Magdalene, a prostitute who came from some horrible little village and had been possessed by seven demons, and another Mary equally unknown, probably a peasant woman, and others of equally no account'.[95] So it was not in the early

---

[93] *PG*, 13.1722.

[94] Thomas P. Scheck (trans.), *Commentary on Matthew*, 26.7 (Washington, DC: The Catholic University Press of America, 2010), p. 293. We can assume that Jerome here is identifying the woman in Matthew 26.7 with the fallen woman in Luke.

[95] Quoted by Bas van Os, 'A Whore from Bethany? A Note on Mary Magdalene in Early Non-Christian Sources, in Lupieri (ed.), *Mary*

Church's interest to have identified Mary Magdalene with a prostitute. It would have been grist to the mill for the opponents of Christianity were they able to suggest that the early Church endorsed the view that its key witness to the resurrection was a sometime harlot.

All that said, neither in the Eastern nor the Western Church was there any witness prior to Gregory the Great who identified the three women as the same person. The Eastern Church followed the majority of the early Church Fathers in keeping the three women separate and eventually celebrating the 'feasts' of Mary Magdalene and Mary of Bethany on separate days.[96] But the Western Church was to follow Gregory the Great in conflating the three and remembering their 'life' on 22 July. This conflation was the beginning of a biography. The woman who first witnessed the resurrection had not come out of nowhere. She was not only a faithful disciple of Jesus from whom he had driven seven demons and not only the first to speak to the risen Christ, but she was also the sinful yet penitent prostitute and his beloved Mary of Bethany who both sat contemplatively at his feet and anointed him in preparation for his burial. As Jansen writes, 'Gregory's composite saint ordained the agenda of Magdalen veneration for the entire Middle Ages and

---

Magdalene from the New Testament to the New Age and Beyond, p. 130. That by the 'horrible little village' is meant Bethany and that therefore, as Os suggests, we have here the first identification of Mary Magdalene with both Mary of Bethany and the sinful woman seems to me too much of a speculative stretch.

[96] 4 June 4 for Mary of Bethany, variously on 30 June, 22 July, and 4 August, for Mary Magdalene.

well beyond. So great was the pontiff's authority that the Roman Church accepted his identification of Mary Magdalene with the penitent prostitute for almost fourteen hundred years, until the liturgical calendar reform of 1969'.[97]

---

[97] Jansen, *The Making of the Magdalen: Preaching and Popular Devotion in the Later Middle Ages* (Princeton, NJ: Princeton University Press, 2000), p. 35.

2

The 'Lives' of Mary Magdalene

~

Among the daughters of men, only the Queen of Heaven is equal to and greater than Mary Magdalene.

Pseudo-Rabanus, *The Life of Mary Magdalene*

The Many Lives of Mary

The three Marys combined by Gregory the Great – the penitent sinner, the Mary who sat contemplatively at the feet of Jesus, and the Mary who was commissioned to preach the Gospel – became the key themes of the 'Lives' ('Vitae') of Mary Magdalene that were produced during the medieval period. While the three Marys interwove with each other in the Lives, each of the Lives arose from a specific take on the primary relationship between Mary Magdalene and Jesus.

There was no biblical account of the life of Mary Magdalene after she had told the followers of Jesus of his resurrection. After the ascension of Jesus into heaven from Mount Olivet, as told in the Acts of the Apostles, a number of the disciples gathered together in Jerusalem. With them, we read, were 'certain women, including Mary the mother of Jesus, as well as his brothers' (Acts 1.14). Although we might reasonably assume Mary Magdalene to have been there, she received no special mention. Outside of the Gospels, Mary Magdalene received no other mention in the New Testament texts. Effectively therefore, after the resurrection of Jesus, she disappeared from view. Thus, there was a gap in the story of Mary Magdalene waiting to be filled.

After Gregory the Great had conflated Mary Magdalene, Mary of Bethany, and the sinful woman, it was possible to create a richer narrative of the life of Mary Magdalene up until the time of the resurrection. But it was only in the ninth century that stories of her life after the time of Jesus began to circulate. The accounts of Mary Magdalene during the medieval period, both of her life at the time of Jesus and afterwards, form part of the writings about the Christian saints more generally (the genre of hagiography). These stories of the saints were the most significant literary form of the medieval period. Like the stories of other saints, those of Mary Magdalene included not only 'Lives' of Mary, but also stories of her miracles both during her life and after her death, of the visions had of her, of the discovery and movements of her relics, and of the places where she was believed to have lived.[1]

The 'Lives' and the 'Afterlives' of Mary will comprise the themes of the next two chapters of this book. In this chapter we will see how, for the most part, the stories of her life after the death of Jesus were ineluctably constructed around her identification with both the sinful woman and Mary of Bethany, so much so that the single Mary virtually disappears, so absorbed is she into both the repentant sinner and Mary of Bethany.

The textual history of the Lives of Mary Magdalene is an exceedingly complex one with a complicated textual

---

[1] For an excellent introduction to the genre(s) of hagiography, see Thomas Head, (ed.), *Medieval Hagiography: An Anthology* (London: Routledge, 2000).

history. But, disentangling the narrative records, we can identify the five key moments. First, there is the development in the early ninth century of the *vita eremitica*, or the *hermit life*. It comprises an account of the life of Mary after the ascension of Christ when she retired to a life of ascetic solitude in the wilderness. Second, there is the first coherent pre-ascension life of Mary in 'A Sermon in Veneration of Saint Mary Magdalene', traditionally attributed to Odo, the Benedictine Abbot of Cluny (879–942). Third, we find, in the early eleventh century, the beginnings of a new post-ascension life of Mary Magdalene, the *vita apostolica*, that includes her exile from Palestine, her arrival in France, and her role in the conversion of the French. Fourth, in the late twelfth century, *The Life of Saint Mary Magdalene and of Her Sister Saint Martha* combined a detailed account of Mary's pre-ascension life with all the features of the post-ascension *vita apostolica*. Finally, with virtually no attention to the pre-ascension life of Mary, there is the *vita apostolica-eremitica* that combines the apostolic and the eremitic, exemplified in *The Golden Legend* of the Dominican Jacobus de Voragine (c. 1230–c. 1298).

The Vitae Eremiticae

The Old English Martyrology, written somewhere between the years 800 and 900, contains some 200 entries giving details of the lives and deaths of individual saints.[2] So it is

---

[2] See Christine Rauer (ed.), *The Old English Martyrology: Edition, Translation and Commentary* (Cambridge: D. S. Brewer, 2013).

a kind of ninth-century version of a dictionary of the saints. The entries are arranged in a calendrical sequence. Among the feast days of saints that span the ecclesiastical year, Mary Magdalene appears on 22 July. It was a date that the *Martyrology* had derived from the *Martyrologium* of the Venerable Bede (c. 672–735), written around 720.[3] Thus, within the West, we can say that devotion to Mary Magdalene dated from at least this time, although her inclusion in Bede's *Martyrologium* suggests that her popularity in Britain was already well established. Bede may also have been influenced by Greek liturgical texts that were also, by this time, recognising 22 July as her feast day.[4]

The first half of the entry in *The Old English Martyrology* for 22 July reads,

On the twenty-second day of the month is the feast of St Mary Magdalen, who was first a sinful woman, and she had seven devils inside her, that was all the vices. But she came to our Lord when he was a man on earth, where he was receiving hospitality in the house of a Jewish scholar. And she brought her alabaster [i.e., 'perfume bottle'], that is, her glass bottle, with precious ointment, and she then wept onto the Saviour's feet, and dried [them] with her hair and kissed [them] then and anointed them with the precious ointment. Then the Saviour said to her: 'Your sins are pardoned; go now in peace.' And she was afterwards so beloved by Christ that after his resurrection

---

[3] See PL vol. 123, col.1037. Mary Magdalene appears on 22 July in most (and possibly in all) of the extant manuscripts of the martyrology that circulated under Bede's name. I am indebted for this point to Felice Lifshitz of the University of Alberta.

[4] Victor Saxer, *Le Culte de Marie Madeleine en Occident* (Paris: Librairie Clavreuil, 1959), pp. 41–42.

he appeared first to her among all men, and she announced his resurrection to his apostles.[5]

The first half of this life of Mary Magdalene is now familiar to us. It is primarily derived from the biblical texts that we examined in the last chapter. Mary was she out of whom had gone seven demons (Luke 8.2), who had brought ointment in an alabaster jar (Luke 7.37), who had anointed the feet of Jesus and dried them with her hair (Luke 7.38), who had been forgiven her sins by Jesus (Luke 7.48), and who had been the first to see the risen Christ and to announce it to his apostles.[6] It is not clear from this text that Mary Magdalene is conflated with Mary of Bethany, although it is probably intended. But she is clearly identified with the sinful woman of the Gospel of Luke. This identification, along with the declaration that 'she had seven devils inside her, that was all the vices' suggests that Gregory the Great was the key source for this biography, either directly or via Bede.[7]

The second half of the *Martyrology's* entry on Mary Magdalene concerns her life after the resurrection and ascension of Christ. It is a version of the life of Mary Magdalene known now as the *vita eremitica*:

And after Christ's ascension her longing for him was so great that she never wanted to see another man again. And so she went into the desert and lived there for thirty years, unknown to all men. She never ate human food, nor drank. But at every prayer-time God's angels came from heaven and lifted her up

---

[5] Rauer (ed.), *The Old English Martyrology*, p. 143.

[6] The only addition here to the biblical texts is the explanation that the 'alabaster jar' was a 'glass bottle' ('glæsfæt').

[7] See Rauer (ed.), *The Old English Martyrology*, p. 143.

into the air, and there she heard some of the heavenly bliss, and then they carried her back to her cave, and for that reason she was never hungry or thirsty. And then after thirty years a holy priest came across her in the desert, and he led her to his church and gave her the Eucharist. And she gave up the ghost to God, and the priest buried her, and great miracles often happened at her tomb.[8]

The focus of the *vita eremitica* was the retirement of Mary Magdalene from society to take up the life of the solitary ascetic. As someone who 'never ate human food, nor drank', she was also a holy anorexic, although, unlike many female saints who survived on the Eucharist alone, it seems in her case to have brought about her death. In this case, by absorbing the body and blood of Christ, her physical body was able to begin its process of transformation into a spiritual body fit for heaven. By the end of the fifth century, the so-called Assumption of Mary – the belief that Mary the mother of Jesus had ascended into heaven after (or before) her death – had become part of the mainstream Christian tradition.[9] In *The Old English Martyrology*, at least some 300 years later, Mary Magdalene seems to have topped this, making a number of ascensions on a daily basis. Unlike Mary the mother of Jesus, however, after her death, Mary Magdalene seems to have kept her feet firmly planted upon this earth.[10] The presence of her body upon earth after her death will make

[8]   *Ibid.*, p. 143.

[9]   See Stephen J. Shoemaker, *Ancient Traditions of the Virgin Mary's Dormition and Assumption* (Oxford: Oxford University Press, 2003), ch. 1.

[10]   The consequence of the assumption of Mary the mother of Jesus is the absence of any bodily relics (except perhaps for some hair). The relics

her more accessible, both in physical and spiritual ways, to both the clergy and the laity than the more aethereal mother of Jesus.

The life of Mary Magdalene contained within *The Old English Martyrology* was derived from an early ninth-century text that probably originated in Southern Italy, was quickly transmitted to Europe, and then found its way to England. The earliest version of the *vita eremitica* closely parallels that of *The Old English Martyrology*, but it significantly elaborates Mary Magdalene's encounter with the priest.[11] Its authority in the medieval period was the consequence of its having been attributed in several early manuscripts to the Jewish historian Josephus (37–100).[12] This was a spurious attribution. But what we can say is that the *vita eremitica* is the oldest Latin account of the life of Mary Magdalene after the ascension of Christ.

According to the *vita eremitica*, it was the custom of a certain priest with the charge of a small parish to retire into the wilderness during Lent. While at prayer, it was revealed to him in a vision that, in that same desert, angels always came at the canonical hours, took something up

---

are consequently 'second order' – garments, rings, veils, shoes, breast milk, tears, nail parings, even her house.

[11] The earliest Latin text may be found in BHL 5453. A critical version of the Latin text can be most easily accessed in J. E. Cross, 'Mary Magdalen in the *Old English Martyrology*: The Earliest Extant "Narrat Josephus" Variant of her Legend, *Speculum* 53 (1978), pp. 20–22. I am particularly grateful to David M. Foley for the first English translation of this text and also for those of BHL 5454 and BHL 5455. These two versions may also be found in Cross, 'Mary Magdalen in the *Old English Martyrology*,' pp. 22–25. They are pretty much identical with BHL 5453.

[12] See BHL 5454 and 5455.

with them from there into heaven, and then returned it to the desert. He began to imagine that, at those times when the saints on earth were wont to pray, one of them was being visited by the angels of the Lord. He then began to make for the place where, in his vision, he had seen the angels dwelling.

There he found a cave and cried out, 'I adjure you, through the Father and the Son and the Holy Spirit, that, if you be a man who dwell in this cave, you speak with me, or if you be a spirit, make some response to this my entreaty'. Out of the cave there came a voice that replied, 'For that thou hast sworn by the Holy Trinity, I respond and say to you what I am. Thou hast heard in the holy Gospel or hast read that there was a wretched and sinful woman who was named Magdalene, from whom the Lord cast out seven demons'. To this, he responded: 'I did hear and did read about her who, thirty years after the Lord's ascension, is now preached through the holy Gospel over the entire face of the earth'. And she said,

I am she, and for ardent love for my Lord Jesus Christ I could neither look upon a husband nor any man. Therefore, after His ascension I withdrew into this solitude and now have dwelt here for thirty years, during which time I have neither seen any man nor heard the voice thereof. But now I perceive by your voice that you are a holy man, and it is for this that I tell you that at every hour the angels of my Lord come to me and take me up into heaven to prayer, and then they reveal to me a glimpse of that celestial delight, and thereafter, being satisfied with such exultant sweetness, they return me once more to my cave. For His account I never took human food nor had any thought of it, and yet never have I hungered nor thirsted these thirty years owing to that celestial sweetness and the sight of the angels. And now I know that soon I shall prevail to be led out from this body and eternally to enjoy the vision of my Lord. Thus I ask you that you receive my prayer as I do yours. Come to me after seven days and bring me human garments, for I cannot dwell among men without raiment. For the Lord has manifested to me that I must end my days among men.

Seven days later, the priest returned bringing the garments, left them at the mouth of the cave for the naked ascetic Mary, and departed. He returned three days later and Mary asked him to lead her to whatever human habitation he wished so that she might there end her days. The priest took her to his own congregation and the church where he was accustomed to celebrate the Eucharist. 'And so', we read, 'Mary Magdalene received the communion of the Body and Blood of our Lord Jesus Christ, and she remained standing next to the altar with her hands upraised in prayer until she sent forth her holy spirit, and thus did the priest bury her honourably in this same church. And there at her tomb great wonders were wrought for cause of her holy merits'.

The Mary Magdalene of the *vita eremitica* stands in the tradition of the so-called desert fathers. From around the beginning of the fourth century, Christians had begun to retire from 'the world' to seek God in poverty, celibacy, and solitude. It is perhaps no coincidence that, as Christianity became legitimized in the Roman Empire and was fast becoming fashionable, many men and some women perceived the church as becoming increasingly corrupted. They headed into the deserts, first of Egypt, then later of Palestine, Syria, and parts beyond to seek salvation apart from the world and each other. They were the first monks (from *monachos* – solitary), hermits (from *eremos* – desert), and anchorites (from *anachorein* – to withdraw from the world).

While the vast majority of hermits were men, there were also 'desert mothers' leading lives of ascetic solitude. There are clear parallels, for example, between the eremitic life of Mary Magdalene and the story of the aged holy virgin in the desert of Scêtê in Egypt:

Two great elders were travelling in the desert of Scêtê. On hearing someone muttering out of the ground, they looked for the entrance of a cave. When they entered they found an aged holy virgin lying down. 'When did you come here, old lady,' they said to her, 'and who is looking after you?' – for they found nothing other than her alone, lying there, sick. She said: 'I have been in this cave for thirty-eight years, satisfying myself with weeds and serving Christ. And I never saw a man until today, for God has sent you to bury my remains.' When she had said this, she fell asleep. The elders glorified God then departed when they had buried the body.[13]

Naked and living, as we might say, on the smell of an oily rag was typical of the desert saints. Another eremitic life tells us of an unnamed woman living naked in a hole in the desert who had fled from Jerusalem having had sex with a monk. One basket of food and a bottle of water had lasted her for thirty years. Although her clothes had worn out, her hair had grown sufficiently long to cover her nakedness. She had not seen a man for thirty years until a monk discovered her. At her request, he went to fetch clothes for her, but on his return, he could not find her.

[13] BHG 1322eb. Quoted by John Wortley, *An Introduction to the Desert Fathers* (Cambridge: Cambridge University Press, 2019), p. 126.

Later, other anchorites saw her and fed her from their supplies. Next morning they found her dead.[14]

Mary Magdalene also fits this type of the fallen woman who sought redemption in the desert. As Marina Warner puts it, 'Mary Magdalene leads a Christian company of harlot saints'.[15] In the eighth century, James the Deacon wrote the Life of Pelagia the harlot who, disguised as a man, was known until her death as Pelagius.[16] According to this, the bishop of Antioch called together all the local bishops, among whom was Nonnus, a monk from a monastery called Tabennisis. While Nonnus was preaching to the others, Pelagia the chief actress of Antioch arrived sitting on a donkey, 'dressed in the height of fantasy, wearing nothing but gold, pearls and precious stones'.[17] When the bishops saw her 'bare-headed and with all her limbs shamelessly exposed', there was not one that did not avert his eyes, except for Nonnus.[18] After she had gone, he asked his fellow bishops several times, 'Were you not delighted by her great beauty?'[19] They did not answer. Retiring to his bedchamber, Nonnus was filled with remorse. And beating his breast, he wept saying, 'Lord Jesus Christ. I know I am a sinner and unworthy, for

---

[14] BHG 1449x. See Wortley, *An Introduction to the Desert Fathers*, pp. 126–127.

[15] Warner, *Alone of All her Sex*, p. 233.

[16] For other 'desert mothers' disguised as 'desert fathers', see Wortley, *An Introduction to the Desert Fathers*, pp. 124–125.

[17] Benedicta Ward (trans.), 'The Life of St. Pelagia the Harlot', in Benedicta Ward, *Harlots of the Desert: A Study of Repentance in Early Christian Sources* (Kalamazoo, MI: Cistercian Publications, 1987), p. 67. The Latin text may be found in PL 73, 663–672.

[18] *Ibid.*, p. 67.   [19] *Ibid.*

today the ornaments of a harlot have shone more brightly than the ornaments of my soul'.[20]

The next day, Pelagia had a change of heart and begged to see Nonnus. He refused to see her on his own, but had her brought to him and the other bishops. When she arrived, she threw herself on the floor, seized his feet, and begged him to baptize her. When he refused, she threw herself on the floor again, seized his feet, washed them with her tears, and dried them with her hair. Nonnus relented and baptized her. She then gave away all her possessions to the poor, freed her slaves, disguised herself as a man, and built herself a cell on the Mount of Olives in Jerusalem. Nonnus comforted her godmother Romana with the words, 'Do not weep, my daughter, but rejoice with great joy, for Pelagia has chosen the better part [Luke 10.42] like Mary whom the Lord preferred to Martha in the Gospel'.[21]

Three or four years later, James the Deacon travelled to Jerusalem and was told by Nonnus there to seek out 'a certain brother Pelagius, a monk and a eunuch, who has lived there for some years shut up alone'.[22] He found her 'with a face so emaciated by fasting . . . that her eyes had sunk inwards like a great pit'.[23] He returned on another day and called her name but received no reply. Warned by God, he broke open the little window to her cell and saw that she was dead. Having reported this to the holy fathers and monks in Jerusalem, they broke into her cell, retrieved her body, and anointed it with myrrh. Only then did they all realize that Pelagius was in fact Pelagia. The people thronging around cried out, 'Glory to you Lord

[20] *Ibid.*, p. 68.   [21] *Ibid.*, p. 73.   [22] *Ibid.*   [23] *Ibid.*, p. 74.

Jesus Christ, for you have hidden away on earth such great treasures, men and women'.[24]

The *vita eremitica* of Mary Magdalene was thus part of a genre of lives of saintly women who had retired from the world. But the eremitic woman to whom Mary Magdalene was most assimilated was Mary of Egypt. We know of her from the seventh-century *The Life of Mary of Egypt* attributed to Sophronius, the Patriarch of Jerusalem (560–638), although the text gives us no clues as to when (and therefore whether) she flourished (or, as with ascetic saints generally, didn't). However that may be, it was undoubtedly a popular legend in the medieval period with translations of the original Greek text into Syriac, Armenian, Ethiopic, Slavonic, and Latin.

The Life of Mary of Egypt was bookended by her encounters with a monk by the name of Zosimas. He first encountered her while on a spiritual retreat in the desert across the River Jordan. One day, while performing his prayers, he saw 'a naked figure whose body was black, as if tanned by the scorching of the sun. It had on its head *hair white as wool*'.[25] She asked him to throw her a garment that he was wearing to cover her nakedness (see Plate 3).

At Zosimas's request, Mary of Egypt, now covered with his garment, began to pray while Zosimas, trembling with fear, bowed down towards the ground. As she prolonged her prayers, he raised his head 'and saw her elevated about one cubit above the earth, hanging in the air

---

[24] *Ibid.*, p. 74.

[25] Alice-Mary Talbot (ed.), *Holy Women of Byzantium: Ten Saints' Lives in English Translation* (Washington, DC: Dumbarton Oaks, 1996), p. 75. This is a translation of the Greek version. For other versions of the story, see Ward, *Harlots of the Desert*, ch. 3.

and praying this way'.[26] Mary had to assure him that she was not a demonic spirit.

Mary then told him the story of her life. She was from Egypt, she said. When she was twelve years old she lost her virginity and threw herself 'entirely and insatiably into the lust of sexual intercourse'.[27] For more than seventeen years, she lived a life devoted to sexual promiscuity. Having encountered a group of men going to Jerusalem for the feast of the exaltation of the Holy Cross, she joined them, offering sex in lieu of payment for the journey by ship: 'There is no kind of licentiousness, speakable or unspeakable, that I did not teach those miserable men', she declared.[28]

Upon arrival in Jerusalem, she sought entry to the church in which the cross was housed. Three or four times she tried to enter the church but was held back by an overwhelming power. When she finally realized that 'it was the filth of my actions that was barring the entrance to me', she prayed to an icon of Mary the mother of Jesus to help her enter the church, promising to repent, to immediately renounce the world and all worldly things, and to go wherever she might be sent.[29] She entered the church, saw the Holy Cross, repented of her sins, and by sunset she had reached the bank of the River Jordan. There she took the sacraments in a church dedicated to John the Baptist, ate half a loaf of bread, and drank water from the river. The next morning, she crossed the Jordan and began her life in the desert. When Zosimas first encountered her, she had been living there for forty-seven

---

[26] Talbot (ed.), *Holy Women of Byzantium*, p. 79.   [27] *Ibid.*, p. 80.
[28] *Ibid.*, p. 81.   [29] *Ibid.*, p. 82.

years, fighting the desires of the flesh for the first seventeen years, living on wild plants, and enduring extremes of heat and cold without clothing.

At her request, he met her a year later on Good Friday on the edge of the River Jordan, having brought her the sacraments. She eventually appeared on the opposite bank and walked on the water across the river to him to receive the sacraments. She then asked him to return in a year's time to the place where they had first met and, once again, she walked across the water to the other side. A year later, he returned, seeking her 'like a most experienced hunter seeking a sweet prey'.[30] Eventually he found her lying dead, her hands folded in prayer and her body facing towards the east. After he had wept and recited appropriate psalms, he noticed writing impressed on the ground beside her head. There he read that he should bury her body. 'I died', it went on to say, 'on that very night of the Passion of our Savior [twelve months earlier] after I received the holy Last Supper'.[31] That her body had been preserved for a year was a sure sign of her sanctity. As with Mary Magdalene and other female ascetics, the receiving of the sacraments brought about her death. Lacking the strength to bury her himself, he noticed a huge lion licking the soles of her feet. At his request, the lion dug with its paws a pit deep enough for the burial of her body.

In another version of the life of Mary of Egypt, her nakedness was hidden by her hair having grown long enough to cover her body.[32] The image of Mary of Egypt with long hair sufficient to hide her nakedness

---

[30] *Ibid.*, p. 90.   [31] *Ibid.*, p. 91.
[32] See Ward, *Harlots of the Desert*, pp. 31–32.

was to be transferred to the eremitic Mary Magdalene. This idea of a very hairy Mary Magdalene may also have been influenced by the legend of Agnes of Rome (fourth century). According to tradition, Agnes was a young woman of around twelve years of age who, because of her devotion to Christ, refused to marry. Arraigned before the authorities, she refused to abjure her faith. Stripped of her clothing, she was led naked to a brothel. There, God 'made her hair to grow in such abundance that it covered her better than any garments'.[33] The image of Mary Magdalene, covered in hair or fur, ascending to heaven with the angels to feed on heavenly food was to become a staple of medieval art. Ironically, long flowing hair, a symbol of female promiscuity, here became a symbol of its radical denial.

The message of the *vitae eremiticae* was a clear and obvious one. No one, however heinous their sins, was beyond repentance, nor beyond the redemption brought about by the death of Christ and the salvation that effected by his body and blood of Christ in the Eucharist.

'A Sermon in Veneration of Saint Mary Magdalene'

The *Sermo in veneratione sanctae Mariae Magdalenae* is a major landmark in the development of the legend of Mary Magdalene in the West. Although we cannot determine who wrote it, it has been traditionally attributed to the Benedictine Odo, the Abbot of Cluny. It was written

---

[33] Ryan and Ripperger (trans.), *The Golden Legend of Jacobus Voragine*, p. 111. Jacobus's version was based on the fifth-century *Acts of the Martyrdom of Saint Agnes*.

somewhere between the years 860 and 1050, perhaps in Vézelay in France, a town which was to become a major site of the cult of Mary Magdalene.[34] It is important evidence of the increasing significance of Mary Magdalene within the religious life of the Western church at the end of the first millennium. It becomes the major source for later accounts of the life of Mary Magdalene before the ascension of Christ, both in terms of the events in Mary's life and the order in which they are presented.

The sermon followed Gregory the Great's composite picture of Mary Magdalene, as well as making large borrowings from the sermons of Haimo of Auxerre (d. c. 865). But its significance lies in its being the first text to combine the Gospel stories of Mary Magdalene, Mary of Bethany, and the sinful woman of the Gospel of Luke into one coherent *vita*. It was written for a monastic audience who, listening to this sermon, would have learnt of an historical Magdalene who foreshadowed the Church, modelled the inner life of contemplation, and was next to Mary the mother of Jesus as an exemplar of the spiritual life. His sermon was intended, as he rather colourfully put it, as a brief taste of those things that 'illuminate the pages of Holy Scripture with the impression of her splendor in the likeness of precious stones, and render them verdant as it were with the blossoms of her virtues'.[35]

---

[34] See Dominique Iogna-Prat, 'La Madeleine du *Sermo in Veneratione Sanctae Mariae Magdalenae* attribué à Odon de Cluny,' *Mélanges de l'École Française de Rome. Moyen Age* 104 (1992), pp. 37–90.

[35] *Sermo in veneratione sanctae Mariae Magdalenae*, PL 133, col. 714A. I am indebted to David Foley for his translation of this work.

His inventiveness was apparent from the beginning. For the sermon began with an account of the early life of Mary that was not present within the Gospels or for that matter, until this sermon, anywhere else. It is notable not only by virtue of her noble origins (*germinis dignitas*), but also on account of her wealth, her parents having died. The listener was reminded of her wealth throughout the sermon. When she became a follower of Jesus, we read, she gave 'food and vesture unto him of her own riches, inasmuch as she was exceedingly wealthy'.[36] Later, at the time of the death of her brother Lazarus, we read that the loftiness of her lineage and the dignity of her worldly honour was discernible through the fact that 'so great a multitude of noble and eminent Jews assembled to lighten her grief'.[37]

Because of her great wealth, however, she gave herself over to 'lascivious occupations, having loosed the reins of her modesty'.[38] Pseudo-Odo quickly identified her as the sinful woman of Luke *and* the woman with seven demons, the sum of all the vices. She it was, we read, 'who began to moisten the feet of her creator with tears of contrition and to dry them with the tears of her devotion, and ceaselessly to tend them with the kiss of true humility and to anoint them with the purest ointment of her love' (see Plate 4).[39]

Intriguingly, pseudo-Odo now added to this another anointing story from the New Testament. This is originally to be found in the Gospels of Matthew (26.6–7) and Mark (14.3).[40] There we read that, while in the house of

[36] PL 133, col. 715B.   [37] PL 133, col.717C.
[38] PL 133, col. 714B.   [39] PL 133, col. 714D.
[40] In the New Testament, these stories in Matthew and Mark are probably variations on the story of the fallen women in Luke.

Simon the leper in Bethany, an unknown woman came to Jesus with an alabaster jar of very expensive ointment and poured it upon his head as he sat at table. The stories in Mark and Matthew are distinct from the story in Luke by virtue of the anointing of Jesus's head and not his feet. Although within the New Testament, they are probably variations upon the story in Luke, pseudo-Odo was able to draw another apparently anonymous woman into the story. For he also identified this unknown woman as Mary Magdalene. Pseudo-Odo provided for his readers a prayer of contrition placed in the mouth of Mary Magdalene:

O my Lord, most merciful Jesus, thou Who knowest all things and lookest truly into every heart, Who desirest not the death of sinners but that they be converted and live, thou knowest what my weeping entreats of thee, what the tears welling up from the depths of my soul implore, what my bitter lamentation prays for. I am a sinner and unclean, befouled by the stain of all my deplorable iniquities. But because I have defiled my life from my earlier years, I now take refuge in thee, my lord, who art eternal life, that thou mayest restore a life which was wantonly laid to waste and in thy clemency deliver me from the jaws of the abyss, that thou wouldst mercifully liberate and powerfully deliver me, thou who alone knowest my toil and sorrow.[41]

Pseudo-Odo then made the clear connection to Mary of Bethany, recounting the story of Mary and Martha (see Plate 5). It becomes a story in which the contemplative life is preferred over the active. In Mary was signified the sweetness of the contemplative life 'whose savour is more

---

[41] PL 133, col. 715A.

strongly tasted the more the soul is separated from visible things and the commotion of worldly cares'.[42] Mary Magdalene, as Mary of Bethany, thus provided the ideal exemplar for the superiority of the contemplative life over the active life.

As a matter of routine, the medieval world endorsed the contemplative over the active life. Medieval culture, at least in principle, saw the contemplative versus the active as part of an array of oppositions that valued the heavenly over the earthly, the soul over the body, the spiritual over the material, the poor over the wealthy, and the celibate over the married. Still, pseudo-Odo did make much of the activity of Mary as she courageously sought the tomb of Jesus although, it has to be said, her physical activity was a symbol of the soul's inner seeking for its divine lover. Certainly, she was an example worthy of imitation by everyone, whether active or contemplative.[43] For Pseudo Odo, her journey to the tomb was a sign of the love that he found exemplified in the Song of Songs (3.1–4):

In my bed by night I sought him whom my soul loves. I sought him and found not. I will arise and go about the city, seeking him whom my soul loves. The watchmen who guard the city found me: Hast thou seen him whom my soul loves? And it happened when I had passed them by that I found him whom my soul loves. I will hold him and I will not let him go until I bring him into the house of my father, and into the bedchamber of my mother.[44]

---

[42] PL 133, col. 717A.   [43] See PL 133, col. 719A.
[44] PL 133, cols. 719A–B.

Having found the risen Jesus, she was forbidden to touch his feet because she had not yet come to believe that he was divine. Nevertheless, he appointed her to inform the apostles of Jesus that he was risen from the dead and that he would soon ascend into heaven. As Christ was the new Adam, so she was the new Eve:

Truly, the most tender clemency of God towards womankind is declared in this place. For since death had been borne into the world through a woman, he elected to announce the joy of the Resurrection to men through the female sex, through which the sorrow of death had been announced, lest the female sex should be ever held in reproach. As if it were said: By the hand from whom thou didst receive the cup of death, by her mouth thou hearest the joy of the resurrection. And just as through blessed Mary ever virgin, who is the sole hope of the world, the gates of paradise have been opened to us with the curse of Eve shut out, so through blessed Mary Magdalene the reproach of the female sex was wiped away and the splendour of our resurrection rose up with that of our Lord and by her was pledged. Whence Mary is well interpreted 'star of the sea.' Although this inter-pretation uniquely corresponds with the Mother of God, through whose virgin birth the Sun of Justice shone forth unto the world, it may nevertheless also be fittingly said of holy Magdalene, who, coming to the sepulchre of the Lord with spices, did first announce the splendour of the Lord's resurrec-tion to the world.[45]

Thus, for pseudo-Odo, Mary the mother of Jesus and Mary Magdalene were equally important as exemplars of the Christian life. As the first to witness the resurrection, it was she, and not the mother of Jesus, who could open

[45] PL 133, cols. 721A–B.

the gates of Paradise to the sinner ready to repent. As the repentant sinner, Mary Magdalene was more accessible to the Christian, whether monastic or lay, than the sinless, maternal Virgin Mary. Ironically, the increasing veneration of Mary the mother of Jesus during the high Middle Ages created a devotional space for Mary Magdalene. As Marina Warner remarks, 'the more Mary [the mother of Jesus] was held to be free of all taint of sin, actual and original, the less the ordinary sinner could turn to her for consolation in his weakness, and the more he needed the individual saints whose own lapses held out hope for him'.[46] Unlike Mary the mother of Jesus, Mary Magdalene was a sinner like us and a model of redemption by Jesus. If even she can be saved, so can we. Thus, with the first biography of Mary Magdalene, pseudo-Odo made possible a new role for Mary Magdalene. She was not only the repentant sinner forgiven by Jesus for her devotion, she was able to fill the gap between the sinful Eve and the sinless mother of Jesus. She provided an exemplar for men. Pseudo-Odo was, after all, writing for and preaching to a male audience. In his sinful (feminine) soul (anima peccatrix), each man could find the sinful yet penitent Magdalene.

But pseudo-Odo also suggested that for women she had a greater significance not least because, it was believed, they carried a double burden, one for being sinners that they shared with men, and one for being women, the daughters of Eve, the architect of the Fall of man. For pseudo-Odo, Mary the mother of Jesus seemed to have solved the problem for sinners generally. But

[46] Warner, *Alone of All Her Sex*, p. 235.

pseudo-Odo was carving out a very special place for Mary in the spiritual life of women. Thus, he declared, 'through blessed Mary Magdalene the reproach of the female sex was wiped away'.[47] On the plus side, Mary Magdalene had opened up the path to redemption for women. But, that said, she had also shown that the path to salvation was a steeper one than it was for men.

Sitting at the Feet of Jesus

Pseudo-Odo had emphasized the role of Mary Magdalene as the representative of the contemplative life. This became the central theme of the *vita contemplativa*. If the focus of the *vita eremitica* was Mary Magdalene as the repentant whore, that of the *vita contemplativa* was the contemplative Mary Magdalene who (as Mary of Bethany) sat at the feet of Christ. She became for clergy and laity alike the exemplar of a life devoted to the interior quest of the soul for union with God. In short, the *vita contemplativa* was Mary imagined as the model mystic. This was specially illustrated in the first half of a text entitled *The Life of Saint Mary Magdalene and of her sister Saint Martha*.[48] It was the longest medieval Latin version of the life of Mary Magdalene. And it combined an elaborate narrative of her life before the ascension of Christ with an account of her apostolic life in France.

Traditionally, this work was ascribed to the Frankish Benedictine monk Rabanus Maurus (c. 780–856), one of

---

[47] PL 133, col. 721B.
[48] See David Mycoff (trans.), *The Life of Saint Mary Magdalene and of Her Sister Saint Martha* (Athens, OH: Cistercian Publications, 1989).

the most celebrated teachers of the ninth-century empire founded by Charlemagne. But it was probably written in the late twelfth century by an anonymous monk in the Cistercian monastic tradition. It was certainly composed within a milieu influenced by the mystical theology of the Cistercian Bernard of Clairvaux (1090–1153). His was a theology of both human and divine love centred on the transformation of the self through the soul's love for God, a love that was itself made possible by God's love for the soul. It was a theology inspired by a spiritual reading of the opening verse of the biblical text The Song of Songs: 'Let him kiss me with the kisses of his mouth' (1.2).

This was an ideal theological template for a life of Mary Magdalene as the contemplative Mary of Bethany. As *The Life of Saint Mary Magdalene* makes clear, before Mary could go to the meal at which Jesus was present, Jesus had already come to her spiritually: 'Groaning within her heart and conscience over these things [her sin and loss], she went to the feast, where it was said the Son of God was in attendance. Nor did she escape the notice of the one to whom she had come, and from whom no secrets are hidden; for in truth, he came to her first, through the sevenfold gifts of the Spirit, bringing to her the sweetness of his blessing, drawing her to himself, hastening her on her way'.[49]

The Life of Saint Mary Magdalene consists of two parts – her contemplative pre-ascension life and her post-ascension apostolic life. The pre-ascension life was very much dependent upon pseudo-Odo's account of Mary Magdalene. Like pseudo-Odo's *A Sermon in Veneration*

[49] *Ibid.*, 6.217–24, p. 35.

of Saint Mary Magdalene, pseudo-Rabanus's *The Life of Saint Mary Magdalene* combined into a unified narrative, sometimes awkwardly, all the scriptural passages concerning Mary Magdalene, Mary of Bethany, and the sinful woman of the Gospel of Luke, together with a Gospel-by-Gospel account of her role in the resurrection of Christ. But it was Mary of Bethany around whom the narrative was constructed. It begins with an account of her life before she encountered Jesus. According to this, Mary Magdalene, her brother Lazarus, and her older sister Martha lived in Bethany. Mary's mother Eucharia came from the royal line of Israel, while her father Theophilus was governor and prince of all Syria and of all the regions bordering on the sea. The family owned the greater part of Jerusalem, Bethany, and Magdala in Galilee. In short, they were people of enormous wealth.

All the children were gifted (as we would say) – talented in Hebrew, beautiful, perfectly mannered, and lucid in speech. The virtues of Martha, physical and spiritual, were only outshone by Mary who 'shone in loveliness and bodily beauty: handsome, well-proportioned, attractive in face, her hair a marvel, sweet in mind, decorous and gracious in speech, her complexion a mixture of roses and the whiteness of lilies. All graces shone in her form and beauty so much so that she was said to be a master-work of God'.[50] She was the ideal of womanhood, at least as imagined in the late twelfth century. Unfortunately, with great wealth and great beauty came great temptations. She perverted what God had given her 'to the service of a lascivious and pandering life'.[51] Taking a leaf

---

[50] *Ibid.* 2.5–62, p. 30.   [51] *Ibid.*, 2.82, p. 31.

out of Jerome's book, pseudo-Rabanus tells us that she took the name of her own country Magdalo, meaning 'the tower'. Like Gregory the Great, pseudo-Rabanus equated demons with vices. Thus, we are told, so great was Mary's fall into sin, that she was said to be possessed by seven demons.

When she realized that she had become destitute of all the virtues, she desired to return to her former ways. Fortuitously, she heard of a kind and holy man whom some believed was the Son of God and the Christ. She sought him out in the house of Simon the Pharisee in Magdalo where Jesus was dining. It was at this time and in this place that pseudo-Rabanus now located Mary's exorcism. The seven demons that tormented her were replaced by the seven gifts of the Spirit – wisdom, understanding, knowledge, counsel, fortitude, piety, and fear of God. Mary was filled with gratitude for Jesus's forgiveness of her: 'with the tears of her eyes ... she washed his feet; with her hair, which had before enhanced the beauty of her face, she dried them; with her mouth, which she had abused in pride and lasciviousness, she kissed them; and with the perfumes she had brought, she anointed them, as once ... she had anointed her own flesh to make it more seductive'.[52]

From that time on, she so changed her life that there was no evil, but only good. She now became a devoted follower of Jesus. Her great family wealth now explains her capacity to provide for Jesus and his followers out of her own resources. She became 'the first servant and special friend of our Lord and Saviour'.[53] The love

---

[52] *Ibid.*, 7.243–51, p. 36.   [53] *Ibid.*, 9.351–52, p. 39.

between Mary and Jesus was a mutual one. Later, when Jesus wept at news of the death of her brother Lazarus, we read, 'Oh lively tenderness, testimony of great love, sign of ineffable friendship! Who can, after that, form a just notion of the mutual love that burned between the Lord and Saviour and his friend Mary, proof of which we see in those sweet tears? I believe, with reverence, that that love is incomprehensible to all humanity and to all angels'.[54]

When Mary Magdalene re-entered the story, pseudo-Rabanus tells of the dinner at the house of Martha and Mary that Jesus attended. It was the key moment in the creation of the mystical contemplative Mary over against her active sister Martha. Mary, we are told, said nothing about her sister's complaints that she was doing all the work. She remained silent, leaving her defence to Jesus while pondering a verse from The Songs of Songs (2.3): 'For it is written, "I sit in the shadow of my beloved, and the fruit of his lips is sweet to my taste." Remembering this in my heart, I shall hope in the same'.[55] Jesus loved Martha for her life of activity. But the contemplative life was preferable. As in the Gospel of Luke (10.42), Jesus told Martha that Mary had chosen the better part: 'that which shall not be taken from her – the part of contemplation, love, and devotion. And she shall never abandon what she has faithfully begun here, a service which shall have its final consummation in heaven'.[56]

Pseudo-Rabanus then picked up the story in the Gospel of John (12.1–8) of Mary of Bethany's anointing of Jesus six days before the Passover at her home in

---

[54] *Ibid.*, 15.726–33, pp. 50–51.   [55] *Ibid.*, 10.413–16, p. 41.
[56] *Ibid.*, 10.425–29.

Bethany. In this case, Mary anointed the feet of Jesus with precious nard and dried them with her hair. Following pseudo-Odo, pseudo-Rabanus now adds to this the other anointing story – that of the unknown woman who came to Jesus with an alabaster jar of very expensive ointment and poured it upon his head as he sat at table. Like pseudo-Odo, he identified this woman as Mary Magdalene. He gave the both of the anointings a spiritualized if highly eroticized theological meaning, one that always seemed on the verge of sliding from the spiritual into the physical:

Drawing back with her fingers the hair of Almighty God, she broke the alabaster vessel and poured the remains of the nard over the head of the Son of God. Then, massaging his hair with her hands, she dampened his curls with nard. With her delicate finger, she skillfully spread the consecrated perfume over his forehead and temples, his neck, and adjacent areas, as though it were the unction of nobility. In this way, Mary fulfilled the works of religious devotion that Solomon in his person once sang of in the Song of Love: 'While he was on his couch, my nard gave forth its fragrance' [Song of Songs 1.12] .... . Now was the house filled with the scent of the perfume, as the world would be filled with the fame of this deed.[57]

In the Gospel accounts, no more was heard of Mary until her presence at the crucifixion. Pseudo-Rabanus did not have Mary present at the Last Supper. But he did give her a much embellished role in the life of Jesus after it. Thus, she was there in the Garden of Gethsemane when Jesus was betrayed and his disciples fled. She alone remained courageous – 'The skin of her flesh adhered to

---

[57] *Ibid.*, 18.889–900, pp. 55–56.

the bones of the Saviour'.[58] This is an obscure statement. But pseudo-Rabanus was drawing upon pseudo-Odo's sermon. 'And thus was it accomplished', declared Odo, 'at the time of the Lord's Passion what had formerly been spoken by blessed Job: "The flesh being consumed, my bone has cleaved to my skin, and nothing but my lips are left about my teeth [Job 19.20]". For just as, when his flesh was consumed, the skin cleaved to the bone, holy Mary Magdalene persevered with the Lord after the disciples had fled'.[59] This, in turn, was an idea that pseudo-Odo had picked up from Gregory the Great who applied it to *all* the women who stuck with Jesus when the disciples fled in fear.

Mary was also present when Jesus was led before Pontius Pilate and then Herod Antipas. She saw him flogged, dressed in purple, crowned with thorns, ironically worshipped, and spat upon. Along with Jesus's mother, his mother's sisters, and other women, she followed him through Jerusalem as he carried his cross. She was present at his crucifixion. 'Christ was raised on the cross', we read, 'Mary wailed and choked on her tears. Christ was pierced with nails on the cross; the soul of Mary was pierced with sharp grief .... In all this, what sorrow was in the soul of Mary, what sobbing, what sighing, what grief, when the lover saw her beloved hung among thieves'.[60]

As for Mary's role in the resurrection, it all seems to have got too complicated for pseudo-Rabanus.

---

[58] *Ibid.*, 20.1031–2, p. 60.   [59] PL 133, col. 718B.

[60] Mycoff (trans.), *The Life of Saint Mary Magdalene and of Her Sister Saint Martha* 21.1089–98, p. 62.

Recognizing the variations in the Gospels and the disparities among the commentators in accounting for them, he presented the resurrection accounts Gospel-by-Gospel. Of her role as the first witness of the risen Christ, we read,

Mary, seeing herself elevated by the Son of God, her Lord and her Saviour, to such a high position of honour and grace; seeing herself alone favoured with the first and the most privileged of his appearances, as being among all women (except for the Virgin Mother of God) the most tenderly loved, the most cherished, and the dearest, could not do otherwise than exercise the apostolate with which she had been honored.[61]

She immediately went and told the apostles of the resurrected Christ and his forthcoming ascension.

Pseudo-Rabanus also picked up on the long tradition of Mary Magdalene as the second Eve. Just as Eve had given her husband a poisoned draft to drink, Mary presented the apostles with the chalice of eternal life. Unlike Eve who was the first to bring death, Mary was the first to see victory over death in a garden devoted to burial. As Eve had persuaded her husband with the serpent's promise of the knowledge of good and evil, so Mary announced to the apostles the good news of the resurrection and prophesied the ascension: 'She came to the sepulchre', we read, 'laden with perfumes and aromatic herbs to embalm a dead man; but, finding him alive, she received a very different office from that which she had thought to discharge – messenger of the living Saviour, sent to bear the true balm of life to the apostles'.[62] Her apostolic life had begun.

---

[61] *Ibid.*, 27.1468–75.   [62] *Ibid.*, 27.1503–08, p. 74.

A Vita Apostolica

Once the exemplar of the eremitic life, then the model for the contemplative one, Mary Magdalene now becomes the preacher of the Gospel of the resurrected Jesus. Thus, in the early eleventh century, a new life of Mary Magdalene, now known as the *Vita apostolica Mariae Magdalenae*, began to circulate in Europe. This work described the evangelization and conversion of France by Mary Magdalene and her companions. It provided a key source for the *vita apostolica* of Mary Magdalene that pseudo-Rabanus created in the second part of his *The Life of Saint Mary Magdalene and of Her Sister Saint Martha*. It was fitting, he there declared, 'that just as she had been chosen to be the apostle of Christ's resurrection and the prophet of his ascension, so also she became an evangelist for believers throughout the world'.[63] Was this an endorsement of the active over the contemplative life? Partly. What is clear is that pseudo-Rabanus was writing for a monastic audience seeking to find the right balance between the active and contemplative lives.

As we will see, it was something of a narrative balancing act. Mary Magdalene maintained a contemplative life but turned it towards an active life of ministry. In comparison, her sister Martha continued her life of active service. But it was one that now arose out of her newfound commitment to contemplative asceticism. In both cases, the contemplative life was the better part. But pseudo-Rabanus was clearly arguing for the position that the contemplative life alone was not sufficient. Rather, he

---

[63] *Ibid.*, 38.2262–2265, p. 96.

endorsed, as a religious ideal, the active life in service of others that flowed from the contemplative life.

In effect, pseudo-Rabanus's *The Life of Saint Mary Magdalene and of Her Sister Saint Martha* was endorsing a third way. This was the *vita mixta* (the 'mixed life'), the synthesis of both the contemplative and the active life that was central to both Franciscan and Dominican spirituality and was grounded in the lives of their respective founders, Francis (c. 1181–1226) and Dominic (1170–1221). Thus, for example, as the Franciscan Bernardino of Siena (d. 1444) put it, 'Having first the knowledge of nature through the active life, comes the knowledge of glory through the contemplative life; from these two lives comes a third, namely the mixed life which comprises both God and man'.[64] The Dominican preacher Giovanni da San Gimignano saw Mary Magdalene as the ideal exemplar of this mixed life. 'There is also a third life', he declared,

composed from each one. And this is considered the best because it embraces each of them . . . and the Magdalen selected the best life for herself because sometimes, as it were, she was active and she ministered to him [Christ], washing his feet, both ministering to him on the journey and pouring out her precious oils on him . . . . She was also a contemplative, as it were, when she was meditating, listening to his words. This was an admirable life made best through the exercise of both lives.[65]

For pseudo-Rabanus, nevertheless, the *vita apostolica* was incompatible with the *vita eremitica*. Pseudo-Rabanus

---

[64] Quoted by Jansen, *The Making of the Magdalene*, p. 51.
[65] Quoted by *ibid.*, p. 52.

knew the latter in detail and rejected it completely. Although willing to admit that Mary Magdalene conversed with angels, he was having nothing of them literally carrying her into heaven on a daily basis and feeding her with heavenly food. He rejected the authority of Josephus for the eremitic story, knew that it was influenced by that of Mary of Egypt, and saw it as nothing more than a pious invention. It was false and a fabrication of storytellers, he wrote, 'that after the ascension of the Saviour, she immediately fled to the Arabian desert; that she remained there without any clothing in a cave; and that she saw no man afterwards until she was visited by I know not what priest, from whom she begged a garment, and other such stuff'.[66]

According to pseudo-Rabanus, Mary's life immediately after the ascension of Christ was much more domestic than hermitic. Her contemplative and eroticized spiritual life continued. 'In her meditation', declared pseudo-Rabanus, 'she burned with the fire of love, the inextinguishable fire in which she was daily consumed in the holocaust of insatiable desire for her Redeemer'.[67] But she lived quietly in Jerusalem with Martha, Mary the mother of Jesus, and other female followers of Jesus.

Thirteen years later, Mary the mother of Jesus was assumed into heaven, the church in Jerusalem was persecuted by Herod, and the faithful that remained were dispersed to preach the Gospel to the gentiles. Mary, Martha, and Lazarus, along with a large number of others, embarked with Maximinus, one of the seventy-two

---

[66] Mycoff (trans.), *The Life of Saint Mary Magdalene*, 39.2315–2321, p. 98.
[67] *Ibid.*, 34.1991–1994, p. 88.

disciples appointed by Jesus before his death (Luke 10.1–20).[68] Landing at Vienne, Mary established herself at Aix with Maximinus. From time to time, we read, Mary left the joys of contemplation and preached to the unbelievers or confirmed believers in their faith. She performed miracles to establish the truth of her words and to provoke faith in her listeners. She cared · little for food and clothing but the women who were with her provided for her needs. Although she remained on earth in the flesh, 'she was nonetheless permitted to walk in spirit amid the delights of Paradise, on whose ineffable sweetness she feasted as much as possible for a mortal'.[69] Mary Magdalene died on 22 July after having a vision of Christ summoning her to heaven: 'Come my beloved, and I shall place you on my throne, for the king desires your beauty, more lovely than any of the sons of men'.[70]

In the history of the story of Mary Magdalene, pseudo-Rabanus's was crucial. From this time, her life and the cult that developed around her within the Western church became inescapably connected to her life in France. But the story of Mary Magdalene in France was, effectively, that of Mary of Bethany. For it is she who travels there accompanied by her sister Martha and her brother Lazarus.

---

[68] Neither Maximinus nor anyone else was named in the Gospel of Luke as one of the seventy-two or seventy that were sent out. Pseudo-Rabanus is presumably following Jerome's translation which has 'seventy two'. He is not named in a very early list of the seventy in pseudo-Hippolytus' *On the Seventy Apostles of Christ*. See *ANF* 5.254–256.

[69] Mycoff (trans.), *The Life of Saint Mary Magdalene*, 45.2594–97, p. 107.

[70] *Ibid.*, 45.2610–2613, p. 107.

As its title showed, the work attributed to Rabanus was also a life of Martha. For the practical Martha, preaching and working miracles was, perhaps not surprisingly, her forté. She healed lepers, cured paralytics, revived the dead, and bestowed her aid on the blind, the deaf, the lame, the mute, the invalid, and the sick. She drove a dragon out of the wilderness of Tarascon, along with all the other reptiles (see Plate 6). This enabled her to embark on a contemplative life for seven years, eating only roots, bitter herbs, apples, and other fruit once a day. Her clothing was rough, made of sackcloth. She wore a girdle of horsehair, full of knots, 'until her flesh became putrid and worm-infested'.[71] In spite of that, she still went into the cities and towns, preaching to the people and then returning to her solitude. She too died, eight days after Mary, following a vision of Christ summoning her to heaven: 'Come then, my hostess, come out of your exile. Come and you shall receive your crown'.[72]

A Wedding in Cana

In the Gospel of John, we read that Jesus, his mother, and his disciples were invited to a wedding in Cana of Galilee. During the course of the party, the wine ran out. Jesus's mother reported this to Jesus who rather haughtily replied, 'Woman, what concern is that to you and to me. My hour is not yet come' (John 2.4). His mother then told the servants to do whatever Jesus said. Jesus ordered the servants to fill stone jars with water and to take some to the chief waiter. After tasting it, without knowing where it

---

[71] *Ibid.*, 41.2427–2428, p. 101.   [72] *Ibid.*, 47.2696–2697, p. 110.

had come from, he told the bridegroom that everyone keeps the inferior wine until last, 'but you have kept the good wine until now' (John 2.10). This was, according to the Gospel of John, the first of the miracles of Jesus (see Plate 7).

But who were the bride and groom? The Gospel is silent. It can be inferred that, since Jesus and his mother were there, that they were close friends of Jesus's family. As early as the fourth century, we get a hint of a tradition that the husband-to-be was John, the author of the eponymous Gospel, the apostle of Jesus, and the one to whom Jesus committed the care of his mother at his crucifixion (John 19.27). Tantalizingly, there is the suggestion that he left his bride 'at the altar' before the marriage, followed Jesus, and remained a life-long virgin. Thus, for example, he was named as the groom in the so-called fourth-century *Monarchian Prologue* to the Gospel of John. 'This is John the evangelist', we read, 'one from the twelve disciples of God, who was elected by God to be a virgin, whom God called away from marriage though he was wishing to marry, for whom double testimony of his virginity is given in the gospel both in that he was said to be beloved by God above others and in that God, going to the cross, commended his own mother to him, so that a virgin might serve a virgin'.[73] Similarly, the unknown author of the preface to a collection of Augustine's homilies on the Gospel of John declared that the author of the Gospel, 'is, indeed, the John whom the

---

[73] *The Latin Prologues: The Anti-Marcionite and Monarchian Prologues to the Canonical Gospels*. Available at www.textexcavation.com/latinprologues .html.

Lord called away from the hazardous storm of marriage and to whom, a virgin, he entrusted his virgin mother'.[74]

The suggestion that John remained a lifelong virgin was to provide something of an exegetical problem for the church. On the one hand, Christ's presence at the wedding in Cana provided evidence that he was not opposed to marriage. On the other hand, he called the bridegroom away before the ceremony to embrace a life of chastity. However that may be, this identification of John as the groom became something of a commonplace within Europe. Thus, for example, the Benedictine grammarian Ælfric of Eynsham (c. 995–c. 1010) declared in a homily on the wedding in Cana, that John was so impressed by the miracle of turning water into wine 'that he forthwith left his bride in maidenhood, and ever afterwards followed the Lord, and was by him inwardly beloved, because he had withdrawn himself from fleshly lusts'.[75] Even Thomas Aquinas (c. 1225–1274) noticed in passing, in a discussion on the desirability of perpetual chastity, that John's wedding was disrupted by Jesus.[76]

In the fourteenth-century *The Life of Christ*, traditionally ascribed to Bonaventure (c. 1217–1274), the author

---

[74] John W. Rettig (trans.), *St. Augustine: Tractates on the Gospel of John 1–10* (Washington, DC: The Catholic University of America Press, 1988), p. 38. For his part, Augustine suggested that John never married and lived in perfect chastity from early boyhood.

[75] Benjamin Thorpe (trans.), 'The Assumption of Saint John the Apostle', *The Homilies of the Anglo-Saxon Church: The First Part Containing the Sermones Catholici, or Homilies of Ælfric* (London: The Ælfric Society, 1844), p. 59.

[76] *Summa Theologiae*, 2a, 2ae, q. 186, art. 4, ad. 1. For a more extended discussion by Aquinas, see P. Raphaelis Cai O. P., *Thomas Aquinas: Super Evangelium S. Ioannis Lectura* (Rome: Marietti, 1952), pp. 4–5, n. 13.

admits that, although it is uncertain whose marriage it was, 'we may suppose, for meditation, that it was of S. John the Evangelist himself'.[77] Its meditative purpose was soon to become clear for, in the light of John's jilting of his bride, the reader was encouraged to contemplate the virtues of spiritual over physical marriage: 'When the feast was ended ... the Lord Jesus called John apart, and said to him, "Leave your wife, and follow Me, for I will lead you to higher nuptials". And John followed Him'.[78] Who the bride was and what her fate might have been were not mentioned.

It was different, however, with Honorius of Autun (early twelfth century). In a commentary on the feast in Cana, although the bride remained anonymous, he named the groom as John the disciple.[79] But elsewhere, in a sermon on Mary Magdalene, he named her as a woman who was given to a husband (*marito traditur*) in Magdala but fled from him into Jerusalem where she became a common prostitute. 'After she freely gave herself over to the brothel of disgrace, she was justly made a temple of demons, for at once seven demons entered into her and continually belaboured her with unclean desires'.[80] In not directly linking Jesus to the marriage of Mary, Honorius was taking Jesus off the hook as the cause of Mary's

---

[77] W. H. Hutchings (ed. and trans.), *The Life of Christ by S. Bonaventure* (London: Rivingtons, 1888), p. 92. The work has more recently been ascribed to the Franciscan John of Caulibus. See C. Mary Stallings-Taney, 'The Pseudo-Bonaventure "Meditaciones Vite Christi: Opus Integrum"', *Franciscan Studies* 55 (1998), pp. 253–280.

[78] *Ibid.*, p. 96.   [79] See PL 172, col. 834.

[80] PL 172, col. 979. I am grateful to David Foley for his translation of Honorius's sermon on Mary Magdalene.

decline into promiscuity. At the same time, however, he was able to fill in the gap in the Gospel narratives about Mary Magdalene. The narrative of the woman fleeing from a marriage provided a seemingly good explanation of how Mary became both a wanton woman and a demoniac. In fact, Honorius was again following in the footsteps of the composite Mary Magdalene of Gregory the Great. For the Mary Magdalene who had seven demons was the sister of Martha of Bethany and Lazarus. And it was her sister Martha who, Honorius informs us, led the possessed Mary to Jesus 'by whom the seven demons were immediately cast out'.[81]

For Honorius, again following Gregory the Great, she was also the 'sinful woman' of the Gospel of Luke. For Honorius went on to relate that it was Mary Magdalene who bathed the feet of Jesus with her tears and dried them with her hair. All those things

which she had once sensually produced in the service of the flesh she now penitently turns towards the service of the Lord; and since she was not formerly ashamed to be immersed before the sight of the angels like a swine in the slough of her uncleanness, now she does not fear to be abased before the men present at the banquet. And thus she discovered there the true fount of mercy, and thence withdrew being cleansed of every stain (see Plate 8).[82]

Later, now following pseudo-Odo, Honorius identified her also as the woman who anointed Jesus's head with oil. As a result, she became a follower of Jesus who supported him financially although, against the

---

[81] PL 172, col. 979.   [82] PL 172, col. 980.

developing tradition of her wealth, Honorius informs us that she was only a person of modest means.

In sum, Honorius endorsed the tradition of Mary Magdalene as Mary of Bethany and as the sinful woman of the Gospel of Luke created by Gregory the Great. He went along with pseudo-Odo's identification of her with the unknown woman who anointed Jesus's head with oil. To these, he added an account of the cause of her sinfulness, namely, that she was a woman who fled from a marriage into sexual promiscuity. As for her life after being the first witness to the resurrection and after seeing Christ ascend into heaven, Honorius gave a summarized version of the *vita eremitica*. For love of Jesus, he declared, she refused to look upon any man again and,

entering into a desert-place she dwelt in a cave for many years. And when a certain wandering priest happened upon her and inquired who she was, she responded that she was Mary the sinner and reported that he had been sent to bury her body. Having said these things, in triumph she obediently departed from this world, which she had long since abhorred, and offering up a hymn with the angels she entered unto the Lord, whom she loved greatly and who had forgiven her many things, and thence he granted her to gather lilies in his garden of sweet aromas together with the virgins in gleaming white.[83]

For Honorius's listeners then, she was the perfect exemplar of the repentant sinner. 'If hitherto, my dear friends,' he declared,

we have laboured in evils, at least today we may strive by the example of this woman to change the things of the past into

[83] PL 172, col. 981.

good works which are to come. For blessed are they whose iniquities are forgiven and whose sins are covered ... . Therefore, dearly beloved, by imitating blessed Mary Magdalene, let us cast off from ourselves the cruel yoke of servitude to the devil, and let us take up the sweet yoke of the Lord's true liberty; and let us render our service to Him, to serve Whom is to reign, with sanctity and justice, so that we might prevail to be granted that freedom which is the glory of the sons of God.[84]

It is unlikely that Honorius believed that the husband from whom Mary Magdalene fled was the beloved disciple John.[85] He failed to mention the name of John's wife in his account of the wedding in Cana, and the husband of Mary Magdalene from whom she fled remained anonymous. But the conclusion that it was John and Mary that were married at Cana was drawn sufficiently often for us to believe that the intended, if thwarted, marriage of John to Mary was something of a medieval commonplace. Thus, for example, the fourteenth century Franciscan author of *The Life of Mary Magdalen* constructed a highly elaborated and romanticized account of her life before Jesus exorcized her seven demons. It combined the tradition of John as the groom who left his bride at the altar with a Mary who turned to 'loose living' in despair at his behavior.

According to this *Vita*, and following pseudo-Rabanus, Mary Magdalene was, with the exception of the mother of Jesus, the most beautiful woman in the world. Her father Siro, having done much for the emperors of Rome, was

---

[84] PL 172, col. 982.   [85] But cf. Haskins, *Mary Magdalen*, p. 159.

rewarded with one third of Jerusalem, along with two castles, Magdalo and Bethany. At his death, Mary came heir to the castle at Magdalo. The Church neither affirmed nor denied, the author of this Life declared, that she was the intended spouse of John the Evangelist. That said, he admits, 'it delights me much to think in my thoughts that this was so'.[86] For his part, although she was much wealthier than John, and he only the son of a humble fisherman, he was nonetheless of a family more noble than hers and, to boot, a youth of virtue, beautiful in person, and the son of the sister of the mother of Jesus. In short, she was 'marrying up'. Those were the good old days; by contrast, he declared, 'in these days it would not be thus, since those who are rich are held great and noble, and those who labour to live are despised and abased, although they be of gentle blood'.[87] Perhaps, it was the genteel poverty of the author's own family that led him to embrace the life of a Franciscan friar.

Be that as it may, the wedding of John and Mary, we are then told, was the one in Cana at which Jesus turned the water into wine. After the feast, Jesus took John away with him, 'wishing that he should remain pure'.[88] When Mary found that John had disappeared, not surprisingly, 'her heart was troubled with great grief, although she did not yet lose the hope that he might return'.[89] As it turned out, this was a forlorn hope. She failed 'to understand that John had another love more comely, more beautiful,

---

[86] Valentina Hawtrey (trans.), *The Life of Saint Mary Magdalen Translated from the Italian of an Unknown Fourteenth Century Writer* (London: John Lane, The Bodley Head), p. 2.
[87] *Ibid.*, p. 3.   [88] *Ibid.*, p. 4.   [89] *Ibid.*

and of high price, that is, the charity of God, so that he had cast her out of his mind, the love of her and of any other earthly thing'.[90] This was a medieval endorsement of the virtue of the celibate over the married life which those of us of a more secular bent find harsh and cruel. Even more so, when we read that Mary turned to a sinful life so as not to die of grief. She did it to dishonour him, although she did more dishonour to herself. Seeing her heart thus prepared, devils entered into her, 'not one but seven, with seven mortal sins'.[91] She became a woman of ill repute.

Honorius, we recall, simply reported that it was Martha, Mary's sister, who had taken Mary to see Jesus. How Mary came to see Jesus was now told at length in this Life. Martha suffered from a long-term illness. She grieved so deeply for her sister Mary, we read, that it made her illness worse. Fortunately, her handmaiden Martilla had heard of Jesus. She went to hear his teaching and to see his miracles and told Martha of them. Martha determined that she too would go to Jesus, convinced that if she could but see him or touch him, she would be healed. When she heard that Jesus was nearby, she headed out with a number of friends to see him.

In the Gospels of Mark, Matthew, and Luke, there is the story of an anonymous woman who had been suffering from haemorrhages for a dozen years.[92] Having heard about Jesus, she joined the large crowd around him. She came up behind him in the crowd and touched his cloak for she believed that, if she but touched

---

[90] *Ibid.*, p. 5.   [91] *Ibid.*, p. 6.
[92] Mark 5.25–34, Matthew 9.20–22, Luke 8.43–48.

his clothes, she would be healed. Immediately, after touching him, she felt in her body that she was healed. When Jesus asked who in the crowd around him had touched him, she confessed that it was she. Jesus said to her, 'Daughter, your faith has made you well; go in peace and be healed of your disease' (Mark 5.34).

It was Ambrose of Milan in the fourth century who first identified Martha with the woman who had the issue of blood. He has Jesus healing Martha at home at the same time that he exorcized her sister Mary of her demons.[93] It was this early identification of Martha with the bleeding woman that facilitated the narrative of *The Life of Mary Magdalen*, although the healing took place, not in the home of Mary and Martha as Ambrose had it but, following the Gospel story, in the middle of a large, jostling crowd. It was Martha, we read, who 'knelt with great reverence in her heart, and touched the hem of His garment and kissed it, and pressed it against her face with all the desire of her heart'.[94] And it was Martha to whom Jesus said, 'Go in peace'. Martha, like the anonymous woman in the Gospels, returned home healed of her illness.

Mary was so shocked to see her sister in such good health that she became ashamed of her sinful life. The devils within her were equally surprised: 'they lost their strength, and scarcely could hinder her more, though ... they did not yet depart out of her'.[95] In fact, the demons

---

[93] See PL 17, col. 697. On the woman who bled, see Barbara Baert, ''Who touched me and my clothes?' The Healing of the Woman with the Haemorrhage (Mark 5: 24b–34parr) in Early Mediaeval Visual Culture', in *Annual of the Antwerp Royal Museum*, 2009, pp. 9–51.

[94] Hawtrey (trans.), *The Life of Saint Mary Magdalen*, p. 20.

[95] *Ibid.*, p. 24.

conspired to persuade Mary that Jesus was one of theirs: 'let us praise Jesus for His great power, His virtue, and His rare excellence, so that she may not dare even think of desiring to go to him; and if we can do this, she will despair, and then maybe it will be permitted to us to kill her; or if not, we will stimulate her to kill herself, and we cannot believe that thus she would be received of God'.[96]

When the devils realized that the now contrite Mary was determined to go to Jesus, they tried to persuade her that her sinfulness was too great for her to approach a man renowned for his purity. She was comforted, however, by a divine light in her room that told her that the greater the illness, the more the gentle physician strives to heal. Mary remained determined to place her faith in Jesus and to go to him. As day broke, she went out to look for Jesus. She found him dining, bathed his feet with her tears, and dried them with her hair. When Jesus told her that her sins were forgiven, 'then all the devils were cast out from her, and all the guilt of sin taken from her, and she was filled with the love of charity, and with greater gladness than I can tell'.[97] She returned home where Martha and Lazarus waited for her with great gladness.

Unable to take vengeance on her soul, Mary Magdalene now determined to punish her body. Mary now provided a model for the Franciscan punishment of the body for the love of God. As Francis of Assisi's early biographer had said of him, 'Christ's strenuous knight never spared his body, but exposed it as something alien

---

[96] *Ibid.*, p. 28.   [97] *Ibid.*, p. 42.

to himself, to all ill-treatment both in deed and word'.[98] In this vein, Mary scratched her face until the blood came. She tore out her hair and struck her eyes and her face with her fists. Taking a stone, she struck herself on the breast, feet, legs, and arms until the blood came. Removing her clothing, she whipped herself with her girdle from head to foot until the blood flowed. She resolved that she would discipline her body until the blood flowed every night, as much as she could bear. She determined to take only bread and water all her life and to clothe herself in the roughest sackcloth. 'Oh sorrowful and guilty sinner', she cried, 'who can make this vengeance great enough? Can it ever be sufficient? No. never! Let heaven and earth, and fire and water, and all the creatures combine to chastise me, and let my Lord preserve me, that I do not therefore die, but suffer a thousand deaths every hour! And even if such punishment endured to the end of the world, still it would not be enough'.[99] All in all, to us, if not to its original readers, a somewhat unedifying account of the victories of the spirit over the flesh, the contemplative over the active life, and the celibate over the married life. In short, it was an endorsement of the virtues of absolute renunciation of the world and of desire for any part of it.

A *Vita Apostolico-Eremetica*

Jacobus de Voragine, a Dominican like Thomas Aquinas and his exact contemporary, was having none of this. He

[98] A. G. Ferrers Howell (trans.), *The Lives of S. Francis of Assisi by Brother Thomas of Celano* (London: Methuen & Co., 1855), p. 164.

[99] Hawtrey (trans.), *The Life of Saint Mary Magdalen*, p. 50.

rejected the suggestion that Mary and John were espoused and that she, 'indignant at having been deprived of her spouse, gave herself up to every sort of voluptuousness'.[100] 'These tales', he declared, 'are to be considered false and frivolous'.[101] Jacobus was not rejecting the tradition that John was the groom at the wedding in Cana, but rather that Mary was the jilted bride who went on to a life of sexual promiscuity. And he cited a Brother Albert whose introduction to the Gospel of John 'says firmly that the lady from whose nuptials the same John was called away persevered in virginity, was seen later in the company of the Blessed Virgin Mary, mother of Christ, and came at last to a holy end'. He seems to have no knowledge or perhaps no interest in the tradition that has Mary Magdalene also keeping company with the mother of Jesus between the ascension of Christ and the forced departure of Mary Magdalene from Jerusalem, although he did write of a fourteen-year gap between these two events. Perhaps he thought it stretching credulity too far to have created a narrative in which both the jilted bride of John and Mary Magdalene kept company with the mother of Jesus.

The most likely person for the 'Brother Albert' mentioned by Jacobus is an older contemporary of his, namely, the Dominican scholar Albert the Great (c. 1200–1280). In the Prologue to his commentary on John, Albert did more or less endorse the tradition that it was John who was called away from his marriage in

---

[100] William Granger Ryan (trans.), *The Golden Legend: Readings from the Saints* (Princeton, NJ: Princeton University Press, 2012), p. 382.

[101] *Ibid.*, p. 382.

Cana of Galilee.[102] But there was no mention there of his deserted wife-to-be. So Jacobus's memory was leading him astray there. Nevertheless, in that section of Albert's commentary dealing with the wedding in Cana in Galilee, we do find the probable source of Jacobus's statement. There, Albert gave what he called the more popular opinion on who the bridegroom was, namely, 'that John himself was the bridegroom, and that afterwards the bride, among the virgins who were consecrated to God, persevered [i.e., in the virginal state] along with the mother of Jesus'.[103] Albert the Great, and Jacobus too for that matter, perhaps thought it a bad look to have Jesus's action in calling John away from his wedding to be seen as the cause of Mary's fall into disrepute.

From the time of the publication of Jacobus's *The Golden Legend* in the 1260s, the Life of Mary Magdalene contained within it was to become the gold standard for her life story. This was the result of the enormous success of *The Golden Legend*. It was a work 'that touched a contemporary nerve', as Eamon Duffy puts it, one that 'was seen and seized on for three centuries as an indispensable pastoral resource, as well as a source of entertainment and of inspiration and source material for poets, dramatists, and painters'.[104] It has survived in almost a thousand manuscript copies of the Latin text and, all or in part, in another five hundred manuscripts in European languages. The advent of print saw it become a medieval

---

[102] Auguste Borgnet (ed.), *Opera Omnia* (Paris: Vivè, 1890–99), vol. 24, p. 13.

[103] *Ibid.*, vol. 24, p. 99.

[104] Eamon Duffy, 'Introduction to the 2012 Edition', in Ryan (trans.), *The Golden Legend*, pp. xi–xii.

best seller. Between 1470 and 1500, with at least eighty-seven Latin editions and sixty-nine in other languages, it outsold the Bible.[105] Readers of English were most familiar with it in the editions from 1483–1527 of William Caxton (c. 1422–1491).

The Golden Legend, or *Legenda Sanctorum* (*Legends of the Saints*) as it was originally called, is a collection of lives of the saints, along with liturgical and doctrinal instruction, arranged more or less into the divisions of the liturgical year.[106] Among the lives of the major figures of the New Testament was that of Mary Magdalene, combining both a *vita apostolica* and a *vita eremetica*. Jacobus constructed his account of Mary Magdalene from an array of pre-existing sources. These enabled Jacobus to arrange the story of Mary Magdalene in five parts: (1) her pre-ascension life; (2) her voyage to Marseilles; (3) the story of the governor of Marseilles; (4) the account of her thirty years of solitude, death, and burial; and (5) the miracles after her death along with the translation of her relics.[107]

The story of Mary's pre-ascension life is, for us, now pretty familiar territory. She was a woman of great wealth, renowned for her beauty and riches, and equally famous 'for the way she gave her body to pleasure'.[108] Following the tradition of Gregory the Great, Jacobus identified

---

[105] See *ibid.*, p. xx.

[106] "Legend' then meant 'a text to be read aloud', rather than its modern meaning of 'a fictional story'.

[107] For a discussion of the complex possible sources of Jacobus's life of Mary, see David A. Mycoff, *A Critical Edition of the Legend of Mary Magdalena from Caxton's* Golden Legende *of 1483* (Salzburg: Institut für Anglistik und Amerikanistik, Universität Salzburg, 1985), pp. 74–88.

[108] Ryan (trans.), *The Golden Legend*, p. 375.

Mary Magdalene with both the sinful woman of Luke and Mary of Bethany. It was she who anointed Jesus's feet with a precious 'suntan lotion' – 'because of the extreme heat of the sun the people of that region bathed and anointed themselves regularly'.[109] It was she whom Martha implied was lazy and whose brother, Lazarus, Jesus raised from the dead (see Plate 9). Like pseudo-Odo, Jacobus also saw her as the unknown woman who anointed Jesus's head with oil. He followed Ambrose in conflating Martha with the woman with the issue of blood. And he followed pseudo-Rabanus in naming Martha's maidservant Martilla (or Marcella).[110]

It was Mary's post-ascension life, however, in which Jacobus showed more interest. He passed over the fourteen years of her life after the ascension of Christ. He picked up the story when, as a result of persecution by unbelievers, Mary was herded onto a ship without pilot or rudder with Maximin, Martha, and Lazarus, her sister's maid Martilla, and Cedonius (also known as Celidonius and Sidonius), whom, when a child, Jesus had cured of the blindness with which he had been born (see Plate 10).[111] The intention was that they would all be drowned. But they eventually landed in Marseilles. There Mary preached to the people who had come to a pagan shrine to sacrifice to the idols. Her listeners admired her beauty and eloquence and 'no wonder, that the mouth which had pressed such pious and beautiful kisses on the Savior's feet

---

[109] *Ibid.*, p. 376.
[110] Mycoff (trans.), *The Life of Saint Mary Magdalene*, 35.2124, p. 92. 45.2610–2613, p. 107.
[111] See John 9.1–38.

should breathe forth the perfume of the word of God more profusely than others could' (see Plate 11).[112]

As we know, Mary Magdalene, unlike the Virgin Mary, was neither a virgin nor a mother. So it is ironic that, as a consequence of the story of the governor of Marseilles, Mary Magdalene became, like the mother of Jesus, a maternal saint. Taking up around a third of Jacobus's Life, this story began with the visit of the governor and his wife to the pagan shrine to pray for a child. Mary dissuaded them from sacrificing. She then appeared in two visions to the governor's wife on two consecutive nights to berate her for letting Christians die of hunger and cold. In a further vision, she appeared to both of them and chastised the governor for being 'sated with a bellyful of all sorts of food while you let the saints of God perish from hunger and thirst'.[113] The governor and his wife, fearful of the wrath of Mary's God, then provided shelter and food to the Christians.

Subsequently, the governor and his wife decided they would convert to Christianity were Mary able to obtain a son for them. Following Mary's prayers to Christ, the woman conceived. Mary told the governor that her faith was strengthened by the miracles and teaching of Peter in Rome. This was a reminder to readers that the locus of Christian power and authority was male and in Rome. In a much later and much different context, the battle between Mary and Peter was continuing. For the governor then wished to visit Peter in Rome to find out whether what Mary preached was true. This was also a reminder to readers of the virtues of pilgrimage. It was, after all, the

---

[112] Ryan (trans.), *The Golden Legend*, p. 377.   [113] *Ibid.*

great age of pilgrimage and Rome was a favourite destination.[114] Mary 'put the sign of the cross on their shoulders against the Enemy's interference on their journey'.[115] From this point on, Jacobus called the governor 'Peregrinus' ('Pilgrim').

Pilgrim and his wife set out for Rome by ship but, in transit, were caught in a storm. Pilgrim's wife went into labour. Fortunately, the child was delivered safely, an 'ethereal' Mary doing a 'midwife's service'. Unfortunately, the woman died as the boy was born.[116] The sailors wished to throw the woman and the child overboard, but the governor eventually persuaded them to leave the dead mother and the baby on a nearby shore. There he left the body of his wife, lying on his cloak with the baby between her breasts. Although he blamed Mary Magdalene for their plight, he nonetheless prayed to her, 'If it be in your power, be mindful of the mother's soul, and by your prayer take pity on the child and spare its life'.[117]

The governor continued his pilgrimage to Rome. There he spent two years with Peter, being instructed in the faith. On the journey home, by the will of God, the ship came close to the coast where he had left his son and he persuaded the crew to put him ashore. As his skiff came close to the beach, he was astounded to see his son alive and playing there. Having never seen a man before, the child was terrified and ran to his dead mother's bosom, hiding under the cloak that Pilgrim had left for her. Pilgrim followed and found the child, feeding at his dead

---

[114] See Jonathan Sumption, *Pilgrimage: An Image of Medieval Religion* (London: Faber & Faber, 1975), ch. 13.
[115] Ryan (trans.), *The Golden Legend*, p. 378.   [116] *Ibid.*, p. 379.
[117] *Ibid.*, p. 378.

mother's breast. Lifting the boy up, he cried to Mary Magdalene, 'O Mary Magdalene, how happy I would be, how well everything would have turned out for me, if my wife were alive and able to return home with me! Indeed I know, I know and believe beyond a doubt, that having given us this child and kept him alive for two years on this rock, you could now, by your prayers, restore his mother to life and health'.[118] Immediately, his wife came back to life (see Plate 12). She told her husband that she had actually been on pilgrimage with him in spirit all the time, an 'ethereal' Mary Magdalene having been her guide and companion. Having returned to Marseilles, they found Mary and told her all that had happened. They were baptised by Maximin, destroyed the temples of all the idols in the city of Marseilles, and built churches to Christ. Maximin was made bishop of Aix.

Thanks to Mary Magdalene, the child was conceived, delivered safely, nurtured at his dead mother's breast for two years, and looked after until the governor returned. It was not the only incident of Mary's concern for expectant mothers. For Jacobus also told the story of a pregnant woman on a sinking ship who, in danger of drowning, called upon (a now deceased) Mary to save her. She vowed that, were she to escape drowning and bear a son, she would give him up to the saint's monastery. A woman immediately appeared to her, held her up by the chin and, while the rest drowned, brought her unharmed to land.[119] In due course, the woman bore a son and fulfilled her vow to Mary Magdalene. Mary had become the saint of childbirth.

[118] *Ibid.*, p. 379.   [119] See *ibid.*, p. 382.

That Mary Magdalene could become a maternal figure is to be explained, at least in part, by the medieval belief that promiscuity created sterility while virginity produced fertility. The chaste were sexually powerful. Mary was no virgin in body, but her post-conversion chastity meant she was a virgin in spirit. According to the Franciscan François de Meyronnes (1285–1327), for example, Mary received the quadruple crown, the third of which was the floral one 'which is given to virgins, not because she was a virgin: but after her conversion she maintained the highest purity of body and mind'.[120] Like many virgin saints, her virginity was heroic, albeit rather late in the day. It was this potent spiritual fecundity that made her the patron (or perhaps matron) saint of gardeners and winemakers.[121] For reasons that are not always clear, she was also to become the patron saint of pharmacists, glove makers, perfume manufacturers, podiatrists, hairdressers, comb makers, foundrymen, sailors, barrel makers, and weavers. Mary, as we would say, was a celebrity, and she had a large fan base.

It is after the story of the governor of Marseilles that Jacobus inserted his *vita eremitica*, its only significantly different feature to those we looked at earlier being that of her death in Aix and not somewhere in the Holy Land. As we will see later, this matters. Be that as it will be, Mary, we read, wishing to devote herself to heavenly contemplation, retired to an empty wilderness, there to

---

[120] Quoted by Jansen, *The Making of the Magdalen*, p. 242.
[121] See Marjorie J. Malvern, *Venus in Sackcloth: The Magdalen's Origins and Metamorphoses* (Carbondale: Southern Illinois University Press, 1975), p. 76.

remain for thirty years, eating only of 'the good things of heaven'.[122] Seven times every day, she was carried aloft by angels where she heard the chants of the heavenly host (see Plate 13). Satisfied with this supernatural food, she required no material nourishment. One day, a priest who lived nearby saw how the angels descended to Mary and lifted her into the upper air and returned her to earth an hour later. Eventually, Mary revealed herself to him as Mary Magdalene.

She asked him to go to Bishop Maximin and tell him that, on Easter Day in one year's time, the bishop was to go to his church where he would find Mary waited upon by angels. On that day, Maximin saw her in the church, raised a metre above the floor, attended by angels, and with her hands raised in prayer to God. So radiant was her face, due to her daily vision of the angels, that 'one would more easily look straight into the sun than gaze upon her face'.[123] After she received the sacraments from Maximin, she laid down full length before the altar and her soul migrated to God. A powerful odor of sweetness pervaded the church for seven days afterwards. This was the odor of sanctity, olfactory proof of exemplary holiness, and a sign that God had placed the saintly body beyond the putrid decay of death. It signified the fragrance of salvation in heaven compared to the sulphurous aromas of damnation in hell. Her body was buried there in Aix.

Jacobus's Life of Mary Magdalene concluded with a brief account of the translation of her remains from Aix to Vézelay, along with several stories of miracles that occurred through her intervention with God – of a knight

[122] Ryan (trans.), *The Golden Legend*, p. 380.   [123] *Ibid.*, p. 381.

who briefly rose from the dead in order to confess his sins, of the pregnant woman whom Mary saved from drowning, of a man who regained his sight, of another whose sins were erased from the paper upon which he had written them, and of still another who, having committed extortion, was freed from his chains. The final miracle reported by Jacobus was that of a clerk from Flanders who had committed every conceivable sin and yet was devoted to Mary Magdalene. Once on a visit to her tomb, she appeared to him 'as a lovely sad-eyed woman supported by two angels'.[124] Mary told him that she would never leave him until he was reconciled with God. He soon felt so great an inpouring of divine grace that he renounced the world and entered the religious life. At his death, we read, 'Mary Magdalene was seen standing with angels beside the bier, and she carried his soul, like a pure-white dove, with songs of praise into heaven'.[125] This was a fitting end to Jacobus's Life of Mary Magdalene. The ascent to heaven of the clerk's soul carried by Mary was an end of life to which all her devotees aspired.

Alongside the story in *The Golden Legend* but never as influential, there is a number of other versions that have Mary and her companions arriving at a town called Saintes Maries de la Mer in southeastern France. According to one version of these stories of the seaborne Marys, Mary Magdalene, Mary of Salome (the mother of James and John), and Mary of James (the mother of James the younger) set sail from the Holy Land. They took with them the bones of the Holy Innocents and the head of James the younger, all of whom had been killed by King Herod. They landed at the

[124] *Ibid.*, p. 383.   [125] *Ibid.*

place where a church now stands dedicated to them in the town named after them. Another version aligned the story of the seaborne Marys with the Provencal story adding in Martha and Lazarus, while yet other versions included Sarah the Egyptian, Maximin, Sidonius, Marcella, and Joseph of Arimathea.[126] Both Mary of James and Mary of Salome stayed by the sea where their remains were unearthed in the fifteenth century, while Mary Magdalene moved inland.[127]

By the end of the thirteenth century, Western Christianity had created an array of Marys. Her life before the ascension of Christ had been much embellished and elaborated into a coherent biography. She was not only the sinful woman of the Gospel of Luke and Mary of Bethany, but she was also the unknown woman who anointed Jesus's head with oil. She was the exemplar of the penitent person and the repentant woman. She had become a model for the contemplative life and an exemplary missionary saint who converted France. She was a patron saint of fertility and childbirth and a miracle worker. Among the saints in heaven, she was available to intercede to God on behalf of those in need in a variety of circumstances. Yet, she remained present on earth in her bodily remains and in the development of the cult of Mary Magdalene around them. The battle over her relics could begin.

---

[126] See David A. Mycoff, *A Critical Edition of the Legend of Mary Magdalena from Caxton's* Golden Legende *of 1483* (Salzburg: Institut für Anglistik und Amerikanistik, Universität Salzburg, 1985), pp. 8, 49.

[127] For a discussion on the complexity of identifying (aside from Mary Magdalene) the other two Marys with the biblical Marys, see Warner *Alone of All Her Sex*, pp. 344–345. See also pp. 228–229.

3

The 'Afterlives' of Mary Magdalene

~

Lay not up for yourselves treasures upon earth, where moth and dust
doth corrupt, and where thieves break through and steal.

Matthew 6.19 (KJV)

Remains to Be Seen

Around the year 326, the dowager Empress Helena, the
aging mother of the Emperor Constantine (c. 246–c. 330)
and an avid Christian, visited Jerusalem. By the end of the
fourth century, her visit there had been elaborated into
her search, with the help of Macarius the bishop of
Jerusalem, for the cross of Christ and the nails with which
he had been crucified, buried deep beneath the rubble of
Golgotha. Thus, in the *Church History* of Rufinus of
Aquileia (c. 344–411), we read that, upon her arrival in
Jerusalem, Helena made inquiries among the local inhabitants about the place where Christ had been crucified.
Hastening to the place to which eventually divine
guidance led her, she discovered three crosses, indistinguishable from one another.

Macarius had all three crosses brought before a high-
ranking woman with a serious illness and close to death.
He prayed to God to show clearly which one was the
True Cross. The first two crosses had no effect upon
her. But when he moved the third of the crosses towards
her the woman was healed and began to 'run about all

over the house magnifying the power of the Lord'.[1] Helena built a church on the site where she had found the Cross. She took part of it with her, leaving the remainder in a silver casing where it is still honoured, declared Rufinus, on the feast day 'with passionate veneration'.[2]

The cult of relics within Christianity began in the middle of the fourth century. It developed rapidly. By the beginning of the fifth century, it had spread throughout Christendom. It remained at the heart of Christian piety until, at the time of the Reformation in the sixteenth century, the rejection of relics became a distinguishing feature of the Reformed churches.[3] The surge in the popularity of relics from the middle of the fourth century was the consequence of the growing belief in their miraculous power. As Robert Wiśniewski notes, in the fourth century, the remains of the saints and martyrs 'became depositories of miraculous power able to chase away demons, heal the sick, reveal hidden things, protect communities, punish the impious, and remit sins'.[4] The miraculous capacity of the remains of the saints was the result of the divine power that they could manifest. Their

---

[1] Head (ed.), *Medieval Hagiography*, p. 129.
[2] *Ibid*. Rufinus is referring to the feast of the dedication of the Holy Sepulchre, 14 September, when the Cross was exhibited to the faithful.
[3] On the beginnings of the cult of relics within Christianity, see Robert Wiśniewski, *The Beginnings of the Cult of Relics* (Oxford: Oxford University Press, 2018). The cult of relics is sometimes thought to have begun with the martyrdom of Polycarp in the middle of the second century. Wiśniewski argues that the reverence paid to the bones of Polycarp reflects more a respect for the bodies of the dead than the beginnings of the cult of relics.
[4] *Ibid*., p. 12.

relics were *numinous* entities. In the words of the German religionist Rudolf Otto, they were encountered as a *mysterium tremendum et fascinans*. They were a 'wholly other' mystery revealed in the here and now. They were awe-inspiring, even terrifying, but they were also fascinating and captivating.[5] This belief in the miraculous powers of relics was enhanced by the stories told by pilgrims of the miracles that were brought about by them, the advertising of their acquisition in solemn ceremonies, and the construction of sites in which to house and display them. These sanctuaries, Wiśniewski writes, 'attracted pilgrims, almsgivers, beggars, and above all the sick and demoniacs, and provided the necessary conditions for the relics to display their power – a stage, actors, and audience'.[6] Supernatural power radiated out from the relics and the sanctuaries in which they were housed.

It was only in the late second century that the doctrine of the immortality of the soul was absorbed from the Greek Platonic tradition into Christianity. From that time on, Christianity held to a dualistic understanding of the human person as consisting of an immortal soul and a mortal body.[7] This enabled, or perhaps forced, Christianity into a new understanding of the afterlife. On the one hand, immediately after death, souls continued their conscious life. The souls of the saints were in heaven enjoying the fruits of eternal life. On the other hand, Christianity also held to another view of the

---

[5] See Rudolf Otto, *The Idea of the Holy* (Oxford: Oxford University Press, 1958).

[6] Wiśniewski, *The Beginnings of the Cult of Relics*, p. 47.

[7] See Philip C. Almond, *Afterlife: A History of Life after Death* (London: I. B. Tauris, 2016), ch. 3.

afterlife that had been present from its beginning, namely, that on the Last Day bodies would arise from their graves and be reunited with their souls, then to be judged by God for eternal happiness or eternal misery in heaven or hell.

In short, despite a philosophical dualism of body and soul, both soul *and* body remained integral within the Christian tradition to the understanding of human persons. As the Church Father Athenagoras put it around the year 180, 'Man therefore, who consists of the two parts, must continue for ever. But it is impossible for him to continue unless he arise again ... . The conclusion is unavoidable, that, along with the interminable duration of the soul, there will be a perpetual continuance of the body'.[8] The bodies of the saints on earth would be rejoined with their souls on the day of resurrection. And the relics of each saint, available on earth for the faithful to see, even to touch, would then be reunited with their other relics to form a resurrected body. Thus, on the one hand, the doctrine of the resurrection of the body was key to the centrality of the relics of the saints in medieval religion. On the other hand, as Caroline Walker Bynum has pointed out, until the time of Gregory the Great, late in the sixth century, 'Western discussions of resurrection would occur mostly in the context of the relic cult'.[9]

Thus, while the souls of the saints were in heaven, in their bodily remains they were still very much on earth.

---

[8] Quoted by *Ibid.*, p. 45.
[9] Caroline Walker Bynum, *The Resurrection of the Body in Western Christianity, 200–1336* (New York: Columbia University Press, 2017), p. 107.

That said, the relics of the saints were much more than merely earthly reminders of the saints already in heaven, available to transmit the prayers of the faithful to God. Thus, for example, Peter the Venerable (c. 1092–1156) had 'confidence more certainly than in any human thing that you ought not to feel contempt for the bones of the present martyrs as if they were dry bones but should honor them now full of life as if they were in their future incorruption'.[10] Peter even went so far as to suggest that the bodies of the saints were *already* living with God: 'And that they live with God', he declared 'innumerable miracles everywhere on earth demonstrate, which miracles are frequently experienced by those who come to venerate their sepulchres with devout minds'.[11] It is not at all obvious what he might have meant by this. He may have meant that the sites of relics were cosmic centres – highly sacred spaces at which heaven touched earth. Moreover, the saints' bodies were considered to have the same influence with God as they had had in their lifetimes. 'Stay beside the tomb of the martyr,' declared John Chrysostom (c. 347–407),

There pour out fountains of tears. Have a contrite mind; raise a blessing from the tomb. Take her [the tomb] as an advocate in your prayers and immerse yourself perpetually in the stories of his struggles. Embrace the coffin, nail yourself to the chest. Not just the martyr's bones, but even their tombs and chests brim with a great deal of blessing. Take

---

[10] Quoted by Caroline Walker Bynum, *Fragmentation and Redemption: Essays on Gender and the Human Body in Medieval Religion* (New York: Zone Books, 2012), p. 264.
[11] Quoted by *Ibid.*, p. 265.

holy oil and anoint your whole body – your tongue, your lips, your neck, your eyes.[12]

From the beginning of the cult of relics in the middle of the fourth century, there arose a significant industry based around the locating of the relics of a previously known or unknown saint and accounts of their discovery ('*inventio*'). Along with this there developed a large trade in the import and export of relics along with accounts of their movement ('*translatio*'). Relics were sought after by bishops, monks, and laity in both East and West. The practice of dismembering the body of a saint began in the sixth century.[13] The value of the relics of particular saints, both spiritual and monetary, was thereby increased. Subdividing the remains did not decrease their power. Each part retained the power of the whole. Thus, for example, Theodoret, Bishop of Cyrrhus (c. 393–c. 458) proclaimed, 'in the divided body the grace survives undivided and the fragments, however small, have the same efficacy as the whole body'.[14] Moreover, each part had equal efficacy in enabling the penitent's access to the heavenly saint. As Peter Brown reminds us, 'the fullness of the invisible person could be present at a mere fragment of his physical remains'.[15] In this way, the number

---

[12] Quoted by Georgia Frank, 'From Antioch to Arles: Lay Devotion in Context,' in Augustine Casiday and Frederick W. Norris (eds.), *The Cambridge History of Christianity: Constantine to c.600* (Cambridge: Cambridge University Press, 2014), p. 542.

[13] See Wiśniewski, *The Beginnings of the Cult of Relics*, ch. 9.

[14] Quoted by Sumption, *Pilgrimage*, p. 28.

[15] Peter Brown, *The Cult of the Saints: Its Rise and Function in Latin Christianity* (Chicago: The University of Chicago Press, 1981), p. 89. See also, Bynum, *The Resurrection of the Body in Western Christianity, 200–1336*, pp. 105–06.

of communities that could share in the saint's power and presence could be multiplied. Moreover, the fullness of the saint could even be present in those things with which the saint had had contact or in those things that had contacted any of their remains (a kind of spiritual DNA). Relics had the power to infuse other materials – cloth, stone, liquid, and skin. As with many other saints, so too with Mary Magdalene – her relics came to be distributed piecemeal both far and wide.

The spread of her relics was fostered by the growing importance of Mary Magdalene within the Western church. In turn, the presence of relics of Mary Magdalene throughout Western Christendom inspired the growth in her cult. Mary Magdalene was the focus of the most egregious account of the attempted subdivision of a saintly bodily part. This was the determined attempt by Bishop Hugh of Lincoln (1186–1200), an avid collector of relics, to have a piece of Mary Magdalene. Adam of Eynsham informs us that, on a visit to the monastery of Fécamp, Hugh undid the wrappings from a bone of Mary and tried unsuccessfully to break it with his fingers. Finally, he broke off two fragments with his teeth and handed them over to Adam. The abbot and the monks were, not surprisingly, outraged, accusing the bishop of gnawing on the bones as if he were a dog. Hugh assuaged their anger with an analogy to the Eucharist:

If, a little while ago, I handled the most sacred body of the Lord of all the saints with my fingers, in spite of my unworthiness, and when I partook of it, touched it with my lips and teeth, why should I not venture to treat in the same way the bones of the saints for my protection, and by this commemoration of them increase my reverence for them, and without profanity acquire them when I have the opportunity.[16]

Fair point. But, in spite of Adam's suggestion that they were mollified, I doubt if the abbot and his monks bought it.

Whether whole, or in bits and pieces, the bodily remains of saints were powerful sites of the miraculous and what we would be inclined to think of (although they wouldn't) as the magical. The *Book of Miracles of Blessed Mary Magdalen* exemplified this. The book was compiled by Jean Gobi the Elder, the Dominican prior of the convent at Saint-Maximin from 1304 to 1328. It contained accounts of eighty-six miracles, grouped according to the affliction remedied or the danger averted. It intended to establish Saint Maximin as the absolute centre of Mary Magdalene's power on earth.[17] According to miracle number ten, there was a man who, although lewd and unclean in his body, was moved nevertheless to go to Saint-Maximin to visit the relics of Mary Magdalene located there. At the time, he wore a ring that, out of devotion to Mary, he touched to the bone of her arm that was commonly shown to pilgrims so that they might kiss it. When he later attempted to have sex, he found that he was sexually powerless. When asked by his lover whether he was wearing anything that prevented him from sexual completion, he responded that it was perhaps the ring with which he had touched the relics of Mary

---

[16] John Shimmers (ed. and trans.), *Medieval Popular Religion 1000–1500: A Reader* (Canada: Broadview Press, 2007), p. 182.
[17] See Head (ed.), *Medieval Hagiography*, p. 684.

Magdalene. Setting aside the ring, he was able to complete his sexual act. He then found that he was unable to replace the ring on his finger.

Ashamed and repentant, he immediately returned to Saint-Maximin and asked forgiveness of his sins. After confession and absolution, he commended himself devotedly and humbly to Mary. He found that he could then place the ring on his finger again. Because 'the original slimness was restored to the finger which had become inflated from carnal knowledge, he was able to place the ring (the material of which was consecrated through contact with the relics of the Magdalen) on his finger easily and without any difficulty just as before'.[18] The moral of the story was a fairly simple one. Sinners should mend their ways, at least before thoughtlessly approaching the relics of a saint. There were serious consequences for not so doing.

The power embedded within the relics also radiated out from them concentrically. Miracle number forty-one tells us of a man from Corsica living in Marseilles who travelled to Saint-Maximin in hopes of a cure to his total paralysis. Because of his many sins and insufficient faith, he gained only the ability to move his hands and his feet, the rest of his body as immobile as before. Five years later, with greater confidence and a firmer faith, 'he began to implore the aid of the Magdalen repeatedly with his whole heart, promising her and God to return to Saint-Maximin to visit her relics'.[19]

Immediately, he began to stand up by his own power and, with the aid of crutches, began to walk to Saint-

[18] *Ibid.*, p. 695.   [19] *Ibid.*

Maximin. The closer he came to the relics of Mary Magdalene, the easier it became for him to move, and he was able to throw away one of the crutches. When he finally entered the church in which the body of the saint lay, each of his limbs was restored to its original function. That man, we read, 'fully and perfectly cured by God through the merits of the Magdalen, gave praise to God and the Magdalen, as he ought'.[20] He left the cart in which he was brought the first time and the crutches with which he came the second time in the church. These joined the many other now redundant reminders as physical testimonies to past miracles and as sources of hope to those in search of one.

Relics were big business. They inspired the faithful, encouraged financial support to, and increased the prestige of, the institutions that housed them. As a result of their ability to attract pilgrims, they were the focus of the medieval tourism industry. But their capacity to generate wealth depended on the miracles that they could produce. As Patrick Geary neatly puts it, 'they provided the only recourse against the myriad ills, physical, material, and psychic, of a population defenseless before an incomprehensible and terrifying universe. The miraculous power of the saint was the basis on which his other power rested, and from this ability and willingness to perform miracles developed his following, his *famuli*, his devoted slaves'.[21] Miracles were the proof of the authenticity of the relics.

---

[20] *Ibid.*, p. 696.
[21] Patrick J. Geary, *Furta Sacra: Thefts of Relics in the Central Middle Ages* (Princeton, NJ: Princeton University Press, 2011), p. 22.

Wealth could also be increased by the purchase or theft of relics from other communities. The value of the relics of one community could also be enhanced by the discrediting of those located elsewhere. Miracle number eighty-four in the *Book of Miracles of Blessed Mary Magdalen* served to prove that the relics of Mary housed in Vézelay, unlike those in Saint-Maximin, were unable to produce miracles and were therefore inauthentic. According to this account, the church in Vézelay gave some relics to the Dominican house at Lausanne, claiming that they were from the body of Mary Magdalene and guaranteeing their miracle-working power. Among those who sought help there from Mary was a man possessed by a demon. His friends asked that the relics of Mary Magdalene be presented to the demoniac. The brother who brought the relics attempted to exorcise the demon: 'I adjure you through blessed Mary Magdalen, the relics of whose body we have here, that you leave this body and do not vex it any more!' To which the demon responded 'you truly speak falsely because there is nothing there of the body or relics of the Magdalen, and that is why I will not leave this person'.[22] With the failure of the exorcism, we are told by the Saint-Maximin apologist, there was a loss of faith in the authenticity of the relics in Lausanne and in those from which they came. The brothers in Lausanne 'were forced to believe that the body in Vézelay from which the brothers had received the relics was not the Magdalen's'.[23]

---

[22] Head (ed.), *Medieval Hagiography*, p. 697.   [23] *Ibid.*

Treasures upon Earth

The Dowager Empress Helena was one of many women for whom relic collecting was not so much a cottage as a castle and convent industry. From the sixth to the eleventh century, pious queens, noble women, abbesses, and nuns procured relics for their private collections and/or those of their monastic communities. As Jane Schulenberg notes, like their male counterparts, 'women were involved in all stages of collecting relics: they discovered and created relics; they begged and received them as gifts; they paid exorbitant prices for them; they divided, sold and exchanged relics; they participated ... in the stealing of relics (the *furta sacra*); and they also gave them as gifts to churches and friends'.[24]

The resident nuns at the monastery at Chelles, a dozen miles east of Paris, were avid relic collectors. Over the period from the time of the monastery's foundation in the mid-seventh up to the end of the ninth centuries, the nuns collected relics mostly from France, but also from Italy, the Holy Land, Byzantium, Egypt, Mesopotamia, and England. Among the most notable relics at Chelles were the stone upon which Moses was standing when he saw God, dirt from Bethlehem, a stone from Calvary, water from the River Jordan, and a piece of Jesus's cradle. It also had relics of Peter and Paul from Rome and a garment of Mary the mother of Jesus from Constantinople. It had also acquired, somewhere during the eighth century, the

---

[24] Jane Schulenberg, 'Female Religious Collectors of Relics: Finding Sacrality and Power in the "Ordinary"', in Michael Frassetto et al. (eds.), *Where Heaven and Earth Meet: Essays on Medieval Europe in Honor of Daniel F. Callahan* (Leiden: Brill, 2014), p. 155.

earliest datable relic of Mary Magdalene, one that had made its way to Chelles from Ephesus.[25]

Relics were not mere pieces of curiosity contained in cabinets, but items of devotion often displayed in ornate reliquaries. They were objects around which liturgical practices developed. Thus, the presence of a relic of Mary Magdalene at Chelles in the eighth century suggests that her cult was already up and running by that time.[26] As we recall from the last chapter, the earliest versions of the life of Mary Magdalene were those in the sermon of pseudo-Odo after 860 and in the *vita eremitica* from the early 800s. Ironically perhaps, therefore, the 'afterlife' of Mary Magdalene began in the West before her Lives had been written. Although we cannot be certain, it was probably the cult that provided the key impetus for the creation of the Lives. The developing cult of Mary Magdalene demanded a coherent biography of her life, both during and after the time of Jesus, and there was a 'boomerang' effect. The Lives, for their part, came to play a significant role in the development of the cult.

Other relics of Mary Magdalene began to appear in Europe from around the beginning of the tenth century. They attest to the spread of the cult devoted to her. Aethelstan, King of the Anglo-Saxons and later of the English (924–939), was a notable collector and generous donor of relics, inspired by the hope that, in spite of Jesus's suggestions to the contrary, perishable earthly treasures might bring him heavenly rewards. The prologue to an

---

[25] See Michael McCormick, *Origins of the European Economy* (Cambridge: Cambridge University Press, 2002), ch. 10.
[26] See *Ibid.*, table 10.13, p. 311.

eleventh-century relics list of Exeter Cathedral noted that Aethelstan gave relics to Exeter 'for the deliverance of his own soul and for the eternal salvation of all those who seek out and worship the holy place'.[27] Among the relics listed was a fragment 'from the finger-bone of St Mary Magdalene who, while alive here, washed our Lord's feet with her tears'.[28] A century later, in 1039, we read of relics of Mary Magdalene held in the abbey of Saint Willibrord in Echternach in Luxembourg.[29] An eleventh-century catalogue of relics from Oviedo in Spain listed 'hair with which Mary Magdalene had dried the feet of Jesus' among its collection.[30]

The period from around 1000 to 1400 was the 'golden age' of relics. Those of Mary Magdalene, like those of other saints, proliferated, as did the sites in which they were to be housed. Relics were also taken on tours to increase their market value along with the prestige and wealth of their possessors. They were mobile sites of supernatural power.[31] The monastic chronicler Rodolphus Glaber (c. 980–c. 1046) saw the rise of relics and of the shrines in which they were located as part of the divine providence:

When the whole world was clothed in a white mantle of new churches, a little later, in the eighth year after the millennium of

---

[27] See Sarah Foot, *Æthelstan: The First King of England* (New Haven, CT: Yale University Press, 2011), pp. 201–02.

[28] Quoted by Patrick W. Connor, *Anglo-Saxon Exeter: A Tenth-Century Cultural History* (Woodbridge: Boydell, 1993), p. 185.

[29] Saxer, *Le Culte de Marie Madeleine*, p. 63.   [30] *Ibid.*, p. 84.

[31] On the movement of relics, see Elizabeth Anne Wiedenheft, 'Circulating Saints: A Study of the Movement of Corporeal Relics in Three Regions of Western Europe, c. 800–1200.' PhD thesis, University of Nottingham, 2018.

the Saviour's Incarnation, the relics of many saints were revealed by various signs where they had long been hidden. It was as though they were waiting for a brilliant resurrection and were now by God's permission revealed to the gaze of the faithful; certainly they brought much comfort to men's minds.[32]

From the tenth to the end of the sixteenth century, there was a continual growth in Western sacred places dedicated to Mary Magdalene. The oldest of these was in the crypt of the monastery of Saint Stephen in Halberstadt in Germany. On 5 November 974, an altar was dedicated to some holy virgins amongst whom were included Mary Magdalene and Martha. It was the beginning of a surge in the cult of Mary Magdalene. In the eleventh century, there were forty sites devoted to Mary.[33] The twelfth century saw 139 sites dedicated to her. We can identify 114 places between 1200 and 1278, and 149 between 1279 and 1399. In the fifteenth and sixteenth centuries, there were 166 sites of devotion to her.[34]

As the number of sites devoted to Mary grew, the market demand for her relics correspondingly increased. There was an embarrassment of riches. Thus, for example, there were four bodies of Mary Magdalene within Europe. The Magdalene altar in Saint John

---

[32] John France (ed. and trans.), *Rodvlfi Glabri: Historiarvm Libri Qvinqve* (Oxford: Clarendon Press, 1989), p. 127.

[33] I use the term 'sites' here to include an array of 'sites of devotion' including churches, chapels, and more particular sites such as altars, tombs, and so on.

[34] These figures are derived from the charts in Saxer, *Le Culte de Marie Madeleine*. These are not easy to interpret but they do strongly suggest the continual growth in her cult.

Lateran in Rome claimed to have one (albeit without the head).[35] The Franciscan chronicler Salimbene (1221–1288) knew of three others. He was delighted at the discovery of a body of 'the Magdalene, whole save for one leg' near Aix in Provence in 1283.[36] But he was also aware that Senigallia in Italy claimed to possess one as did Vézelay in Northern France. When the body at Aix in Provence was found, he informs us, her epitaph could scarcely be read with a magnifying glass for the antiquity of the writing. Consequently, as far as he was concerned, this was the authentic body, 'wherefore the contentions and contradictions and cavils and abuses and falsehoods which were of old concerning her body are henceforth ended ... [for] it is manifest that the body of the same woman cannot be in three places'.[37]

Complete (or virtually complete) bodies aside, various parts of Mary Magdalene were to be found across Europe.[38] Even a London parish church in 1480 could contain a sizeable relic collection with a contribution from Mary Magdalene. Kept in a small chest in the church of Saint Stephen Walbrook were twenty-two relics. Amongst these was a relic of the place where Christ appeared to Mary Magdalene, of the rock upon which

---

[35] See Jansen, *The Making of the Magdalen*, p. 327.
[36] G. G. Coulton, *From St. Francis to Dante: Translations from the Chronicle of the Franciscan Salimbene, 1221–1288* (Philadelphia: University of Pennsylvania Press, 1972), p. 311. As we will see, Salimbene has the date wrong and he is referring to the discovery at Saint-Maximin in 1279. Salimbene is the only source to suggest that Mary was missing one leg.
[37] *Ibid.*, p. 311.
[38] I include England, Scotland, and Ireland within the geographical, if no longer political, understanding of Europe.

Moses was standing when God spoke to him, a piece of the stone upon which Christ's body was washed after his crucifixion, a finger of one of the Holy Innocents killed by Herod, a piece of bone from one of the 11,000 virgins slaughtered along with Saint Ursula, and a piece of the stone upon which Jesus was standing, whence he ascended to heaven.[39] Most prolific within the English lists of the relics of Mary Magdalene was, perhaps not surprisingly, her hair. Twelve pieces of her abundant locks were held at various sites, along with a comb or two. Her hair was also abundant in many places all over Europe. Within these English lists, we also find a toe, three fingers, some of the ointment with which she massaged the feet of Christ, rings, four items of her clothing, and a belt.[40]

There was no shortage of fingers either. England, as we noted above, had three. The Franciscans in Sulmona in Italy had one in a silver reliquary.[41] Saint Martha in Tarascon, Saint Victor in Marseilles, and San Marco in Venice all claimed to have fingers. The relic collection in Halle had two fingers (with bones) in a silver reliquary along with some of her hair.[42] Saint-Maximin claimed one arm while Cologne claimed to have two. There were

---

[39] See Charles Pendrill, *Old Parish Life in London* (London: Oxford University Press, 1937), p. 21.

[40] See Islwyn Thomas, 'The Cult of Saints' Relics in Medieval England', PhD thesis, The University of London, 1974, Appendix 2.

[41] Except where otherwise indicated, for this reference and much of what follows on the locations of relics, I am indebted to Jansen, *The Making of the Magdalen*.

[42] See Philipp Maria Halm and Rudolf Berliner (eds.), *Das Hallische Heiltum* (Berlin: Deutscher Verein für Kunstwissenschaft, 1931), p. 46. I am indebted to Dagmar Eichberger from the University of Heidelberg for this reference.

others in Sicily, Hainault, Marseilles, Venice, and Fécamp – the one that Hugh of Lincoln took a bite out of, making a total of eight arms. Saint John the Baptist of the Florentines in Rome possessed one of her feet.[43] Saint-Maximin held a reliquary with her head, Abbeville claimed to have her skull, while the Dominican nuns of Aix had her jaw.

Aside from parts of her body, other relics connected to her life were popular. 'La Nunziatella' outside of Rome had a fragment of the cave in which she did penance; Saint John Lateran in Rome held a piece of her hair shirt. Santa Croce in Gerusalemme in Rome had the stone slab upon which Jesus laid when he forgave her sins. La Trinité de Vendôme held a teardrop of Christ from the tears Jesus wept when he heard of the death of Lazarus, caught by an angel and placed in a container that was given to Mary Magdalene for safekeeping. The Frari in Venice held a drop of Christ's blood mixed with the ointment of Mary Magdalene that had come to it from Constantinople.[44] Saint-Maximin possessed a reliquary that held bits of blood-soaked stones from Golgotha that Mary Magdalene had brought to France. The blood was said to liquify annually on Good Friday.[45] Saint-Maximin also held perhaps the most noteworthy of all. This was an uncorrupted piece of the skin on Mary Magdalene's

---

[43] See *Saints in Rome and Beyond*, Available at www.saintsinrome.com/2013/08/st-mary-magdalene_3.html.

[44] See Haskins, *Mary Magdalene*, p. 278.

[45] On the fascinating scholastic debate around relics of the blood of Christ, see Nicholas Vincent, *The Holy Blood: King Henry III and the Westminster Blood Relic* (Cambridge: Cambridge University Press, 2001), ch. 5.

forehead, which Jesus had touched when he forbade *her* from touching him after his resurrection.

Oriental Imaginings: Mary in Palestine and Ephesus

Perhaps not surprisingly, as we saw above, Salimbene was sceptical of the existence of three bodies of Mary Magdalene. He was unaware that the church of Saint Lazarus in Constantinople also claimed to have one, transferred there from Ephesus. But he was convinced of the authenticity of the body near Aix. As a show of his faith in this body, he went on to describe a miracle that had followed its discovery. According to this, a young butcher was going along a road when an acquaintance asked him from whence he came. He answered that he was coming from the town of Saint-Maximin 'where the body of the blessed Mary Magdalene was; and I kissed her leg'.[46] To which the other answered, 'Thou has kissed no leg of hers, but rather the leg of an ass or a mare, which the clergy show to the simple for lucre's sake'.[47] The argument became so heated that the sceptic struck the believer many times with his sword; yet, with the help of the Magdalene, the believer suffered no harm. He then struck the sceptic with his sword once and killed him. Fearing reprisals from the sceptic's family, he fled to St.-Gilles.

---

[46] G. G. Coulton (ed.), *Life in the Middle Ages* (Cambridge: Cambridge University Press, 1928), p. 311.
[47] *Ibid.*

Cast into prison for murder, he was condemned to be hanged. But in the night before his execution, Mary Magdalene appeared to him assuring him that he would not die. Next day, as he was being hanged, 'there flew down from heaven a dove, dazzling white as snow, and alighted on the gallows, and loosed the knot around the neck of the hanged man ... and laid him on the earth wholly unhurt'.[48] When the officials tried to hang him again, he escaped with the help of his fellow-butchers who were there in numbers, ready armed with swords and staves. When he told his rescuers how he had killed the sceptic while defending his own life and the honour of the Magdalene, they 'praised God and the blessed Magdalene who had freed him'.[49]

It was as clear to our medieval forebears as it is to us that not all of the relics of Mary Magdalene could be authentic. Although, that said, they were perhaps more likely than we to believe that at least some of them might be. Certainly, Salimbene was not alone in worrying about determining which relics were genuine. The Benedictine Guibert of Nogent (1055–1124) was more sceptical than most. Noting that both the people of Constantinople and the monks of Angély claimed to have the head of John the Baptist, he concluded that 'it is obvious that one group or the other has resorted to lies'.[50] Like Salimbene, it was not devotion to relics as such that troubled Guibert, but questions around their authenticity and the willingness of Christians, both educated and uneducated, to engage in

---

[48] *Ibid.*, p. 312.   [49] *Ibid.*
[50] Head (ed.), *Medieval Hagiography*, p. 448.

both pious and impious fraud.[51] As Colin Morris notes, 'All the features which he most disliked, the disentombing and breaking up of the bodies of the saints, the carrying them about and the use of settings of precious metals or ivory, were ultimately, he thought, designed to increase the flow of offerings'.[52] The saints, he thought, ought to be allowed to rest in peace and not in pieces, at least until the day of resurrection.

There was sufficient evidence of fake relics to justify Guibert's concerns about the authenticity of many of them and to warrant his worries about the lack of any evidence to authenticate them. In the middle of the eleventh century, the abbey church at Vézelay in Burgundy in the north of France began to claim possession of relics of Mary Magdalene. Positioned along one of the pilgrimage routes between Germany and the East to the shrine of Santiago de Compostela (housing the relics of Saint James), it was ideal as a site of pilgrimage. The earliest claim to the authenticity of the relics at Vézelay relied upon divine providence, a vision, and miracles. 'Many have wondered,' declared one of the monks, 'how it was possible that the body of St. Mary Magdalen, who was born in Judea, was brought to Gaul [France] from such a distant region. But they can be answered in a few words: because all things are possible for God, and he did what he wished. It is not difficult for Him to do what He

---

[51] On Guibert and relics, see Jay Rubenstein, *Guibert of Nogent: Portrait of a Medieval Mind* (New York: Routledge, 2016), pp. 124–130.

[52] Colin Morris, 'A Critique of Popular Religion: Guibert of Nogent on "The Relics of the Saints"', in G. J. Cuming and Derek Baker (eds.), *Popular Belief and Practice* (Cambridge: Cambridge University Press, 1972), p. 57.

wished'.[53] Moreover, he went on to say, Mary not only punished most of those who doubted that she was in Vézelay, she would often herself appear to verify it. Only last Saturday, he went on, as he placed the cover over the relics after Matins, an image of a virtuous woman appeared before the small door of the shrine in which her bones were housed. As he watched, she said, 'I am she who is thought to be here'. In addition, he declared, what is believed to be there is 'proven plainly by the power of the miracles [that occur there]'.[54]

There were, however, much more 'this-worldly' attempts to authenticate relics, particularly those of the early saints and martyrs, through the creation of narratives of their origins and travels (either before or after their deaths). Like modern antiques, the value of relics was enhanced by credible accounts of their provenance. There were four different legends surrounding the place of origin of the relics of Mary Magdalene, depending on whether her remains were seen as having been laid to rest in Palestine, Ephesus (thence to Constantinople), or Provence.

If Vézelay's first account of the provenance of the body of Mary Magdalene relied upon a divine transport system, there was, by 1024–1025, another account in circulation of how the body of Mary had been brought to Vézelay. It is contained in the *Gesta Episcoporum Cameracensium* (*Deeds of the Bishops of Cambrai*), a work that provided a history of the diocese of Cambrai from the

---

[53] The *Vézelay Miracles [Bibliotheca Hagiographica Latina*, nos. 5471–5472], in Head (ed.), *Medieval Hagiography*, p. 688.

[54] *Ibid.*, p. 689.

late Roman period to the middle of the eleventh century. There we read that there was a monastery in honour of Saints Peter and Paul in Leuze in Belgium. It was the resting place of a monk called Baidilo. We know little of Baidilo except that he was thought to have made the pilgrimage to Jerusalem.[55] 'He is said', remarked the author of the *Gesta*, 'to have carried the body of St. Mary Magdalene from Jerusalem to Burgundy in the place called Vezelay'.[56] We do know too that he did spend a brief time in Vézelay around 880 and that it was later recorded by Hugh of Poitiers (d. 1167) that the body of Mary Magdalene arrived in Vézelay in that year.[57] So it is not unreasonable to suggest that Baidilo was the founder of the cult of Mary Magdalene in Vézelay in the late ninth century.

Although the earliest versions of the *vita eremitica* could be read as implying that Mary retired to the deserts of Palestine, there is no other source in the West or the East that has Jerusalem or Palestine more generally as her resting place. But reading behind the text of the *Gesta*, we can probably conclude that this was a story that was invented in Vézelay in the early eleventh century further to bolster its claims to have the body of Mary Magdalene

[55] As we will see, his role in the afterlife of Mary Magdalene will later be both elaborated and significantly different. I have used the name 'Baidilo' for this monk. There is a variety of different spellings of his name in the medieval sources.

[56] Bernard S. Bachrach, et al., *Deeds of the Bishop of Cambrai, Translation and Commentary* (Abingdon, VA: Routledge, 2018), p. 263.

[57] See John Scott and John O. Ward (eds.), *The Vézelay Chronicle* (Binghamton, NY: Center for Medieval and Early Renaissance Studies, 1992), p. 310.

in its keeping.[58] The entry in the *Gesta* was repeated a century later in another chronicle of the region, the *Chronicon Sancti Andreae Castri Cameracesii*. After that, to all intents and purposes, it was never heard of again.[59]

If the discovery (inventio) of Mary Magdalene's remains in Palestine and their translation to Europe was an 'invention' both in the medieval and the modern sense of the term, the tradition that her remains had originally been in Ephesus was on somewhat firmer ground. Within the East, the first hard evidence of the cult of Mary Magdalene can be found in the mid-tenth century in the liturgical calendar of Constantinople, the *Synaxarion*. We recall that, in the Eastern tradition, Mary Magdalene was not identified either with Mary of Bethany or with the sinful woman of Luke. Thus, the entry for Mary Magdalene on 22 July in the *Synaxarion* tells us only that Christ cast seven demons out of her, that she was among the women who followed Jesus, that she attended his crucifixion and entombment, and that she was the first to see the risen Christ.[60]

However, we also get a different account of Mary's life after the ascension of Christ to those in the West. This was focused on the city of Ephesus. Since the first century, Ephesus had been a major centre for Christianity.

<hr/>

[58] On the Palestinian legend, see Victor Saxer, 'Les Saintes Marie Madeleine et Marie de Béthanie dans la Tradition liturgique et homilétique orientale,' *Revue des Sciences Religieuses* 32 (1958), pp. 19–22.

[59] See PL, vol. 149, col. 254A.

[60] Hippolyte Delehaye (ed.), *Synaxarion Ecclesiae Constantinopolitanum e codice Sirmondiano nunc Berolinensi*, cols. 833–834. Available at https://archive.org/details/DelehayeSynaxariumConstantinopolitanum/page/n3/mode/2up.

By the beginning of the seventh century, when Ephesus was at its height, it was an important pilgrimage site, lying as it did on the main seaway between Constantinople and the Holy Land.[61] The key place for most pilgrims was the Church of Saint John within which the body of Saint John was buried beneath the high altar. Next in importance was the Cave of the Seven Sleepers.

Although there is no Eastern tradition of Mary having married or having been jilted by John, the *Synaxarion* tells us that, after the ascension of Jesus, she went to Ephesus to be with John. There she died and was buried in the entrance to the cave of the Seven Sleepers.[62] Ephesus was thought to be the burial place of the evangelist John by the early fourth century. But the tradition that Mary Magdalene, along with John, was buried in Ephesus is first to be found in the sixth century historian Bishop Gregory of Tours (c. 540–594) in his *Glory of the Martyrs*, completed in the early 590s. Gregory tells of John descending into a tomb while still alive and ordering that it be covered. 'Still today', he declared, 'his tomb produces manna with the appearance of flour', relics of which are sent throughout the world 'and perform cures for ill people'.[63] Gregory was here reflecting the tradition, known to Augustine, that John was buried in Ephesus while still alive, that he was sleeping in his tomb until Christ returned, and that he was often heard snoring.

---

[61] On Ephesus generally, see Clive Foss, *Ephesus after Antiquity: A Late Antique, Byzantine and Turkish City* (Cambridge: Cambridge University Press, 1979).

[62] Delehaye (ed.), *Synaxarion*, cols. 834–835.

[63] Raymond van Dam (trans.), *Gregory of Tours: Glory of the Martyrs* (Liverpool: Liverpool University Press, 1988), p. 47.

This apparently supernatural 'manna' was dust thrown to the surface by the saint's ongoing breath.[64]

Gregory of Tours immediately went on to give a much shorter notice of Mary: 'Mary Magdalene is buried in that city', he wrote, 'having no covering over her'.[65] This brief notice, wedged between long accounts of the tombs of the apostles John and Andrew, looks a little like an after-thought. It is difficult to determine what Gregory might have meant by 'having no covering over her' (*nullum super se tegumen habens*'). The meaning of the term '*tegumen*' ('covering') can range from a garment or a shroud to a sarcophagus cover or the roof of a monument.[66] The most we can probably conclude is that, by the time of Gregory of Tours, while the cult of John was well-established in Ephesus, that of his companion Mary Magdalene was only just beginning at the turn of the seventh century.

This judgement is reinforced by a sermon of Modestos, Patriarch of Jerusalem (d. 630) entitled 'On Women bearing Perfumes'. In this sermon, Modestos gave a longer account of Mary Magdalene than Gregory had, adding that she was martyred in Ephesus. After the death of Mary, the mother of Jesus, he wrote, Mary Magdalene 'went to Ephesus to be with the beloved disciple, where she, the bearer of perfumes, completed her

---

[64] See John Gibb and James Innes (trans.), *St. Augustin: Lectures or Tractates on the Gospel According to St. John*, 124.2, NPNF (first series), vol. 7, p. 448.

[65] PL vol. 71, col. 731.

[66] van Dam (trans.), *Gregory of Tours: Glory of the Martyrs*, p. 47. On various modern interpretations of the phrase '*nullum tegumen super se*'), see Saxer, 'Les Saintes Marie Madeleine,' p. 23.

apostolic life through martyrdom, not wishing up to her last breath to be separated from John, virgin and evangelist'.[67] We can assume that Modestos believed that her remains were in Ephesus where she had been executed. Unfortunately, he gave no information about the place of her remains, perhaps suggestive of there being no cultic activity centred upon them. That said, he clearly placed Mary in the category of sanctity. His was the single Mary, not the composite one identified with the repentant prostitute. On account of her perfect virginity and purity, he declared, she seemed to her executioners to be like 'clear crystal'.[68]

As we noted above, the *Synaxarion* of Constantinople from the mid-tenth century reported that Mary Magdalene died in Ephesus and was buried in the entrance to the cave of the Seven Sleepers. It is difficult to determine where the tradition of Mary's burial site being connected to that of the Seven Sleepers originated. In terms of religious capital – churches, tombs, relics, miracle sites, and so on – Ephesus was a key destination for pilgrims to Asia Minor. As we know from Gregory of Tours, the city contained the tomb of Saint John the evangelist and a memorial of some kind to Mary Magdalene. It also held the tombs of Saint Timothy and Saint Hermione, the daughter of Saint Philip. There was also the stone on which Joseph of Arimathea had washed the body of Christ, a piece of the true cross, a shirt that Mary the mother of Jesus had made for John, and his manuscript copy of the last book of the Bible – the book

---

[67] PG vol. 86, col. 3275.   [68] *Ibid.*, vol. 86, col. 3273.

of Revelation. But second in importance to the tomb of Saint John was that of the Seven Sleepers.

In his *Glory of the Martyrs*, Gregory of Tours gave a long account of the legend of the Seven Sleepers. According to this, during the time of the persecution of Christians in 250 by the Emperor Decius (c. 201–251), seven Christians shut themselves in a cave in order to avoid persecution. During a time of prayer to God to rescue them from their plight, they fell asleep. When the Emperor heard of them, he ordered that the cave be sealed up with stones so that they would die. At least 160 years later, during the reign of the Christian Emperor Theodosius II (401–450), the seven men awoke. When the emperor heard of them, he visited them 'and glorified the Lord who did not allow his people to perish'.[69] The seven men then lay down on the ground again and fell asleep, awaiting the final day of resurrection. 'Even today,' Gregory wrote, 'the men lie asleep in that spot, covered by cloaks made of silk or linen'.[70] The legend of the Seven Sleepers entered the world of Islam through its incorporation into the *Qur'ān*. In this version, a number of young men (only God knew how many) slept for 309 years, accompanied by their faithful dog (see Plate 14).[71]

Although the mid-tenth century *Synaxarion* was undoubtedly drawing on a tradition that Mary Magdalene was buried at the entrance to the cave, there is, to my knowledge, only one earlier reference. It comes from the *Itinerarium of Willibald*, an account of the travels

---

[69] van Dam (trans.), *Gregory of Tours: Glory of the Martyrs*, p. 118.
[70] *Ibid.*, p. 119. [71] See *Qur'ān*, 18.9–26.

of Willibald (c. 700–c. 787), the first English pilgrim to visit the Holy Land. On the way there, somewhere around 724, Willibald stopped in Ephesus. 'There at the tomb of St. John the Evangelist', we read, 'they poured forth their prayers with tears, marveling at the manna that bubbles forth from it; and then they commended themselves to the Seven Sleepers and to St. Mary Magdalene, who rests there'.[72] We can probably conclude, therefore, that the tradition of Mary Magdalene being buried near or at the entrance of the cave of the Seven Sleepers began after the time of Gregory of Tours and Modestos (both of whom we might have expected to have mentioned it) but before that of Willibald, that is, sometime in the seventh century.

Byzantine Travels: From Ephesus to Constantinople

Ephesus was a favourite place for imperial visitors as a site to gather relics, thereby increasing the status of Constantinople. When the Russian Abbot Daniel visited Ephesus in 1106, he saw the tomb of Saint John and the Cave of the Seven Sleepers that, by that time, also contained relics of some 300 holy fathers and of Saint Alexander. In the same cave, he saw the tomb of Mary Magdalene as well as her head.[73] That he should have seen Mary's head is something of a surprise. For by then,

---

[72] Anon., *The Itinerary of St. Willibald*, in Rev. Canon Brownlow (trans.), *The Hodoeporicon of Saint Willibald* (London: Palestine Pilgrims' Text Society), p. 41.

[73] See Foss, *Ephesus after Antiquity*, pp. 127–128.

Mary Magdalene's remains in Ephesus had left there some 200 years earlier. Thus, the *Synaxarion* informs us that her remains were transferred to Constantinople by the philosopher Emperor Leo VI (866–912).[74] There they were buried on the left side of the sanctuary opposite those of Lazarus (that Leo had brought from Cyprus in 898) on the right in the monastery of Saint Lazarus newly built by Leo specifically for monastic eunuchs.[75]

The relics of Mary Magdalene were of sufficient merit for Mary to be worth transferring from Ephesus to adorn the monastery of Saint Lazarus. That said, she was not important enough to merit a church dedicated to her, either in Constantinople or, for that matter, anywhere else in the Byzantine Empire. It is difficult to fathom why she was not particularly important in Constantinople. After all, even as the single Mary, she was the first witness of the resurrection of Christ. Perhaps, it was simply because there was such a wealth of relics in Constantinople. Relics were at the centre of the glory that was Constantinople. As Geoffrey de Ville (c. 1150–c. 1215) remarked in 1203, the relics there 'were beyond description, for there were as many at that time in Constantinople as in all the rest of the world'.[76]

---

[74] Delehaye (ed.), *Synaxarion*, col. 835.

[75] For the key Greek texts on the translation of the remains of Mary Magdalene to Constantinople, see Vassilikia A. Foskolou, 'Mary Magdalene between East and West: Cult and Image, Relics and Politics in the Late Thirteenth-Century Eastern Mediterranean', *Dumbarton Oaks Papers* 65/66 (2011–2012), pp. 295–256. I am indebted to Foskolou for this discussion.

[76] Quoted by John Wortley, 'The Byzantine Component of the Relic-Hoard of Constantinople,' *Greek, Roman, and Byzantine Studies* 40 (1999), p. 353.

Constantinople had been amassing relics from the middle of the fourth century. But the key period was between the Arab conquest of Jerusalem in 637–638 and the conquest of Constantinople by the Ottomans in 1453. It was during these centuries, as Holger A. Klein points out,

that the Byzantine Emperor established and asserted himself as the safekeeper, defender, and distributor of the most sacred relics of Christendom, namely, those associated with the Passion of Christ, the Virgin, and certain Eastern Saints. It was the possession of these relics that confirmed the emperor's close ties with the divine powers, guaranteed his victoriousness in battle, and lent his office a political and spiritual prestige that other Christian rulers could hope to acquire only if they them-selves gained possession of these precious, and truly priceless objects.[77]

They were the objects of envy and desire in the West, 'the Byzantine stuff of which western dreams were made', as Klein neatly puts it.[78] This meant that they could play a significant role in the giving of gifts by the Byzantine Emperor or his diplomatic delegations to worthy Westerners thus enhancing his political and spiritual superiority over them. If the most important relics belonged to the imperial household, they were also held in the city and its environs. In 1200, a Russian pilgrim, Antony of Novgorod, visited seventy-six shrines in the city and twenty-one nearby. At one time,

---

[77] Holger A. Klein, 'Eastern Objects and Western Desires: Relics and Reliquaries between Byzantium and the West', *Dumbarton Oaks Papers* 58 (2004), p. 284. I am indebted to Klein for this discussion.

[78] *Ibid.*, p. 288.

Constantinople held 3,600 relics of 476 different saints.[79] There was no shortage to give to a West keen to receive them. Gifts of relics were sent by Patriarchs from Constantinople to Popes and other episcopal worthies in the West.

Perhaps because of the sheer number of relics in Constantinople, those of Mary Magdalene did not become a key site for pilgrims to visit. Thus, Vassilikia A. Foskolou notes that, of the dozen texts written by foreigners who visited the city before 1204, Mary's relics were only mentioned once.[80] This was in the so-called late eleventh-century *anonymus Mercati*, the earliest list of the relics and sanctuaries of Constantinople. A Latin translation of a late tenth-century Greek original, it was intended as a guide to pilgrims. There we read that, in the monastery of Lazarus, there lies Mary Magdalene, along with Lazarus. Moreover, in keeping with the Eastern tradition of the distinction between Mary Magdalene and Mary of Bethany, the monastery also contained 'relics of Martha and Mary, the sisters of Lazarus'.[81] Among the 295 relics in Constantinople listed by Anthony of Novgorod in the year 1200, the remains of Mary did not appear. Clearly, it was not well known that the body of Mary Magdalene was reposing in the monastery of Saint Lazarus.

---

[79] See Derek Krueger, 'The Religion of Relics in Late Antiquity and Byzantium', in Martina Bagnoli et al. (eds.), *Treasures of Heaven: Saints, Relics, and Devotion in Medieval Europe* (London: British Museum Press, 2011), p. 13.

[80] Foskolou, 'Mary Magdalene between East and West,' p. 282.

[81] Krijnie N. Ciggaar, 'Une Description de Constantinople Tradite par un Pèlerin Anglais,' *Revue des Études Byzantines* 34 (1976), p. 249.

Why did Mary Magdalene not provoke in the East the kind of attention she did in the West? A likely explanation lies in the East continuing to differentiate between Mary Magdalene, Mary of Bethany, and the sinful woman in the Gospel of Luke. Thus, in the Eastern church, Mary Magdalene was merely one of the myrrh-bearing women, along with Mary of Bethany and Martha, present at the death and resurrection of Jesus. And she had not appropriated the Gospel narratives of the penitent prostitute and of the Mary who anointed Jesus's feet. The life of the single Mary as imagined in the East was not enough to build a narrative sufficiently connected to the life of Christ. Moreover, in her life after the ascension, the East only developed a minimalist tradition of her journey to Ephesus and her death there. As we will see later, only around the beginning of the fourteenth century did a burgeoning interest in the East in her cult lead to the construction of a life of apostolic travels by Mary as far West as France before she eventually returned to the East.

Until the beginning of the thirteenth century, the giving of relics as gifts by Eastern authorities was the only way in which the Western lay and clerical elite could obtain them. The only alternative was to steal them. The relics in Constantinople drew the Fourth Crusade towards the city. The relics, 'having as it were consecrated Byzantium as a new Jerusalem', John Wortley writes, 'deflected the Crusade in their direction like some gravitational force diverting an object travelling through space'.[82] When the

---

[82] Wortley, 'The Byzantine Component of the Relic-Hoard of Constantinople', p. 353.

soldiers of the Crusade gained control of Constantinople in April 1204, they looted the monasteries and churches of the city. The 3,600 relics of Constantinople were among the treasures that were at the mercy of the crusaders.

The remains of Mary Magdalene were, of course, among them. If the remains of Mary were of minimal interest in the East, the Crusaders were much keener. The European acquisition of relics from the Fourth Crusade was, at least as far as the West was concerned, a fortuitous outcome from a flawed venture. Bishop Conrad of Halberstadt (c. 1162–1225) in Saxony, who accompanied the crusade, made something of a killing, so to say, in the relics market. Amongst the earthly treasures with which he arrived back in Halberstadt were the blood of Christ, Jesus's crown of thorns, his shroud, his purple garment, and his sandals. He also had some of the Virgin Mary's hair, the skull of Saint John the Baptist, the shinbone of Saint Peter, the arm of Simon the apostle, the head of Saint James, the shoulder of Saint Philip, the arm of Saint Barnabas, and a portion of the skull of Saint Stephen. Leading the relics of female saints was a portion of 'the skull of Mary Magdalene' ['*de craneo Maria Magdalene*'] followed by the hand and arm of Euphemia the virgin, and relics of Lucy, Margaret, Katherine, and Barbara.[83] These were souvenirs with power: 'with the extremely propitious arrival of these saints, Divine Mercy adorned the land with such grace that the schism between the king [Philip of Swabia] and the priesthood [Pope

---

[83] 'The Deeds of the Bishops of Halberstadt', in Alfred J. Andrea (ed.), *Contemporary Sources for the Fourth Crusade* (Leiden: Brill, 2008), p. 262.

Innocent III], already of long duration, was replaced by unity in the Church'.[84]

If Conrad arrived back in Germany with the head of Mary Magdalene, what happened to the rest of her? We have no evidence that, either in Ephesus or in Constantinople, Mary had been divided into parts. Thus, in Constantinople, there was probably a complete body. So, more than likely, he took all of her along with him when he returned from the crusade. On his way back, he detoured from Venice to Rome to visit Pope Innocent III. He kept Mary's head but, we can suggest, he gave the rest to the Pope. For we do know that, eventually, she came to rest, albeit without her head (*sine capito*), in an altar dedicated to her in Saint John Lateran in Rome during the reign of Pope Honorius III (1216–1227).

She was still there in 1297 when the altar was refurbished. The inscription to that altar reads, 'In the name of God, amen. In the year of the Lord 1297, the altar of the chapter was consecrated to the honour of God and the Blessed Mary Magdalene by Lord Gerardo of Parma, Bishop of Sabina, by the order of Pope Boniface VIII. The body of the saint is buried in the altar, without head and arm, along with relics of many other saints'.[85] It is very likely that both Gerardo and Boniface knew that Mary had been buried there without her head at an earlier time, although they might not have known that her head had gone to Halberstadt. But why did they make it very public that she was now 'without head *and* arm' (*'sine capito et brachio'*)?

---

[84] *Ibid.*, p. 262.
[85] For the Latin inscription, see Saxer, *Le Culte de Marie Madeleine*, p. 215, n. 143. See also p. 215, n. 141.

Well, the addition of 'an arm' to the inscription was necessitated by the Pope's awareness that by 1293, there were reliquaries containing both Mary's head *and* her arm at Saint-Maximin in France and, more importantly, that he himself had confirmed their authenticity in April of 1295.

Despite the body of Mary Magdalene having been translated to the West, the East did not give up on its claim to have the body of Mary Magdalene. A replacement body was found. Within the East, there was a growing awareness of the importance of Mary Magdalene in the West because of the Latin occupation of Constantinople from 1204 to 1261. Her status in the East grew. Thus, a long encomium to Mary Magdalene was written by the church historian Nikephoros Kallistos Xanthopoulos (c. 1256–c. 1335), somewhere between 1282 and 1328, to increase her saintly profile in the East and to authenticate her relics there. As well as constructing a coherent account of the life of Mary Magdalene before the ascension of Christ, he also gave an extensive account of her subsequent life. According to this, after the ascension, she lived for a time with John and Mary the mother of Jesus. After a long missionary journey that took in Italy, France, Phoenicia, Syria, and Egypt, preaching the Gospel as she went along, she returned to Palestine and rejoined the Virgin Mary and John. Xanthopoulos's rhetorical intentions are clear. He was aware of the tradition of Mary Magdalene having visited France and, no doubt, knew of the story of her having been buried there. Thus, ignoring the accounts of her death and burial in France, he appropriated the story of her visit to France into his account, and constructed a round trip for her from Palestine to France and back.

Subsequently, he declared, Mary travelled with John and Mary the mother of Jesus from Palestine to Ephesus where she died and was buried. This enabled him then to pick up on the tradition of her translation to Constantinople and to re-establish her remains in the monastery of Saint Lazarus. Thus, Chapter 27 of this work described how the Emperor Leo, after a vision of Mary Magdalene, 'deposited solemnly and with great respect her revered remains in a box wrought of pure gold'.[86] He and his brother Alexander carried the body of Mary from Ephesus to Constantinople on their shoulders and placed it in the church of Saint Lazarus 'at the left side near to the wall'.[87]

Xanthopoulos was not only trying to reestablish the cult of Mary Magdalene in Constantinople. With the loss of the relics of many other saints and the consequent decline in their cults, he was also pushing for a significant increase in her status, along with that of Lazarus, and the standing of the monastery in which they lay. Thus in the final chapter of his tribute, he declared that she and Lazarus 'keep guard of the city, acting as deliverers and dispensers of manifold graces, and as most efficacious advocates before God, for nothing is more worthy of reverence than a friend and disciple'.[88]

The French Correction: A Body in Vézelay

It will be remembered that, according to the *Deeds of the Bishops of Cambrai* (1024–1025), it was a monk by the name of Baidilo who, having made the pilgrimage to

---

[86] PG 147, col. 573–74, n. XXVII.　　[87] *Ibid.*　　[88] *Ibid.*

Jerusalem, returned from there with the body of Mary Magdalene to Europe and deposited it in Vézelay. But by the late eleventh century, a new account of the discovery of the remains of Mary Magdalene and of their translation to Vézelay had come into play. This was the first of a number of accounts of her remains that were derived from those traditions of her life, after the ascension of Christ, which had her travelling to France and dying there. These were part of the creation of a 'Frenchified' Holy Land, recreated in France, in which the burial sites of a number of the original Christian saints – James, Mary, Martha, Lazarus, Maximin, Mary the mother of James, and Mary Salome – had moved from the East to the West.[89] As we recall from the previous chapter, during the eleventh century, the *Vita Apostolica* – which had Mary Magdalene travelling to France, dying, and being buried there – had become dominant. So it was necessary for the Vézelay community to suppress its first story of the Palestinian origin of their body of Mary Magdalene and to construct another story that aligned it with the remains of Mary being in France as a result of her having died there.

This new story was contained in a text written in the mid to late eleventh century entitled '*Sermo de Sancta Maria Magdalenae*'. It began with a brief *Vita Apostolica*. According to this, Mary, Martha, and Lazarus left

---

[89] See Romy Wyche, 'A Provençal Holy Land. Re-Reading the Legend and the Sites of Mary Magdalene in Southern France, *Collegium Medievale* 29 (2016), pp. 111–130. Mary Magdalene, Mary the mother of James, and (Mary) Salome were the three women who, according to Mark 16.1, brought spices to the tomb of Jesus to anoint him. They are known traditionally as the myrrophores or myrrh-bearing women.

Jerusalem and reached Marseilles. Because, following New Testament guidelines (1 Timothy 2.12), it was prohibited for a woman to be heard in public, she gave that task to Lazarus. After persisting in their work for a long time, 'they came to the end of this present life with glorious virtues'.[90] In the time of the Frankish King Carloman II (reigned from 879 to 884), the story went on, Adalgaire, Bishop of Autun (from 875 to 893) visited Vézelay accompanied by a knight called Adelelmus, the brother of Odo, the Abbot of Vézelay (827–911).[91] In conversation with the monks, Bishop Adelgaire mentioned with what great love Mary Magdalene had followed Christ. Adelelmus then declared that, from the time that he was a child, he had seen and had known where Mary was buried. When the Abbot Odo heard this, he knelt to kiss the hands of the bishop and his brother and excitedly to ask for the relics.

Funds were raised and monks were chosen to set out with Adelelmus and his soldiers to retrieve the remains of Mary from Arles in the south. When they arrived in Arles, they learned that the whole region had been ravaged by the 'Saracens' ('Arab Muslims'). The locals had fled, taking the remains of both Mary and Maximin and hiding them. Relying on the prayers of the bishop and the abbot, they continued on, and came to the place in which the bodies of the saints had been concealed. As they were gathering the bodies of the saints, a large number of Saracens came upon them. In terror, they called upon Mary and Maximin to protect them. A great cloud

---

[90] Head (ed.), *Medieval Hagiography*, p. 689.
[91] Adelelmus is unknown outside of this text.

appeared to hide them from the Saracens until they reached their own lands. Our protector Mary, we are told, 'obtained this for us'.[92] Mary's protection was a sign both of the authenticity of the bodies and of her approval of her translation to Vézelay.

This account served two purposes. First, it aligned the possession of the body of Mary in Vézelay to the tradition of Mary's death and burial in France. Second, it served to reflect and strengthen the cordial relationship that existed between the monastic community at Vézelay and the diocesan bishops in Autun who had oversight of it.[93] These relations were to sour during the first decade of the twelfth century during the episcopacy of Bishop Narigald or Norgaut (1098–1112). This provided an opportunity for Vézelay to rethink its account of how the body of Mary Magdalene had come there and to elaborate upon it. In this new story, the monk Baidilo (who had earlier been said to have brought her body back from Jerusalem) reappeared in place of the knight Adelelmus, Bishop Adalgaire was replaced by Gerard de Roussillon (c. 810–c. 877), the founder of Vézelay, and Mary's earlier resting place in Arles became Aix in Provence.

According to this account, it was well established that the body of Mary Magdalene had been handed over by Bishop Maximin for burial in the territory of the city of Aix. It was a city that had been captured by the Saracens from Spain who eventually, after much slaughter of the inhabitants that included skinning them alive, withdrew to

---

[92] Head (ed.), *Medieval Hagiography*, p. 690.
[93] See Scott and Ward (eds.), *The Vézelay Chronicle*, pp. 343–344.

Spain. Count Gerard and Abbot Odo of Vézelay sent one of the monks, Baidilo, to Aix with the mission to find any relic of the body of Mary Magdalene and bring it back to Vézelay. Finding in Aix nothing but death and destruction, he wandered here and there in search of her body. Eventually, he came to a place where there was an elaborate sepulchre that gave promise of containing a 'heavenly treasure'.[94] Its carvings of scenes from Mary's life revealed to Baidilo that it was the sepulchre of Mary Magdalene.

Overcome with uncertainty as to what he should do, Baidilo sought the help of Mary to assist him in discerning how to proceed. Fortunately, we read, divine inspiration came with the result that, one night, he broke off part of the pediment to the sepulchre and peered in. There he saw a body still completely covered in skin with its hands placed over its chest and lying fully extended. A fragrance of ineffable sweetness rushed out of the tomb. This was key evidence: 'For the body of her who was worthy to anoint with spices God in his bodily form ought to have been the most sweet smelling of all'.[95] The body had what was more generally thought of as the odour of sanctity. The bodies of the saints, rather than exuding the smell of corruption, gave forth the sweet aroma of Paradise. During that night, Baidilo had a vision of Mary, clothed in the whitest of garments, who told him not to be afraid 'since the same place has been predestined by God for us as for you'.[96] The following night, he extracted the body from the tomb, wrapped it in fresh cloths, and set off with it for Vézelay. Baidilo's burglary had begun.

[94] *Ibid.*, p. 338.   [95] *Ibid.*, p. 339.   [96] *Ibid.*

The authenticity of the body was further guaranteed by a miracle en route. As they were passing through the town of Salon-de-Provence, a dead man raised himself up from the bier in which he had been lying, and cried out three times, 'Mary Magdalene is passing'. His family and friends set off to see if what he said was true. Coming across Baidilo and his companions, they 'discovered the truth of the matter'.[97] Fearful of being discovered in the city of Nimes with the stolen body of the saint, Baidilo and his companions turned aside to a church and there separated the longer bones of the body and placed them alongside the rest of the body so that they could fit into a smaller space. Within a mile of Vézelay, the body began to become so heavy that, no matter how many tried, they were unable to move further. Mary, in keeping with a tradition of the translation of saints, became immovably weighty until properly welcomed.

They then sent a messenger to the monastery to tell the monks of their inability to go further. With great joy, the brothers streamed out to meet them. They all prostrated themselves on the ground, 'praying to the omnipotence of the divine majesty and fervently beseeching Mary ... to allow the remains of her body to be removed from that place to the monastery. As soon as they rose up from their prayers and tried to go on they were able to proceed with such speed and the weight seemed so insubstantial that it felt as if they were being carried rather than were carrying anything'.[98] Since her arrival in Vézelay, 'the blessed Mary Magdalene, beloved of God, has shone forth in that place through innumerable signs and

[97] Ibid.   [98] Ibid., p. 340.

miracles'.[99] This was to become the standard account of the discovery and translation of Mary Magdalene to Vézelay as shown by its inclusion in *The Golden Legend* of Jacobus de Voragine in the 1260s.[100]

The attachment of Mary Magdalene to Vézelay was a piece of medieval marketing genius. Her connection to that place began with Geoffrey of Cluny who had been elected Abbot of the Benedictine community at Vézelay in 1037. There may well have been relics of Mary Magdalene at Vézelay since the end of the ninth century. But it was during the tenure of Geoffrey that Vézelay began selling its claim that it possessed relics of Mary. In 1058, a papal bull of Pope Stephen IX recognised Vézelay as possessing her remains. Papal accreditation allied with persuasive accounts of the discovery and translation of her remains to Vézelay turned it into a booming place of pilgrimage.

Thus, for example, the Second Crusade was launched there in 1146 by Bernard of Clairveaux. In 1166, it was in the monastery church dedicated to Mary Magdalene (although originally to the Virgin Mary) that Thomas Becket, the Archbishop of Canterbury in exile, preached a sermon threatening the English King Henry II with excommunication. On their way to the Third Crusade in 1190, King Richard the Lionheart rendezvoused there with the French King Philip II. When Hugh of Poitiers was writing his history of Vézelay in the middle of the twelfth century, it was at the height of its success. The church of Vézelay, declared Hugh, grew powerful as 'the chapel of the blessed loved one and servant of God, Mary

---

[99] *Ibid.*   [100] See Ryan (trans.), *The Golden Legend*, pp. 381–382.

Magdalene, whose relics and special seat are there, and whose name, known splendidly to all, is celebrated the world over and adored. Many people as a consequence have flocked to the place from all parts and, as much by their number as by their affluence in worldly goods, have rendered the town of Vézelay illustrious and conspicuous'.[101]

The eleventh to twelfth centuries were the golden age of Vézelay. But the early thirteenth century saw also the beginning of a decline in its fortunes. The abbey's finances were dwindling, and venality and corruption were commonplace. Moreover, the pilgrim market was drying up. With bits and pieces of Mary Magdalene all over Europe, not to mention another body in Rome (albeit sans head), Vézelay's claims to possess the complete body of Mary Magdalene were coming to look increasingly doubtful. Moreover, if her body really was in Vézelay, it was asked, shouldn't she be able to protect it from economic decay?[102]

Word of Vézelay's troubles, spiritual and temporal, reached Rome. Thus, on 29 September 1265, the papal legate in France, Cardinal Simon de Brion received a letter from Pope Clement IV (1265–1268) to undertake a reform of the monastery. The Abbot, John of Auxerre

---

[101] Scott and Ward (eds.), *The Vézelay Chronicle*, p. 154. See also Donald Maddox, 'Du Déclin au Renouveau: Vézelay, Girart de Rousillon, et l'Inventio des Reliques de la Madeleine', in Emmanuelle Baumgartner and Laurence Harf-Lancner (eds.), *Progrès, Réaction, Décadence dans l'Occident Médiéval* (Geneva: Droz, 2003), pp. 95–109; and Victor Saxer, *Le Dossier Vézelien de Marie Madeleine: Invention et Translation des Reliques en 1265–1267* (Bruxelles: Société des Bollandistes, 1975).

[102] See Scott and Ward (eds.), *The Vézelay Chronicle*, pp. 12–13.

(1252–1274), moved quickly. Convinced that the key reason for the decline in Vézelay's fortunes was that no one had seen Mary's remains, he staged a last ditch attempt, before Simon's arrival, to revive them (the fortunes not the remains). Thus, on the night of 4 October 1265, in the presence of bishops Guy of Auxerre, Peter of Caesarea, and the entire monastic community, the bronze coffin under the high altar was ceremoniously opened up. Within the coffin, they discovered bones wrapped in silk and tresses of female hair. And, O happy day, there was an undated letter from a 'King Charles' attesting to the authenticity of the remains. After the ceremony, the bones wrapped in their silk were returned to their coffin and it was put back in its original place. This fortuitous 'invention' only needed some official confirmation. On 24 April 1267, the French king Louis IX (1226–1270) presided over the translation of Mary's remains to a new casket of pure silver.

The king was rewarded for his devotion to Mary with relics of Mary – an arm, and a jawbone with three teeth, while Simon de Brion received a rib. In July of the same year, the king returned the arm in an arm-with-hand shaped reliquary along with the jawbone and teeth in a reliquary held by a silver angel. Along with these, he bestowed relics of Christ upon the monastery – a piece of the true cross, two thorns from the crown of thorns, and fragments of Christ's clothing – that had been brought back from Constantinople in 1204.[103] In 1281,

---

[103] Louis IX had been given the crown of thorns by the Latin Emperor of Constantinople Baldwin II in 1238. In 1801, it was deposited in the cathedral of Notre Dame. On 15 April 2019, it was rescued from the fire in Notre Dame. It is now kept in the Louvre.

Simon de Brion, by then Pope Martin IV, gave his rib to the Archbishop of Sens. Although there were bits and pieces of Mary apparently present in the coffin under the high altar in Vézelay, that there was a full body (corpus) was not authenticated. Only 'certain holy relics' ('*quasdam venerandas reliquias*') were found.[104] Were the remains found in the tomb along with the letter from King Charles all part of an elaborate fraud by the community at Vézelay? You could be forgiven for thinking so.

Relics, Reliquaries, and Remnants in Saint Maximin

Fraud or not, the attempt to revive the cult in Vézelay was not successful. For, in opposition to the Benedictines in Vézelay, the monks in Provence were soon to construct a counter-narrative, one that was not only to establish that the body of Mary Magdalene had never been in Vézelay but also that, as the *vita apostolica-eremitica* indicated, it had *all along* been at Saint-Maximin in the south of France. It was a story that, as we will see, had a ready explanation why the body at Vézelay could not be authentic. We can pick up the story in Provence with the chronicle of the lives of the popes – the *Flores Chronicon* – that the Dominican inquisitor Bernard Gui (d. 1331) wrote between 1311 and 1316. His account was to become a defining one.

According to Bernard, it was on 9 September 1279 that Charles of Salerno (1254–1309), the future Charles II and nephew of Louis IX, was in Saint-Maximin, searching for

---

[104] See Head (ed.), *Medieval Hagiography*, p. 684.

the body of Mary Magdalene in the chapel within the church in which Saint Maximin had laid it. There he discovered the sweetly smelling body of Mary in a marble tomb. It was clearly seen by all present that there was a root with a small branch of fennel stuck in her throat. This emerged from her (still preserved) tongue and extended at some length from her body. A 'divided root with a small branch', he went on to explain, 'is currently used in various places for the preservation of certain relics'.[105] Perhaps the preserved tongue was a recognition of the power of her preaching. Hers, after all, was a mouth that Jacobus de Voragine described breathing forth 'the perfume of the word of God more profusely than others could'.[106] Be that as it may, the preserved tongue did not appear in later accounts, although variations on the branch of fennel did.

Crucially, in the same tomb, next to her body, there was an ancient document enclosed in wood that authenticated the remains. This informed Charles that, during the reign of the French King Odoyno, on 16 December 700, 'this body of the most precious and venerable blessed Mary Magdalen was moved secretly at night from her alabaster sepulcher into this marble [sepulcher] (once the body of Sidonius was moved) so that it might be better hidden during the invasions of that treacherous people the Saracens'.[107] The implications were clear. The body

---

[105] *Ibid.*, p. 691.   [106] Ryan (trans.), *The Golden Legend*, p. 377.

[107] Head (ed.), *Medieval Hagiography*, p. 691. There is no historical figure we can identify as Odoyno. For an excellent overview of the Saint-Maximin relics, see Neal Raymond Clemens Jr., 'The Establishment of the Cult of Mary Magdalen in France, 1279–1543', PhD thesis, Columbia University, 1997.

that had been discovered later by Baidilo in an alabaster tomb could not have been that of Mary Magdalene but, either someone else's, or merely a part of hers:

the recent deeds of Prince Charles (as just mentioned) and truth, uncovered and revealed by such evident signs, clearly indicate and faithfully manifest that the translation of the body of the Magdalen to Vézelay, commonly broadcast and written, is not able to be truly accepted because her body was not then in the sepulchre of alabaster where it was first placed, but [it was a translation] of some other body or perhaps some part of her body.[108]

Having examined all the things found in the chapel, Charles called together the archbishops of Narbonne, Arles, and Aix, together with other bishops, abbots, monks, nobles, clergy, and people. On 5 May 1280, Charles placed the body of Mary in a reliquary made of gold and precious stones. On this occasion, the authenticity of the body was further evidenced by another ancient document found in the tomb that declared, 'Here lies the body of blessed Mary Magdalen'.[109] Charles's father, King Charles I (1226/7–1285) was soon to make Mary the protector of the Angevin dynasty. It is testimony to the importance of Mary at this time that she was able to provide an 'otherworldly' legitimation to the Angevins.

It seems that Charles might have taken a few souvenirs away with him. He may have taken an arm. For, at an early time afterwards, he returned an arm of Mary Magdalene to Saint-Maximin in a silver reliquary. More importantly, he undoubtedly took the most valued relic of

---

[108] *Ibid.*, p. 692.   [109] *Ibid.*

all – her head. On 11 June 1281, he displayed the head in Aix along with the lower jaw that he later presented to the Dominican nuns there. It was his declared intention at the time to construct a gold and silver reliquary, ornamented with precious stones, in which the head would be set, visible through a crystal front. The head was put in the reliquary on 10 December 1283. And eventually it did make its way back to Saint-Maximin. For it was mentioned in an inventory of 261 relics at Saint-Maximin in 1504.[110]

This discovery of Mary's remains was another pious (or perhaps impious) fraud, whether with or without the connivance of Charles we cannot be sure. The supposedly eighth-century document was a fake. But it was a persuasive one. Salimbene, for example, was sufficiently convinced in 1284 to declare the rival claims of both Vézelay and Rome as dead.[111] Simon de Brion as Pope Martin IV held the ground for Vézelay, but the weight of opinion was shifting to Saint-Maximin. In 1295, Charles of Salerno (by then Charles II) was putting pressure on Pope Boniface VIII to declare in favour of Saint-Maximin. Papal approval was not only desirable to invalidate the relics of Mary in Vézelay, it was also necessary. The Roman authorities had become aware of the fraud surrounding the trade in relics. Thus, the Fourth Lateran Council in 1215 forbade the sale of relics, ordered that

---

[110] J. –H. Albanès, 'Inventaire des Objets Précieux Conserves au Couvent de Saint-Maximin, en Provence, en 1504,' *Revue des Sociétés Savantes*, ser. 6, vol. 5 (1877), p. 299. This reliquary was destroyed during the French Revolution.

[111] See Coulton, *From St. Francis to Dante: Translations from the Chronicle of the Franciscan Salimbene, 1221–1288*, p. 313.

all relics should only be displayed in a reliquary, and banned the showing of them publicly 'unless they have previously been approved by the authority of the Roman pontiff'.[112]

How Charles II managed to get papal endorsement from Boniface VIII is something of a puzzle. We do know that the two documents found with Mary Magdalene in her tomb, along with a letter of support from assorted archbishops and bishops, were sent to Pope Martin IV before 1285, not least because Charles is referred to as 'Prince of Salerno', a title that ceased when he became King in that year. 'These two *cartellae*', we read, 'which make mention of the body of blessed Mary Magdalen ... were discovered in the sepulcher. They are enclosed here ... so that, having inspected them and duly considered their age and the form of their writing, the Lord Pope and who[ever] should see them, may judge the certainty of the matter more firmly'.[113] We also know that documentation was provided to Boniface in 1295, so it is probable that these documents were provided to Boniface and his accreditation of the remains of Mary Magdalene was given as a result. In 1295, Boniface was probably also aware of both the arm and the head in their respective reliquaries. As we noted above, the inscription on the altar in Rome that he re-dedicated to Mary Magdalene in 1297 declared that the body was present, although 'without head and arm'.

---

[112] 'Fourth Lateran Council: 1215', *Papal Encyclicals Online*. Available at www.papalencyclicals.net/councils/ecum12-2.htm#62.

[113] Quoted by Clemens, 'The Establishment of the Cult of Mary Magdalen in France, 1279–1543', p. 78

A more picturesque account of the process of accreditation was given in 1355 by the vice-chancellor of the Kingdom of Naples, Cardinal Philippe de Cabassolle (1305–1372), in his *Libellus Hystorialis Marie Beatissime Magdalene*.[114] Philippe believed that Charles II brought the head and the documents to Boniface in Rome. Remembering that he had the jaw-bone of Mary in the chapel in Saint John Lateran, Boniface decided to test whether the jaw that he knew to be Mary Magdalene's fitted the skull. *Et voilà* – a perfect fit. This account was, perhaps, written by Philippe in ignorance of the fact that Charles had given the jaw to the Dominican nuns in Aix. Moreover, the jaw and the head were reunited in 1458 when King René, (1409–1480) returned the jaw held by the nuns in Aix to the head reliquary in Saint-Maximin (although he took the arm reliquary in exchange for it). Documentation and relics aside, there was no doubt sufficient political pressure for Boniface VIII to accede to the king's wishes:

We, therefore seeing that you are known to have shown the exceptional devotion normal to you to the above-mentioned saint, especially through the evidence of this labor, in that once when the place where that body was buried was unknown, you gave yourself to effective study in order to seek and discover it and at length, when the body was found in the above-mentioned church, with fitting devotion and appropriate reverence you ordered it to be buried before a great multitude of

---

[114] On this work, see Victor Saxer, 'Philippe Cabassole et son *Libellus Hystorialis Marie Beatissime Magdalene*', Publications de l'École Française de Rome 245 (1998), pp. 193–204.

clergy and people from those parts. And we intend to accede in this matter to your desires favorably especially because we shall have seen many things about the aforementioned items in eye-witness testimony.[115]

In addition, Boniface gave the Dominicans authority over the site, and granted indulgences to visiting pilgrims. Two years later, the second Dominican prior at Saint-Maximin decreed that Mary's feast day be celebrated throughout the entire order, and she became the patron saint of the Dominicans.[116]

As Oscar Wilde elegantly put it, 'Moderation is a fatal thing. Nothing succeeds like excess'. In their late fifteenth-century embellishment of the account of Charles and the discovery of the body of Mary, the Dominicans were anything but moderate. This was the final act in the writing and rewriting of the history of the relics at Saint-Maximin. This Dominican legend of Saint Mary Magdalene has Charles as already King Charles II and King of Sicily in 1279, although he wasn't until 1285. It also declared that he had been in prison in 1279, although he wasn't imprisoned until 1284. Earlier accounts of Charles's discovery of Mary had failed to give any reason for Charles having looked in Saint-Maximin. The key rhetorical strategy in this final account was to emphasise the miraculous in the whole process by putting Mary Magdalene completely in charge of the discovery of her own body from the outset.[117]

---

[115] Quoted by Clemens, 'The Establishment of the Cult of Mary Magdalen in France, 1279–1543', p. 79.

[116] See Saxer, *Le Culte de Marie Madeleine*, pp. 241–242.

[117] The Latin version may be found in BHL, no. 5512.

In the year 1279, we read, Charles II was captured by the king of Aragon in a naval battle and imprisoned. Totally devoted as he was to Mary, he begged for her aid and support. She came to him in a dream in the middle of a night and asked him what he was seeking from her. He responded that he wished to be free from prison. In response to his prayers, Mary granted his request. In return, Mary demanded of him that he demonstrate to the Pope and the people that her body was in Saint-Maximin and not in Vézelay in Burgundy. She told him that he would find her body in the church of Saint-Maximin to the right of the great altar in a tomb. She also told him that the body that had been moved to Vézelay after the expulsion of the infidels was not hers, but rather that of Sidonius which had also been lying in her tomb. In addition, she told Charles that he would find the bark of a tree above the tomb that would say in the hand of Maximinus, 'Here lies the body of blessed Mary Magdalen'. He would also find her bones, destitute of flesh 'except on the part of my head where our Lord Jesus Christ touched me saying, "Do not touch me", after his glorious resurrection'.[118] Along with these, next to her left jaw, there would also be found a small crystal jar with earth soaked with the blood of Christ, hairs from her head turned into ashes except for those that had touched the feet of Christ when she dried them, and 'a palm branch with green leaves, proceeding from my mouth'.[119] She then declared that Charles should build a convent and a church and that the Dominicans had her authority to oversee these.

---

[118] Head (ed.), *Medieval Hagiography*, p. 698.   [119] *Ibid.*

In this account, Mary's tongue with the branch of fennel to preserve it, as Bernard Gui had reported, has disappeared to be replaced by a palm branch. If the preserved tongue was a sign of her eloquence in preaching after she arrived in France, it may have been deliberately omitted. While a number of accounts of Mary's life in France were content to emphasize the eloquence of her tongue, others were uncomfortable with the idea of a woman preaching. As early as the mid to late tenth century, the '*Sermo de Sancta Maria Magdalenae*' had Mary, upon reaching Marseilles, handing preaching duties over to Lazarus because it was prohibited for a woman to be heard in public.

Philippe de Cabassole, upon whom the Dominicans were relying for their account, did see the palm branch as a sign of her preaching. But he nonetheless did not endorse it, declaring in 1355, 'After she heard the decree of the apostle that *to teach is not the office of women* (1 Timothy 2.12), she immediately ceased preaching lest she should usurp the duties of another and, content with her limits, she renounced the world, giving herself up completely to contemplation, and thus she did not steal the obligations that rightly belonged to another'.[120] In spite of the Dominicans being an order of preachers, Mary became rather a model of conversion and penance, and not an exemplar of preaching. Or perhaps, it was precisely *because* they were an order of preachers. Preaching was their forte, and they were reluctant to

---

[120] Quoted by Clemens, 'The Establishment of the Cult of Mary Magdalen in France, 1279–1543,' p. 249. I am indebted to Clemens for this discussion.

allow any visiting lay pilgrims – particularly female pilgrims – to encroach on this prerogative.

The Dominican friars were also reliant upon Philippe de Cabassolle for their claim that there was a piece of uncorrupted flesh on Mary's forehead. He declared,

On the right side of her forehead, above the place of her temple, He preserved the flesh from corruption, with the sacred touch of the master, the same master whose [prerogative] it is to be able to dissolve anything natural and to preserve anything corruptible (against the statutes of the laws of nature), in which the properties of the touch of the sacred hand is clearly evident to all those who see it.[121]

Cabasolle's was the earliest mention of the incorruptible flesh on Mary's forehead. The bodies of the saints were thought to be resistant after death to decay. Theodore of Echternach put it succinctly around 1104: 'From nature it is putrid and corruptible, but from grace and merits it remains for a long time without rot even contrary to nature, and it repels the greedy worms'.[122] In short, the incorruptibility of the bodies of the saints was a divine gift and an anticipation of the imperishability of the resurrection body.

This piece of Mary's uncorrupted flesh came to be mentioned in almost every fifteenth-century description of the relics at Saint-Maximin. Visible through the crystal face of the reliquary, it was genuinely numinous. The pilgrim Jerome Münzer in 1494 wrote of it,

---

[121] Quoted by *Ibid.*, pp. 103–104.
[122] Quoted by Bynum, *The Resurrection of the Body*, p. 210.

Finally we saw in that place [the crypt of Saint-Maximin] secured behind bars and metal barriers the head of the most holy Magdalen, covered with gold and silver work. It was terrible to see this face: on the front part of the skull on the left side the flesh and skin remained on the bones, [it was] on this part [of her head] on which Christ after his resurrection touched her with his glorified body, and said 'Do not touch me'.[123]

In Charles's dream, Mary also ordered him to give the Dominicans authority over a grotto, a few miles away from Saint-Maximin. High up in a massif known as Sainte-Baume, this was where Mary had purportedly spent the thirty years of her eremitic life. We do not know when the grotto began as a place of pilgrimage. But it was already a well-established site for devotees of Mary – and a nice spot for a picnic – when Salimbene visited it in 1248. 'Now the Magdalene's cave' he wrote,

wherein she did penitence thirty years, is five miles distant from Marseilles, and I slept there one night immediately after her feast. It is in a high rocky mountain, and great enough, if I remember well, to contain a thousand men. There are three altars and a dropping well of water like unto the well of Siloa, and a most fair road to it, and without is a church hard by the cave, where dwells a priest ; and above the cave the mountain is as high again as the height of the Baptistery of Parma, and the cave itself is so far raised above the level ground that three towers like that of the Asinelli of Bologna could not reach it, if I remember aright : so that great trees which grow below show like nettles or bushes of sage ; and since this

---

[123] Quoted by Clemens, 'The Establishment of the Cult of Mary Magdalen in France, 1279–1543', p. 104.

region is utterly uninhabited and desolate, therefore the women and noble ladies of Marseilles when they come thither for devotion's sake bring with them asses laden with bread and wine, and pasties and fish, and such other meats as they desire.[124]

When Charles did arrive in Saint-Maximin, accompanied by a number of bishops, he dug in the place revealed to him by Mary and 'at length found, with the greatest fragrance, the most sacred body of St. Mary Magdalen with the foretold signs'.[125] He then evicted both the nuns of Saint-Zacharie who had been living at Saint-Maximin and the monks of Saint-Victor who were looking after Sainte-Baume. The Dominicans were appointed protectors of the cult of Mary Magdelene and he provided funds to build a cathedral and support the monastery.

Mary Magdalene was herself soon to become the site of a further controversy. In the sixteenth century, the question of her identification with Mary of Bethany and the sinful woman was to be raised by Christian humanists. Her remains in Saint-Maximin were to become a focus of the ensuing debate.

---

[124] Coulton, *From St. Francis to Dante: Translations from the Chronicle of the Franciscan Salimbene, 1221–1288*, p. 311.
[125] Head (ed.), *Medieval Hagiography*, p. 699.

4

Mary Divided

Sacred and Profane

~

Magdalene was not well, and Jesus had to chase seven devils out of her body. Thus, the mercy of God was manifested through her. From the fact that she was more constant than the apostles, and acted as the messenger of the resurrection of her master, one can easily conclude that women can often be more trustworthy than men. Love, when loyal, makes faith and trust more perfect.

François Demoulins de Rochefort, *Vie de la Magdalene*

Three Marys, Two, or One? The Quarrel of the Magdalene

The Italian Dominican friar Silvester Mazzolini, better known as Prierias (1456–1527), is most remembered as the theologian of the Catholic Church officially designated to respond to Martin Luther's (1483–1546) ninety-five theses – that list of propositions critical of the Church that fanned the flames of the Reformation. He was also, along with his inquisitorial interests in witchcraft and demonology, an ardent devotee of Mary Magdalene and an avid supporter of the Provencal tradition.[1] In order to fulfil a vow made to the saint, he had made the pilgrimage to Saint-Maximin in the summer

---

[1] On Prierias, see Michael Tavuzzi, *The Life and Works of Silvestro Mazzolini da Prierio, (1456–1527)* (Durham, NC: Duke University Press, 1997).

of 1497. He visited the usual sites and he read the manuscript version of 'The Dominican Legend of Mary Magdalene'. Subsequently, in his popular commentary on the Gospels, the Aurea Rosa, he gave a complete description of what a pilgrim might have hoped to see there at the end of the fifteenth century. 'There was shown to me several times', he wrote,

[H]er sacred and venerable skull, which was large, and completely bare to the bone all around, except on the forehead, where we claim that the Saviour of us all touched her. For there the skin is clearly visible, looking like the skin of an Ethiopian woman, or of a corpse killed long ago: and in the skin two hollows [made by] the tips of two fingers, one of which is much more obvious and much deeper than the other, and under the skin, the flesh, whitish in colour. There was also shown to me some of her hair in a glass vessel, not all of it, but the part which wiped the feet of Christ. And in addition a glass vessel full of earth, in colour between red and black, which Saint Magdalen gathered under the Cross on Good Friday. They all declared to me without hesitation that every year on Good Friday when the Passion is read it bubbles up clearly and visibly, as though blood were bubbling in it. I will leave to others what is to be made of this. I also saw her arm, which was large, and the colour of wax, but I was unable to see her bones, which were locked up in a silver case.[2]

The late fifteenth and early sixteenth centuries were the heyday of the shrines of Mary Magdalene at Saint-Maximin and Saint-Baume, supported by clergy, laity, and royalty alike. They were visited in late 1515, by Louise of

---

[2] Quoted by Sheila M. Porrer (ed. and trans.), *Jacques Lefèvre D'Étaples and the Three Maries Debates* (Geneva: Librairie Droz, 2009), p. 39.

Savoy (1476–1531), mother of the French King Francis I (1494–1547), accompanied by her daughter Marguerite of Angoulême (1492–1549) and Francis's wife Claude (1499–1524). This journey was taken in fulfilment of a vow made by Louise to Mary Magdalene a year earlier when she had asked the saint to ensure the safety of the king and to accord him victory over the Swiss at the battle of Marignano. With the Swiss defeated and King Francis safe, the queen and her entourage passed through Tarascon where they visited the tomb of Martha, and Arles where they saw relics of Mary the mother of James and Mary Salome, before arriving at Saint-Baume on 31 December 1515 to visit the shrine of Mary Magdalene. Having joined up with the king on his return trip from Italy, they visited the cathedral at Saint-Maximin on 20 January 1516 to view the relics there and then proceeded on a return visit to Saint-Baume.

It was one of the most significant visits in the history of these sites. For what came out of them was a debate about the identity of Mary Magdalene that was to rage from 1518 into the early 1520s and generate some twenty works. It was an argument about both the life and the afterlife of Mary Magdalene at a time when the West was thinking its way through how to balance the traditions of the Western Church against the revival of the traditions of classical antiquity in Renaissance Humanism.

It began when Louise, moved by her visit to the Provencal sites and intrigued by the identity of Mary Magdalene, commissioned the Franciscan priest and Humanist scholar François Demoulins de Rochefort (fl. 1501–1526) to create an illustrated Life of Mary Magdalene. It was to be a personal book of devotion, a souvenir of her visit to Provence, and a response to the questions her journey had provoked about the identity of Mary Magdalene. Demoulins certainly wanted to please the queen, not least because he was angling for an appointment as bishop. Collaborating with the Flemish illustrator Godefroy le Batave (fl. 1516–1526), Demoulins presented the tiny, illustrated volume entitled *Vie de la Magdalene* to Louise in 1517.[3] This was a work that reflected the dilemma faced by its author. As Anselm Hufstader neatly puts it, 'The obedient Humanist soon found himself perplexed. To edify Madame as well as flatter her, he must praise the saint by retelling her legends. To maintain Humanist standards, however, he had to cast a more critical eye on conflicting Gospel narratives and spurious traditions'.[4] Thus, underlying the debate about the identity of Mary Magdalene was a rift within Christendom that was to become crucial during the Reformation. The question of the composite versus the single Mary reflected a division between the general consensus of the Church and the critical awareness of a few individuals who, focusing on a new philological reading of the New Testament, defended their *individual claims* to truth against the traditions of the Church.

---

[3] The text was slightly smaller than a pack of cards. On the *Vie de la Magdalene*, see Barbara Jean Johnston, 'Sacred Kingship and Royal Patronage in the *Vie de la Magdalene*: Pilgrimage, Politics, Passion Plays, and the Life of Louise of Savoy', PhD thesis, Florida State University, 2007. This thesis contains an English translation of the *Vie de la Magdalene*.

[4] Anselm Hufstader, 'Jacques Lefèvre D'Étaples and the Magdalen', *Studies in the Renaissance* 16 (1969), p. 35.

Apart from the New Testament Gospels, Demoulins's key sources for his Life of Mary Magdalene were *The Life of Saint Mary Magdalene* of pseudo-Rabanus and the account of Mary Magdalene given by Jacobus de Voragine in his *Legenda Aurea*. Thus, the Mary Magdalene of the first major part of Demoulins's Life is the composite Mary – she who is the Mary Magdalene dispossessed of seven demons, Mary of Bethany, and the sinful woman who washed Jesus's feet and dried them with her hair. It is the story which we now know pretty well. Demoulins described Mary's pleasure-seeking youth, followed by the events in her life as related in the Gospels. He included Mary in the descent of the Holy Spirit at Pentecost (Acts 2.1–4). After that, according to him, she began to preach in public until she was put to sea with Lazarus, Martha, Marcella, Maximus, and Sidonius by the Jews, finally arriving at Marseilles. After a time of preaching in Marseilles, Mary retired to La Baume where, Demoulins told Louise, 'you took the pain to climb … with the best and sweetest little queen [Claude] that ever was in France'.[5]

Demoulins went on to describe the death of Mary Magdalene. It is the point at which some Humanist scepticism began to creep into his text. 'Some say', he declared,

[T]hat when Saint Maximus presented the sacrament to the Magdalene, the host flew to her mouth, but I believe this is a

---

[5] Johnston, 'Sacred Kingship and Royal Patronage', p. 368. This section of the text was accompanied by images depicting the grotto at Saint-Baume.

fable. However, it is possible. Besides, I do not know what mad one wrote that, once, she looked at her hands and was annoyed to see them black and wrinkled. I believe none of it. I do not believe either that she went to Aix to receive the Body of God. [I think instead] that Maximus went to La Baume, and that after the Magdalene died, he had her body carried to Aix, and he ordered a beautiful tomb for her.[6]

Well, not surprisingly, Demoulins rejected the claims of Vézelay to have the remains of Mary in favour of those of Saint-Maximin. But he was doubtful about some of the details of the relics held there. Thus, while he accepted that the hair in the reliquary could be the hair of Mary Magdalene, he doubted that it was the *actual* hair with which she had wiped the feet of Jesus. Of the reliquary containing the skull of Mary, he declared,

Madame, you have seen it with great devotion and it is because of you that so many people, following your example of humility, have honored and invoked the Magdalene. I remember well that, on one occasion, you devoutly talked about this precious fragment of flesh, which is on her forehead, and has been called 'Noli me tangere', 'Do not touch me', by the Jacobin [Dominican] brothers. But as far as I am concerned, I call it 'Noli me credere', 'Do not believe me', for although the evangelists wrote that the Magdalene had touched the feet of Jesus Christ, they never said that Jesus Christ had touched her forehead.[7]

Demoulins repeatedly emphasized his desire to be a faithful son of the Church. Nevertheless, as a Humanist *and* therefore a 'critical' reader of the New Testament, he

---

[6] *Ibid.*, p. 376.
[7] *Ibid.*, p. 380. I have slightly altered the punctuation in this passage.

had noticed that the Gospels, along with at least some of the early Church Fathers, did not identify Mary of Bethany with the sinful woman. He recognized too that the resurrection accounts seemed to be in contradiction if there were a composite Mary Magdalene. The Gospel of John had Jesus say to Mary Magdalene 'Touch me not' (John 20.17) while the Gospel of Matthew had Mary touching and holding Jesus's feet (Matthew 28.9). And Demoulins *was* aware that there were those who supported the idea that there were two Magdalenes as against those who held to one, arguing that 'Jesus appeared to her on two occasions'.[8]

In order to sort all this out, Demoulins demonstrated that he was still very much a man of his time. He turned to a revelation given to a Franciscan visionary Amadeus Menez de Silva (1420–1482) who had separated the Mary Magdalene who was a public sinner from the Mary Magdalene who had been possessed by demons. 'Both indeed were from the castle that is called Magdalum', Amadeus had declared, '[t]herefore the two Marys are confused by their names'.[9] Demoulins also quoted several passages from the fifth-century Christian poet, Coelius Sedulius, that distinguished the sinful woman from Mary Magdalene. For her part, Louise was keen to resolve the issue of 'the two Magdalenes' asking Demoulins if there was anything that would support the idea. With Louise's encouragement, Demoulins now declared that he thought that he 'could demonstrate, with the help of an honest and good man, that there were three Marys whom we call "Magdalene"'.[10]

---

[8] *Ibid.*, p. 385.   [9] *Ibid.*, p. 387.   [10] *Ibid.*, p. 398.

This 'honest and good man' was the Catholic Humanist Jacques Lefèvre D'Étaples (c. 1460–1536). He was to become the key player in the ensuing debate about the three Marys that began in earnest with the publication of his *De Maria Magdalena* in 1517, along with two subsequent works in 1518 and 1519.[11] By the time of these works, Lefèvre had long been a celebrated scholar in Europe, renowned not only for his work on the Aristotelian and Neo-Platonic philosophical traditions but also, from 1508, for his critical studies of the Bible that were to occupy him until the end of his life.[12] Crucially, for Lefèvre, it was the account of the Marys given in the Gospels that counted for more than the opinion of Gregory the Great and the cumulative weight of learned opinion and liturgical practice since that time. 'This is the method of inquiry', he wrote, 'to draw conclusions from no other source than the gospels. If any other elements are introduced, I will not draw the principal arguments from them. And I will proceed in the

---

[11] The full title of the 1517 work was *De Maria Magdalena & Triduo Christi*, consisting of one tract on Mary Magdalene and another on the issue of whether Christ arose after three days or on the third day. The second work in 1518 was a slightly revised edition of the 1517 version with an additional tract on the daughters of Anne, the supposed grandmother of Jesus, entitled *De Maria Magdalena, Triduo Christi, et ex Tribus una Maria, Disceptatio Secunda Emissio*. It also contained a prefatory epistle by Josse Clichtove. The third work in 1519 was a new work devoted only to Mary Magdalene entitled *De Tribus et Unica Magdalena Disceptatio Secunda*. For the discussion of Lefèvre, I have used the 1518 second edition of *De Maria Magdalena* and the 1519 *De Tribus et Unica Maria Magdalena*.

[12] For an introduction to the life and works of Lefèvre, see Guy Bedouelle, 'Jacques Lefèvre D'Étaples', in Carter Lindberg (ed.), *The Reformation Theologians* (Oxford: Blackwell, 2002), pp. 19–33.

manner of dialecticians: by setting down certain propositions which I will attempt to prove from the light of the
gospel alone, aided by the laws of reason'.[13] This was, as
close as makes no difference, the *'sola scriptura'* ('scripture
alone') of the Protestant Reformation.

As Demoulins expected, Jacques Lefèvre D'Étaples did
accept that Mary Magdalene, Mary of Bethany, and the
sinful woman of Luke were three separate women. Unlike
Demoulins, however, he thought that only two of them
were named Mary Magdalene and that the sinful woman
was anonymous. Be that as it may, in the main part of his
1518 *De Maria Magdalena*, a slightly revised version of the
1517 text, Lefèvre undertook a systematic analysis of the
biblical evidence. According to this, Mary of Bethany was
the unnamed woman who anointed Jesus's head with oil
in the house of Simon the leper (Mark 14.3–9, Matthew
26.6–13). It was also Mary of Bethany, the sister of
Martha and Lazarus who, as the Gospel of John declared,
anointed Jesus's feet and dried them with her hair when
Jesus came to a meal in their home (John 12. 1–8). Mary
of Bethany, he argued, was called 'Magdalen', meaning
'fort, citadel and tower' because she lived in such a 'castle'
in Bethany or owned one elsewhere in Judaea.

This 'Mary Magdalene' was, however, to be distinguished from the so-named Mary Magdalene, out of
whom Christ had cast seven devils, and who had then
become his devoted follower. In her case, the name
'Magdalene' was derived from the town whence she
came – Magdala in Galilee on the shore of the sea of

---

[13]   Quoted by Hufstader, 'Jacques Lefèvre D'Étaples and the Magdalen',
p. 42.

Tiberias. One Mary Magdalene was alone when she encountered the risen Christ. To this 'Mary Magdalene' Jesus had said 'Touch me not' (John 20.17). The other 'Mary Magdalene', in the company of another Mary, met Jesus, embraced his feet and worshipped him (Matthew 28.9). This idea of two Mary Magdalenes within the text was always going to be an exegetical bridge too far. Telling which Mary was which within the variety of Gospel accounts was fraught with interpretative difficulties. Lefèvre himself came to think so too. Thus, in his third work in 1519, he has given up the struggle of arguing that two different women were called 'Mary Magdalene'. The only Mary Magdalene, he then conceded, was the one so-called and not the Mary who was the sister of Martha and Lazarus, that is, Mary of Bethany. 'It is quite pointless,' he declared, 'to enquire where in the Gospel Mary the sister of Martha is called Magdalen'.[14] That said, his argument that Mary Magdalene and Mary of Bethany were different women (even if only one was called 'Magdalene') still held.

There remained, of course, the question of the identity of the unnamed sinful woman in the Gospel of Luke who anointed Jesus's feet with ointment and dried them with her hair. Was she Mary of Bethany or Mary Magdalene? In short, she was neither: '[T]his Mary Magdalene, from Galilee, was not that public sinner in the city. And even less so, that most noble Mary, the sister of Martha, who had towers, villages and towns'.[15] For Lefèvre, the

---

[14] Porrer (ed. and trans.), *Jacques Lefèvre D'Étaples and the Three Maries Debates*, p. 425.

[15] *Ibid.*, p. 212.

Biblical evidence clearly pointed to three different women. Moreover, he argued, the majority opinion of the early Church Fathers was with him and even Augustine who was uncertain was not against him. In the end, it was for him an argument between the truth of the Gospel that pointed to three different women and the error of a long tradition that had held to one.[16]

As for Gregory the Great, he it was whom Lefèvre blamed for perpetrating false teaching. And he it was who bore the blame for placing the stain of sin on Mary of Bethany by identifying her with the sinful, if repentant, woman. All this was not so much about the separation of Mary Magdalene from the others. It was about the separation of Mary of Bethany from Mary Magdalene and the sinful woman, and Mary of Bethany's rehabilitation as a woman of virtue and not of vice. For Lefèvre and his supporters, the virtuous contemplative Mary represented a higher ideal than the sinner who repented. No one must ever believe, Lefèvre declared, 'that Mary Magdalen, the sister of Martha, was ever that sinner in the city, and woman of notorious reputation'.[17] The Flemish Humanist Josse Clichtove (c. 1472–1543), made the point even more clearly in his defense of Lefèvre in 1519. 'Which is the higher condition', he asked,

[T]hat of innocence and sinlessness or that of repentance and sorrow for the acquired stains of sin? Here is one [Mary of Bethany] who is said never to have sunk into the stains of vice. Is she not given greater praise for virtue than the one who, after a fall, is said to have been raised up by the merciful grace of God and washed from her filth? Surely one's life becomes finer

---

[16] See *Ibid.*, p. 488.   [17] *Ibid.*, p. 206.

and more praiseworthy to the extent that it is assimilated to divine perfection. Truth itself, speaking in the gospel, declares that each one will be perfect if he is like his master. A life lived without falling into serious sin appears to be more similar to divine perfection and purity, which is totally foreign to sin, than one which, after the downfall of sin, is cleansed and washed by the help of divine mercy.[18]

Lefèvre's argument had momentous implications. First, it threw into question the liturgical practice of the Church that had celebrated both Mary of Bethany and Mary Magdalene as the same person on the same day – 22 July – for at least 800 years. Second, it brought into question the viability of the cult of Mary Magdalene that had been focused on the identification of Mary of Bethany with Mary Magdalene. Third, it raised questions about the authenticity of the relics in Provence. This seriously threatened the economies of Saint-Maximin and Saint-Baume that were dependent on the relics being those of Mary Magdalene.

Who was it then whose remains were in Saint-Maximin? It could only be Mary of Bethany. For it was she who, according to the *Vita Apostolica* and the *Vita Apostolica-Eremitica*, had travelled to France with her sister Martha and her brother Lazarus, both of whose remains were also to be found in that land. Lefèvre was happy with this solution. '[W]e shall not deny', he declared, that it was Mary of Bethany, the sister of Martha, who 'brought the faith to the inhabitants of Marseilles and Provence'.[19]

---

[18] Quoted by Hufstader, 'Lefèvre D'Étaples and the Magdalen', p. 57.
[19] Porrer (ed. and trans.), *Jacques Lefèvre D'Étaples and the Three Maries Debates*, p. 237.

As for her retirement to Saint-Baume, this was a further sign that she was Mary of Bethany, for she withdrew, not to do penance, but 'in order to exercise the contemplative life'.[20]

All this meant that it was the skull of Mary of Bethany in the reliquary in Saint-Maximin and not that of Mary Magdalene. But *then* there was another problem, one that had already been raised by Demoulins. How could the piece of flesh on the forehead of this woman (whoever she might be) be the result of Jesus's touching her when he is said in the Gospels *never* to have touched her? Lefèvre appears to be heading over the precipice of Demoulin's scepticism about the piece of skin known as the 'noli me tangere'. But he pulls up short. 'And how that happened it is not for us to pronounce; God himself knows, to whom alone all things human and celestial are open'.[21]

Mention of the 'noli me tangere' led Lefèvre into a discussion of the veneration of relics more generally. And he developed a theory of relics that gave them validity *regardless* of their authenticity. For this, he drew upon a justification of relics that combined piety with a gentle skepticism. It was developed, he said, by an unnamed close friend and travelling companion.[22] Simply put, relics were to be viewed as no more than outward and visible signs of higher spiritual realities. This was a significant shift in the theory of relics. As we have seen earlier, traditionally, *they themselves* were objects of power.

---

[20] *Ibid.*, p. 239.   [21] *Ibid.*, p. 243.
[22] This may have been Guillaume Farel (1489–1565). Farel embraced Protestantism in the early 1520s and became a leader of the Swiss Reformation.

Now they were no more than symbols of power *beyond them*. This new view of the nature of relics was one that undoubtedly appealed to the Platonically inclined Lefèvre for whom *all* earthly things were but passing and pale reflections of eternal and heavenly realities. Thus, his friend told him,

And so if sometimes people press on me visible objects for me to look at, out of pure humanity on their part, and if they tell me that here is the sandal of St. Anne, here the milk of the spotless Virgin, here the hair of St. Andrew, here the tooth of Apollonia, or something similar, I certainly do not place my faith in these things which are shown, and I neither respect them too much, nor disdain them (for CHRIST does not require my faith in these things). But I keep my faith centred on what is represented by the things I am told, especially those which I know the church celebrates, and I raise my mind to heaven, to the models on which visible things are patterned, which are evident to the eyes of the mind, not of the body.[23]

This was a theory of relics that enabled Lefèvre himself to get around the fact that, when he himself visited Saint-Maximin, he believed that he was venerating one woman, although he was actually venerating three. It mattered little. For although they were three in fact, in perfect charity, they were one: 'Nor does it displease the three, to be celebrated in united praise, nor does it displease each one to be celebrated in threefold praise, for all contention and all envy are far away from them, nor does it displease the three, to be venerated under one name. Whom I too venerate under the same name, that is, Mary

---

[23] Porrer (ed. and trans.), *Jacques Lefèvre D'Étaples and the Three Maries Debates*, pp. 243–245.

Magdalen'.[24] Moreover, they could be venerated in *any place* dedicated to their memory, even if there were no remains present. In short, as far as Lefèvre was concerned, whether Mary Magdalene was three persons or one, neither the liturgical practices around her nor her cult needed to be disrupted by his account of them. Nor, he believed, was the issue of the authenticity of her relics problematic. Or so he hoped.

The Church Fights Back

On Friday 23 July 1518, the papal legate to the English court, Cardinal Lorenzo Carpeggio (1474–1539), arrived in England. The following Tuesday, he dined with the Bishop of Rochester, John Fisher (1469–1535). Fisher was a Humanist and not unsympathetic to the kind of critical analysis of Mary Magdalene that he had found in Lefèvre's *De Maria Magdalena*. Carpeggio was fully aware of the debate about Mary Magdalene, and he asked Fisher for his opinion. At this time, Fisher had found Lefèvre's position a reasonable one. But later that year, the French ambassador to England and Bishop of Paris, Stephen Poncher (1446–1524), wrote to Fisher asking him to reconsider his opinion. It was Poncher, Fisher later wrote, who had awakened him to what great peril lay hidden, and what great confusion and disgrace could arise for the whole Church of Christ from this difference of opinions.[25] Poncher's choice was an astute one. Fisher did

---

[24] *Ibid.*, p. 251.
[25] Quoted by Edward Surtz, S. J., *The Works and Days of John Fisher* ... (Cambridge, MA: Harvard University Press, 1967), p. 5.

not pull his rhetorical punches in the three works he produced in 1519 arguing for the composite Magdalene. Europe's leading Catholic Humanist, Desiderius Erasmus (c. 1466–1536), wrote to Poncher, 'I am sorry that Lefèvre has to deal with the Bishop of Rochester [ie. Fisher], a man of outstanding piety and erudition, but of such a character that he does not easily give up once he has warmed to the fight'.[26]

For Lefèvre and his supporters, a virtuous and contemplative Mary of Bethany, one who fitted the Church's ideals of chastity, was to be preferred to the repentant sinner Mary Magdalene. By contrast, Fisher emphasized the pastoral desirability of a Mary Magdalene who, in moving from a state of sinfulness to a repentant, active, and finally contemplative life, was a better role model for the everyday Christian: From a prostitute on the streets to a contemplative on a mountain top was at the core of the story of Mary Magdalene. 'It stands to reason,' declared Fisher, 'that for those who are immersed in the vices of the flesh, the gospels should be held up as a model, not only of repentance but also of the ascent to the peak of virtue'.[27] Thus, for Fisher, this was no mere academic debate about the interpretation of Scripture. It had

---

[26] Quoted by Porrer (ed. and trans.), *Jacques Lefèvre D'Étaples and the Three Maries Debate*, pp. 105–106. Erasmus was right. On the matter of Henry VIII's divorce from Catherine of Aragon, Fisher (who was Catherine's confessor) was unbending in his support of the queen and unceasing in his opposition to Henry's desire to be acknowledged Head of the English Church. It was to cost him his head. Upon the scaffold, he declared that 'I am come hither to die for the faith of Christ's holy catholic church.' He was executed on 22 June 1535. In 1936, he was declared a Catholic saint.

[27] Quoted by Hufstader, 'Lefèvre D'Étaples and the Magdalen,' p. 55.

implications beyond the academy for the whole Church. 'I reflected often', he wrote,

How many disadvantages for the whole Church would arise from this opinion of Lefèvre's, should it be accepted, how many authors would have to be censured, how many books would need amending, how many sermons formerly preached to the people would now have to be revoked. Furthermore, I considered the serious scruples many people would entertain from this, how many excuses for bad faith they would seize upon, placing henceforward too little trust in either books or histories, but entertaining wholly unjustifiable doubts even about their common mother, the Church, which has sung and taught this very thing through so many centuries.[28]

Against the lone individual critically reading the Scripture and coming to their own conclusion, Fisher put the weight of the tradition of the Church, its authority, and its pastoral responsibility to the sinners under its care. Little wonder that, with the odds so stacked against Lefèvre, Erasmus wrote to Fisher that 'everyone admits that you have the upper hand across the board'.[29]

That said, Erasmus would have been in no doubt that opponents of Lefèvre did not have it all their own way. Thus, for example, the German Humanist Willibald Pirckheimer (1470–1530) wrote to Erasmus in 1520, condemning those who 'snatch Mary Magdalene from her deliverer Lefèvre and thrust her with most disgraceful harlots into a stinking brothel – when it would rather be

---

[28] Quoted by Porrer (ed. and trans.), *Jacques Lefèvre D'Étaples and the Three Maries Debate*, p. 105.

[29] *Ibid.*, p. 110.

more becoming in such a doubtful matter to follow the opinion which approaches closer to piety'.[30]

So, to bring this all together. There is a character in the New Testament called Mary Magdalene, possessed of seven demons and delivered from them, a disciple of Jesus and a key witness to his resurrection. She was identified in the year 591 by Pope Gregory the Great with two other women in the New Testament, namely, Mary of Bethany and the anonymous sinful woman of the Gospel of Luke. François Demoulins de Rochefort expressed doubt about this identification and declared to Queen Louise that he could demonstrate, with the help of Jacques Lefèvre D'Étaples, that there were three Marys who were called 'Magdalene'.

Initially, in his first work, Lefèvre distinguished the composite Mary Magdalene into three separate people, an anonymous sinful woman and two other women – the Mary Magdalene so named in the Gospels (named after the town of Magdala) and another Mary Magdalene (named Magdalene after her castle in Bethany), who was the same person as Mary of Bethany, the sister of Martha and Lazarus. Subsequently, in a later work, he gave up his two 'Mary Magdalenes' for one – she who Jesus delivered of seven demons, became his disciple, and was present at the resurrection.

On 9 November 1521, Lefèvre's views on Mary Magdalene were officially censured by the Faculty of Theology at the Sorbonne in Paris. His works were not placed on the Index of prohibited works in France. But

---

[30] Quoted by Surtz, S. J., *The Works and Days of John Fisher...* , pp. 403–404.

they were added to the Spanish Index in 1551 and the Roman Index in 1559. It was a sign to the Humanists that they would do well to leave popular piety alone. In the 1520s, the debate about the role of the individual in the reading of Scripture over against the authority and tradition of the Church was to move away from Mary Magdalene to new ground. The Church was to be far more engaged with the reforms of Lefèvre's friend and Fisher's enemy Martin Luther than with the identity of Mary Magdalene. By the end of the sixteenth century, within what was by then the Catholic side of the Western Church, the 'quarrel of the Magdalene' was relegated to not much more than an interesting historical aberration. The composite Mary Magdalene had won the battle.

A Woman for All Seasons

It was no coincidence that Martin Luther posted his 95 Theses on the door of the Castle Church in Wittenburg on 31 October 1517.[31] It was the Eve of All Saints' Day. When the door was opened on 1 November, the faithful would pass through to view the more than 5,000 relics that would be on display.[32] Of the saints with the most relics, Mary the mother of Jesus and Mary Magdalene shared the podium. Mary the mother of Jesus

---

[31] Whether Luther *actually* did so remains a matter of debate. The 95 Theses were certainly sent to Albrecht of Mainz on 31 October.

[32] Lucas Cranach produced an inventory of the relics in his *Wittemberger Heiligthumsbuch*. For Cranach's 'official catalogue', see Hans J. Hillerbrand (ed.), *The Reformation: A Narrative History Related by Contemporary Observers and Participants* (Grand Rapids, MI: Baker Book House, 1978), pp. 47–49.

topped the list with fifty-six, while Mary Magdalene came second with fifty-four. Luther rejected the cult of the saints along with their relics. He was unimpressed by the supposed head of John the Baptist. 'They show at Rome', he said, 'the head of St. John the Baptist though 'tis well known that the Saracens opened his tomb and burned his remains to ashes'.[33] He also told of a Franciscan who kept some of the hay in which Christ lay in his manger in a wallet that he carried with him. Another fellow replaced the hay with some charcoal. When the monk came to show the people the hay, he found only the wood. He was at no loss, however. 'My brethren', he said, 'I brought out the wrong wallet with me, and so cannot show you the hay; but here is some of the wood that St. Lawrence was grilled upon'.[34] For Luther, relics went with a whole array of papal and devilish lies – 'purgatory, relics, consecration of churches, swarms of decrees and decretals, and many more countless books full of vain, new inventions'.[35] Thus, for Luther, the veneration of relics was a sign of the general corruption of the church:

Oh, what a terrible and heavy reckoning those bishops will have to give who permit this devilish deceit and profit by it. They should be the first to prevent it and yet they regard it all as a godly and holy thing. They do not see that the devil is behind it all, to strengthen greed, to create a false and fictitious faith, to weaken the parish churches, to multiply taverns and harlotry, to

---

[33] William Hazlitt (ed. and trans.), *The Table Talk of Martin Luther* (London: Bell & Daldy, 1872), no. 444, p. 199.

[34] *Ibid.*, no. 435, p. 198.

[35] Quoted by Lyndal Roper, 'Luther Relics', in Jennifer Spinks and Dagmar Eichberger, *Religion, the Supernatural and Visual Culture in Early Modern Europe* (Leiden: Brill, 2015), p. 332.

lose money and working time to no purpose, and to lead ordinary people by the nose. If they had read Scripture as well as the damnable canon law, they would know how to deal with this matter![36]

Luther's Swiss colleague John Calvin (1509–1564) was equally, if not more, scathing in his *A Treatise on Relics* (1543). Calvin did not take prisoners, whether saints or sinners. For him, relics were nothing but a fraudulent imposte upon the gullible. If a total inventory of relics was completed, he declared, 'it would then be seen that every apostle had more than four bodies, and each saint at least two or three, and so on. In short, if all the relics were collected into one heap, the only astonishment would be that such a silly and clumsy imposition could have blinded the whole earth'.[37] Thus, the arm of Saint Anthony in Geneva was the bone of a stag, the brain of Saint Peter a piece of pumice stone. Moreover, if all the pieces of the true cross were collected, 'they would form a whole ship's cargo'.[38] Had Mary the mother of Jesus been a wet-nurse all her life, or a dairy, 'she could not have produced more [milk] than is shown as hers in various parts'.[39] Unlike Lazarus who, Calvin declared, had three bodies in different places, Mary Magdalene 'owns but two bodies, one at Auxerre, and another of very great celebrity, with its head detached, at St Maximin, in Provence'.[40] As for the tradition that Mary Magdalene had come to France, anyone

---

[36] Martin Luther, *Three Treatises* (Philadelphia: Fortress Press, 1970), pp. 75–76.

[37] John Calvin, *A Treatise on Relics* (Edinburgh: Johnstone, Hunter, & Co., 1870), p. 166.

[38] *Ibid.*, p. 173.   [39] *Ibid.*, p. 185.   [40] *Ibid.*, p. 197.

who has read the accounts 'cannot fail to be convinced of the folly of this fable'.[41] For Calvin, simply put, relics were fakes, put forward by imposters who were intent on deceiving the whole world.

Calvin's critique of relics, like that of Luther, reflected a significant shift in religious sentiment – from a spirituality focused on the immanent and the material to one oriented to the transcendent and the spiritual. As Alexandra Walsham nicely puts it,

> Beneath Calvin's vicious outburst against relics was a violent rejection of the assumptions about the immanence of the holy that underpinned traditional Catholic devotion to them. The notion that the body parts and possessions of Christ and the saints were sources of supernatural power and conduits of heavenly grace ostensibly flew in the face of a system of faith that powerfully re-emphasized the *transcendence* of the sacred and the *incorporeality* of the divine.[42]

The saints were no longer supernatural supporters, protectors, or intercessors to God on behalf of their earthly devotees. Nevertheless, they did become moral and spiritual exemplars whose lives could be woven into the fabric of Protestant beliefs and practices. As Margaret Arnold declares, 'Far from being ignored in the Protestant tradition, the saints of the Bible provided evangelical theologians and preachers with irresistible models for their congregations: familiar, time-honoured stories of

---

[41] See *Ibid.*, p. 165.
[42] Alexandra Walsham, 'Skeletons in the Cupboard: Relics after the English Reformation', *Past and Present* (2010), Supplement 5, pp. 121–122 (my italics).

men and women reacting to the presence and instruction of Christ, offering cautionary tales at need, but also examples of faith and obedience to imitate'.[43] Of those saints whose lives provided exemplars of faithfulness from the earliest times, Mary Magdalene was in the top rank.

It would be intellectually neat were we able simply to say that, while Catholicism held to the tradition of the composite Mary Magdalene (that included Mary of Bethany and the sinful woman), Protestantism endorsed the single Mary Magdalene – she who was possessed of demons, was a follower of Jesus, and was present at the resurrection.[44] But Luther seems not to have been persuaded by Lefèvre's debunking of the traditional composite Mary. His Mary Magdalene was identified with both the sinful woman and Mary of Bethany.[45] She was certainly not the jilted bride of John the evangelist at the wedding at Cana in Galilee.[46] The bride and groom, according to Luther, were poor relations or neighbours of Jesus's mother. Moreover, Jesus would not have been party to tempting John away from marriage. For Luther, marriage was the *only* state ordained by God. By his first miracle at the wedding in Cana, Luther wrote, Jesus

---

[43] Margaret Arnold, *The Magdalene in the Reformation* (Cambridge, MA: The Belknap Press, 2018), pp. 4–5. I am indebted to Arnold for this discussion of Mary Magdalene in the Reformation period.

[44] Porrer *does* argue this. See Porrer (ed. and trans.), *Jacques Lefèvre D'Étaples and the Three Maries Debate*, p. 150.

[45] For Mary Magdalene as Mary of Bethany, see Jaroslav Pelikan (ed.), *Luther's Works* (St. Louis, MO: Concordia Publishing House, 1955–1986), vol. 11, p. 541. For Mary Magdalene as the sinful woman, see Pelikan (ed.), *Luther's Works*, vol. 14, p. 151.

[46] See Martin Luther, *Martin Luthers Werke: Kritische Gesamtausgabe [Weimarer Ausgabe]* (Weimar: Hermann Böhlau, 1883–), vol. 17.1, p. 17.

'confirms marriage as the work and institution of God, no matter how common or how lowly it appears in the eyes of men, God none the less acknowledges his own work and loves it'.[47]

How then did Martin Luther appropriate the composite Mary Magdalene for the Protestant cause? Well, simply put, she was the ideal Lutheran. To be sure, she was the sinner who repented. But she was saved, not by her acts of contrition that followed faith but *through her faith alone.* Thus, she exemplified the key Lutheran doctrine of salvation by grace, through faith, and not through works. Thus, in a sermon on Mary Magdalene day in 1527, he declared, 'The hypocrites and work-saints write that such signs or works bring righteousness, but Christ says, "Your faith has saved you". And many sins are forgiven her. For she has loved much'.[48]

The story of Mary of Bethany and her sister Martha provided a further exemplar for Luther of salvation by faith rather than by works. As we know, this story was read within the medieval church as speaking to the contrast between two opposing ways of living – the contemplative versus the active life. But Luther rethought these as complementary parts of the *one* life. On his reading, the active life was one of works, the contemplative that of faith. Luther declared,

We see Mary here doing nothing except sitting still. But the word alone allows her to become godly. If it was different, he

---

[47] John Nicholas Lenker (ed.), *Martin Luther: Sermons*, vol. 2, p. 41. Available at http://sermons.martinluther.us/Luther_Lenker_Vol_2.pdf.

[48] Luther, *Martin Luthers Werke*, vol. 17.2, p. 464.

would have said, 'Mary, go and do something here or there'. But he wants to let her stay. Not only stay but also get nothing done. He does not reject Martha's works, but he says ... 'Martha, understand this – first there is the pure word and faith hangs on this. My word is eternal, your works will pass by in an instant'.[49]

On this reading, the contemplative life was no longer the prerogative of those living a monastic life, secluded from the world, nor was it the preserve of an educated theological elite. Rather, it was for every man and every woman. As Margaret Arnold eloquently sums it up, 'In Lutheran preaching, Mary Magdalene was brought back from her retreat into a hermit's cell and relocated in the hurly-burly of the mundane. Sitting at the feet of Jesus ... does not represent a turning away from the duties of this life but a devotion to the Word as it pierces through the cacophany of market place and nursery, workshop and battlefield'.[50]

For Luther, spiritually, both men and women were equal. In Luther's 'priesthood of all believers', there were both priests and priestesses. And both men *and* women were at the Last Supper. All were disciples of Christ:

And without doubt the women, Mary Magdalene, Martha, Johanna, were at the supper, and went with Him freely, who went together at Passover and on Easter. He does not speak of apostles, of priests, but of disciples, whereupon you should observe this .... Just as the name of Christians and disciples

---

[49] Susan C. Karant-Nunn and Merry E. Wiesner-Hanks, *Luther on Women: A Sourcebook* (Cambridge: Cambridge University Press, 2003), pp. 78–79.

[50] Arnold, *The Magdalene in the Reformation*, p. 57.

is common to all, men and women, so remains this text for our community also.[51]

Mary Magdalene was an exemplar for all men and women in the task of preaching the Gospel. In a Maundy Thursday sermon in 1530, Luther declared that Christ 'makes a preacheress [predigerin] out of her, so that she might be a mistress and teacher of the dear apostles'.[52]

That said, Luther's understanding of Mary Magdalene has to be placed within the context of his understanding of women more generally.[53] This was one that is unlikely to bring joy to the heart of any modern feminist. Simply put, Mary was saved by faith but, like Martha, she was still expected to do the housework under a stern yet benevolent and companionable patriarchal gaze. Women were accordingly expected to be (like Mary) pious, quiet, submissive, and obedient, and (like Martha) to get on with the housekeeping and child rearing. Thus, while Mary Magdalene was 'the preacheress', this was not a role that Luther was comfortable in granting to women in general. Fine in principle, but in practice? In the light of New Testament ambiguity around the issue, Luther steered between reformation and anarchy: 'Therefore, order, discipline, and respect demand that women keep silent whenever men speak; but if no man preaches, then it would be necessary that the women preach'.[54]

---

[51] Quoted by *Ibid.*, p. 61.
[52] Luther, *Martin Luthers Werke*, vol. 32, p. 80.
[53] For an excellent overview on Luther on women, see Karant-Nunn and Wiesner-Hanks, 'Introduction', *Luther on Women*.
[54] Luther, *Martin Luthers Werke*, vol. 8, p. 498.

While Martin Luther accepted the composite Mary, John Calvin opposed it. He was vociferous in his rejection of the identification of Mary of Bethany with the sinful woman. He declared,

The monks and similar pettifoggers ... imagine that this Mary, the sister of Lazarus, is that infamous woman of evil life, whom Luke mentions .... . The anointing supplied a reason for the error: as if it were not sufficiently clear however that Christ was anointed several times, and indeed in different places. The woman who was a sinner, of whom Luke writes, anointed Christ in Jerusalem, where she lived, but Mary did the same afterwards, in Bethany, in her own village.[55]

This meant that the space available for Calvin to interpret Mary Magdalene was significantly more confined than that of Luther. In the absence of Mary of Bethany *and* the sinful woman, Mary Magdalene featured only as the woman from whom Christ drove out seven demons and as the first witness to the resurrection. Calvin's position was a radical attack on the medieval tradition of Mary Magdalene.

Calvin was heir to the Classical tradition that saw women as flawed versions of men and therefore naturally inferior to them. Thus, although the Holy Spirit worked on both men and women equally, it needed to work a little harder in the latter case. Women *ought to* be humble, modest, and honest, but they *are* 'full of dissoluteness, pomp, vanity, and every vain

---

[55] Quoted by Porrer (ed. and trans.), *Jacques Lefèvre D'Étaples and the Three Maries Debate*, p. 151.

excess'.[56] Thus, it is not surprising that, for Calvin, Mary Magdalene served as an instance of sinful and depraved humanity, of the rejection of works, and of the need to surrender to God. 'Moreover', he declared, 'in order that we may be aroused and exhorted all the more to carry this out, Scripture makes known that there are not one, not two, nor a few foes, but great armies, which wage war against us. For Mary Magdalene is said to have been freed from seven demons by which she was possessed'.[57]

To be fair, like Luther, Calvin accepted, in principle at least, the spiritual equality of men and women. Mary Magdalene did provide an exemplar for Calvin (with qualification) of seeking God through faith. 'We will have no profit from the resurrection of our Lord Jesus Christ,' he declared, 'unless we seek him by faith, to be united to him .... And the example for that is offered to us here, when it is said that Mary Magdalene and her companions came to the sepulchre'.[58] The risen Christ's calling Mary by name, Calvin remarked in his commentary on the Gospel of John, is 'a lively image of our calling; for the only way in which we are admitted to the true knowledge of Christ is, when he first knows us, and then familiarly invites us to himself'.[59] That said, Calvin gave Mary no

[56] Quoted by Susan C. Karant-Nunn, *Reformation of Feeling: Shaping the Religious Emotions in Early Modern Germany* (Oxford: Oxford University Press, 2010), p. 180.

[57] John T. McNeill, *Calvin: Institutes of the Christian Religion* (Louisville, KY: Westminster John Knox Press, 2006), vol. 1, p. 173.

[58] Quoted by Arnold, *The Magdalene in the Reformation*, p. 171.

[59] William Pringle (trans.), *Commentary on the Gospel According to John* (Edinburgh: Calvin Translation Society, 1847), vol. 2, p. 258.

credit for recognising Jesus: 'This is a secret and wonderful change effected on the human understanding when God, enlightening her by his Spirit, renders her clearsighted, who formerly was slow of apprehension, and, indeed, altogether blind. Besides, the example of Mary ought to serve the purpose of exhortation, that all whom Christ invites to himself may reply to him without delay'.[60]

In the Magdalene tradition, it had resounded to her credit that, while the male disciples had fled the garden in fear, Mary Magdalene had stayed and was, as a result, the first witness to the resurrection. Calvin, however, cut Mary Magdalene and the other women no slack: 'As for the women remaining *at the sepulchre*, while the disciples return to the city, they are not entitled to great accommodation on this account; for the disciples carry with them consolation and joy, but the women torment themselves by idle and useless *weeping*. In short, it is superstition alone, accompanied by carnal feelings, that keeps them *near the sepulchre*'.[61] Mary's initial failure to recognize Christ was an example of the mistakes into which the human mind frequently falls. Mary remained focused on earthly and not heavenly things: 'Mary has no view of this matter but what is earthly. She desires only to obtain the dead body of Christ, that she may keep it hidden in the sepulchre; but she leaves out the most important matter, the elevation of her mind to the divine power of his resurrection'.[62] In short, her wish to touch Jesus was nothing but a vulgar earthly desire to keep him in this world.

---

[60] *Ibid.*, vol. 2, p. 258.   [61] *Ibid.*, vol. 2, p. 254.
[62] *Ibid.*, vol. 2, p. 257.

In effect, Calvin damned Mary Magdalene, if only metaphorically, with faint and begrudging praise. The only reason Christ had revealed himself to Mary Magdalene and the other women was to shame the male disciples who had been tardy and sluggish in their coming to believe. '[T]hey deserve', he wrote, 'not only to have *women* for their teachers, but even oxen and asses; since the Son of God had been so long and laboriously employed in teaching, and yet they had made so little, or hardly any progress. Yet this is a mild and gentle chastisement, when Christ has sent his disciples to the school of the women'.[63] Thus, unlike Luther, Calvin rejected women preaching in any circumstances. So Mary's preaching to the disciples was only a one-off. Christ 'did not intend that what was done once by a singular privilege should be viewed as an example'.[64] For women generally, this was a case of not preaching what they practised.

A Woman Preaching

The Church's traditional identification of Mary Magdalene with Mary of Bethany provided a Swiss Calvinist like Pierre Viret (1511–1571), Calvin's closest friend, with grist for his anti-papal mill. Viret, like Calvin, was a supporter of the separation of Mary of Bethany from Mary Magdalene. 'This Mary Magdalene', he wrote, 'was not the sister of Martha and Lazarus . . . . On this, we have the testimony of Chrysostom, who says clearly, that this Mary was not a whore [putain] but honest and

---

[63] *Ibid.*, vol. 2, p. 260. [64] *Ibid.*, vol. 2, p. 261.

virtuous, the one who cared for Jesus Christ, and loved him strongly with her sister'.[65] Moreover, Mary Magdalene ought not to have been identified with the sinful woman of the Gospel of Luke. This gave him the chance for a cheap shot at Catholicism. 'I do not know', he wrote, 'if the priests and monks wrote these things of Mary Magdalene ... in order to give greater encouragement to women to prostitute themselves, seeing that such great prostitutes were received in paradise in such honour'.[66] Still, even though Viret wanted to separate the virtuous Mary of Bethany from the others, he was just as dismissive of her role as a preacher. 'I leave aside ... ', he declared, 'that she performed the office of Apostle and minister, preaching the Gospel, and that she had this authority from St. Peter, the pope of Rome. For these are such weighty lies [Car ce sont mensonges si lourds]'.[67] Viret's propagandistic message was clear: Calvinists supported virtue and silence in women, Catholics sex and speech.

In contrast to Calvinism, the seventeenth-century English religious movement known as Quakerism fully endorsed the role of women as preachers.[68] Their

---

[65] Quoted by Arnold, *The Magdalene in the Reformation*, p. 174. See also Pierre Viret, *De la Vraye et Fausse Religion* (Geneva, 1560), p. 594. Available at
    file:///C:/Users/repalmon/AppData/Local/Temp/De%20la%20vraye%20et%20fausse%20religion%20touchant%20les%20voeus%20et%20les%20sermens%20olicites%20et%20oill-1.pdf.

[66] Quoted by *Ibid.*, p. 174. See also Viret, *De la Vraye et Fausse Religion*, pp. 595–596.

[67] Quoted by *Ibid.*, p. 176. See also Viret, *De la Vraye et Fausse Religion*, p. 595

[68] On the differences in theology and tone between Calvinism and Quakerism, see Hugh Rock, 'Quakerism Understood in Relation to

commitment to the preaching of women was immortalized in James Boswell's life of Samuel Johnson. On 31 July 1763, Boswell told Johnson that he had been that morning to a meeting of Quakers where he had heard a woman preach. To this, Johnson responded, 'Sir. A woman's preaching is like a dog's walking on his hinder legs. It is not done well; but you are surprized to find it done at all'.[69]

Support for the preaching of women was to be found within the writings of the founder of the Quakers, George Fox (1624–1691). His endorsement of the equal rights of women to preach arose from a robust doctrine of the Holy Spirit inspiring both men and women equally. For precedents on women preaching he looked particularly to the Biblical examples of women prophesying. Of these women, Mary Magdalene informing the disciples of the resurrection of Jesus was a prime example:

Now you that make a scoff & a wonder at a Womans declaring [preaching], you may see that it was *Mary* that first declared Christ after he was risen, so be ashamed and confounded for ever, & let all your mouths be stopt for ever, that despise the spirit of prophesie in the daughters, and do cast them into prison, and [d]o hinder the women-labourers in the Gospel, and saith the Apostle, Christ in the male and in the female, and if Christ be in the female as well as in the Male, is not he the same? and may not the Spirit of Christ speak in the female as wel as in the male? ... for the light is the same in the male, & in

Calvinism: The Theology of George Fox', *Scottish Journal of Theology* 70 (2017), pp. 333–347.

[69] George Birkbeck, Norman Hill and L.F. Powell (eds.), *Boswell's Life of Johnson, Vol. 1: The Life (1709–1765)* (Oxford: Oxford University Press, 1934), p. 463.

the female which cometh from Christ, him by whom the world was made, and so Christ is one in all, and not divided, and who is it that dares stop Christs mouth?[70]

George Fox's wife, Margaret Askew Fell (1614–1702), was similarly eloquent in her defence of the preaching of women. Against the Biblical prohibitions on women speaking (1 Corinthians 14.34–6, 1 Timothy 2.11–15), Fell argued for the love Jesus showed to them and the love and compassion they showed to him. Were it not for Mary Magdalene and other women, the message of the redemption brought about by the resurrection of Jesus would have been lost. 'What had become', she asked, 'of the Redemption of the whole Body of Man-kind, if they had not believed the Message that the Lord Jesus sent by these Women, of and concerning his Resurrection? And if these Women had not thus... sat watching, and waiting, and weeping about the Sepulchre until the time of his Resurrection, and so were ready to carry his Message, as is manifested; else how should his Disciples have known, who were not there?'[71] Fell's point, as Margaret Arnold notes, is that 'the giving and receiving of love in intimate exchange has ultimately forged a stronger bond between Christ and his female followers than has the intellectual teaching and ecclesiastical debate conducted among the male disciples'.[72] The Magdalene's religion was one of the heart and not of the mind. And there was more than a

---

[70] George Fox, *The Woman Learning in Silence* ... (London, 1656), p. 5.
[71] Margaret Askew Fell Fox, *Womens Speaking Justified, Proved and Allowed of by the Scriptures* ... (London, 1656), p. 7.
[72] Arnold, *The Magdalene in the Reformation*, p. 216.

suggestion in Margaret Fell that not only was the faith of women equal to that of men but superior to it. This was Mary Magdalene's major contribution to the spiritual life of Protestant women.

The devotion of Mary Magdalene and her female companions to Jesus along with their role in preaching the resurrection was also remarked upon by other more mainstream English Protestant commentators. Thus, for example, in a sermon on Easter Day 1608, the Bishop of Winchester, Lancelot Andrewes (1555–1626), wondered why Christ would have made his resurrection known to women rather than men. In this case, he suggested, the women had outdone the men in 'manliness'. While the men had fled, the women had stayed. Truly, he declared, 'there will appeare more *Love*, and *Labour* in these *Women*, then in *Men*; even the *Apostle's* themselves. At this time (I know not, how) *Men* were then become *Women* ... and *Women* were *Men*: Sure, the more *manly*, of the twaine'.[73] Mary's medieval title 'apostle of the apostles' still had resonance in Protestant preaching. Thus, on Easter Day 1622, Andrewes again warmed to his Magdalene theme. In Jesus's commissioning Mary to preach his resurrection, she had been made 'an *Apostle*. Nay *Apostolorum Apostola, an Apostle* to the *Apostles* themselves'.[74] The first Gospel of all, therefore, was '*Marie Magdalen's Gospell* ... the prime *Gospell* of all, before any of the other foure'.[75]

---

[73] Lancelot Andrewes, *XCVI Sermons by the Right Honourable and Reverend Father in God, Lancelot Andrewes, Late Lord Bishop of Winchester* (London, 1629), p. 404.
[74] *Ibid.*, p. 556. [75] *Ibid.*

Mary, Loving and Much Loved

As we have seen in earlier chapters, the action in the life of the medieval Mary took place more after the ascension of Christ than before it. In particular, in her latter days in France (or elsewhere), she had embarked upon a long eremitic life as a demonstration of her repentance. Thus did Mary Magdalene exemplify the later medieval Church's understanding of divine forgiveness as requiring three things: contrition, confession, and acts of penitence, the last imposed at the end of a confessional encounter between priest and sinner. It was the 'works' *after* repentance that held the key to forgiveness and thus salvation.

The Reformation roundly rejected the idea that salvation depended upon actions *after* repentance. Rather, it was the act of repentance itself followed by the divine gracious act of forgiveness that effected salvation. As a consequence, acts of penitence were redundant, and there was no need for the Protestant Mary to engage in a long life of penitential acts. Thus, along with Protestantism's rejection of the cult of Mary Magdalene, there went a rejection of (or at least a disregard for) the traditions of her life beyond the New Testament. The Protestant Mary was, above all, the Biblical Mary. Of the medieval 'quadriga' or four-fold interpretation of Scripture – literal (or historical), moral, allegorical, and anagogical, Protestantism accepted the literal, embraced the moral, but rejected the allegorical and the anagogical.[76] Thus, in

---

[76] Although Protestant interpreters often incorporated non-literal readings into their 'literal' interpretations. On late medieval and early modern theories of biblical interpretation, see Deeana Copeland

the case of Mary Magdalene, *all* the Protestant emphasis was upon the literal story of her repentance within the New Testament and the moral lessons that could be drawn from it.

Was she Calvin's single or Luther's composite Mary? At this point, it didn't probably matter. She was so much a part of lived religion that the quarrel of the Magdalene had little purchase. The Mary Magdalene of Protestantism remained the first witness to the resurrection (although, the Quakers aside, not generally as a model for women preaching). She still sat at the feet of Jesus, although with Protestantism's rejection of the monastic tradition, she was no longer required as the exemplar of the contemplative life. But as the repentant prostitute who wept on the feet of Jesus and wiped them with her hair – saved by grace and not by works, she still had a key role to play.

Repentance now became the central moment in the drama of Mary's life. The repentant person should no longer seek the help of dead saints, Bishop John Hooper (c. 1495–1555) reminded his congregation. No one can incline God to be merciful but his own gentle and compassionate nature. All sinners should therefore resort to God, through Jesus Christ, and to no other. It was this conviction of God's mercy, he declared, that 'made Marie Magdalene creepe under the boorde to his feete with teares: there to receive and eate of his mercie, to quenche

Klepper, 'Theories of Interpretation: The Quadriga and Its Successors', in Euan Cameron (ed.), *The New Cambridge History of the Bible, Volume 3: From 1450–1750* (Cambridge: Cambridge University Press, 2016), pp. 418–438.

the hunger and smarte of her sinnes'.[77] Mary was now defined by her tears of contrition. The Elizabethan John Bishop (d. 1613), for example, asked, 'Who can with words, expresse her immeasurable sorrowe, which so at one instant wroung out of her al the moisture of her bodie, and turned it into repentant teares? whom shee dried with the golden lockes of her head which with their beautie, sweete smell of precious ointmentes, and curious & gorgeous trimming, had allured many great men unto her lewde love, and made them her beastlike bondmen & slaves'.[78] No greater change, it was imagined, could a woman make than to turn from prostitution to contrition. As the popular Puritan preacher Thomas Watson (c. 1620–1686) told his (perhaps slightly embarrassed) congregation with not a little rhetorical relish,

Repentance works a Change in the *Life*. Tho Repentance begins at the Heart, it doth not rest there, but goes into the Life... What a Change did it make in *Mary Magdalen*! She that before did *kiss* her Lovers with wanton Embraces, now kisseth Christ's Feet. She that did use to curl her Hair, and dress it with costly Jewels, now she makes it a Towel to wipe Christ's Feet. Her *Eyes* that used to sparkle with Lust, and with impure Glances to entice her Lovers, now she makes them a Fountain

---

[77] John Hooper, *Certeine Comfortable Expositions of the Constant Martyr of Christ, M. John Hooper, Bishop of Gloucester and Worcester* ... (London, 1580), p. 54. He was burnt to death for heresy during the reign of Queen Mary. On the English Protestant Magdalene, see David M. Whitford, 'The Moste Folyshe Fable of the World: Preaching the Maudlin', in Herman J. Selderhuis and Arnold Huijgen (eds.), *Calvinus Pastor Ecclesiae* (Göttingen: Vandenhoeck und Ruprecht, 2016), pp. 449–464.

[78] John Bishop, *Beautifull Blossomes, Gathered by John Byshop, from the Best Trees of All Kyndes* ... (London, 1577), p. 84.

of Tears to wash her Saviours Feet. Her *Tongue* that used to speak vainly and loosely, now it is an instrument set in Tune to praise God.[79]

Mary, Sacred and Profane

Henry VIII's Protestantism was always a little lukewarm. He had been given the title '*Defensor Fidei*' ('Defender of the Faith') by Pope Leo X in 1521 for a book entitled *Assertio Septem Sacramentorum* (*Defense of the Seven Sacraments*) in which he had defended the supremacy of the Pope. His devotion to the papacy was not to last. Henry VIII was ambiguously to embrace Protestantism so that he might bigamously embrace Anne Boleyn. In effect, however, Protestantism was finally established as England's only legal religion in 1559 by Queen Elizabeth I (1533–1603), soon after her accession to the English throne. In the following century, Catholic religious practices were banned and Catholic priests outlawed in England. Without priests, the Mass could not be celebrated and the body of Christ could not be 'sacrificed' on the altar for the redemption of the faithful.

For English Catholics before the Reformation, the Body of Christ in the Mass was something more to be seen than to be consumed. For the laity, the central moment was when the priest said the words '*Hoc est enim Corpus Meum*' ('For this is my Body') thus transforming the bread into the body of Christ, and then elevated the

---

[79] Thomas Watson, *A Body of Practical Divinity: Consisting of above One Hundred Seventy Six Sermons on the Lesser Confession* (London, 1692), p. 402.

Host above his head. Seeing the Body of Christ thus lifted up provided benefits to both body and soul. 'For glad may that man be', it was said, 'That once in the day may him see'.[80] The abolition of the Mass and, with it, the opportunity to worship the Body of Christ was thus a spiritual catastrophe for Catholics.

The story of Mary Magdalene in the garden on the morning of the resurrection mirrored the new experience of English Catholics similarly deprived of Christ's body. 'Sir', Mary had said to the person she assumed to be the gardener, 'if you have carried him away, tell me where you have laid him' (John 20.15). This deep sense of loss found expression, for example, in the poem of the English Catholic exile Richard Verstegan (c. 1550–1640) 'A Complaint of S. Marie Magdalen. At her not fynding Christ in his sepulchre':

A Las my Lord is gon,
How must I now deplore,
Where may hee bee that is each where,
And I see him no more.

Hope led mee here to seeke
Recure of my destresse,
But sorrow here hath sought mee out,
And found mee comfortlesse.[81]

---

[80] Edward Peacock (ed.), *Instructions for Parish Priests by John Myrc* (London: Trübner & Co, 1868), p. 10. This work also contains a list of the benefits, physical and spiritual, that accrue from seeing the Host. I have modernised the early English in this passage. On seeing the Host, see also Eamon Duffy, *The Stripping of the Altars: Traditional Religion in England c.1400–c.1580* (New Haven, CT: Yale University Press, 2005), pp. 95–102.

[81] Richard Verstegan, *Odes in Imitation of the Seaven Penitential Psalmes . . .* (Antwerp, 1601), p. 89.

The same sense of absence was reflected in the title of the Catholic layman Gervase Markham's (c. 1568–1637) poem 'Marie Magdalens Lamentations for the losse of her Maister Jesus'. Like English Catholics bereft of the body of Christ in the Mass, Mary Magdalene too feared, in the absence of Christ's body, for the loss of her soul. 'For I (poore soule)', we read, 'have lost my Maister Deere,/ To whom my thoughts devoutly were combind,/ The totall of my love, my cheefest cheere,/ The height of hope, in whom my glory shind / My final feare, and therefore him excepted,/ No other hope, nor love, nor losse respected'.[82]

That said, English Catholic writers nevertheless gave their readers the hope that, even in the absence of Christ's sacramental body, Christ was still present for them in their hearts.[83] In the absence of the consecrated body of Christ, Catholics could no longer touch his body. In this context, Christ's words to Mary Magdalene, 'Touch me not' took on a new resonance. Thus, for example, the English Jesuit Robert Southwell (c. 1561–1595) interpreted 'Touch me not' (John 20.17) as Christ's endorsement of inner rather than external religion. '[I]t is now necessarie', Jesus tells Mary, 'to weane thee from the comfort of my external presence, that thou maiest learne to lodge mee in the secretes of thy heart, and teach thy thoughts to supply the offices of

---

[82] Gervase Markham, *Mary Magdalens Lamentation for the Loss of Her Maister Jesus* (London, 1604), p. 9.

[83] See Lisa McClain, '"They have taken away my Lord": Mary Magdalene, Christ's Missing Body, and the Mass in Reformation England', *Sixteenth Century Journal* 38 (2007), pp. 77–96.

outward senses'.[84] We find similar sentiments in Gervase
Markham. Thus, for example, he had Jesus comforting
Mary for the absence of his physical body by the promise
of his inward presence:

> If thou my former promises beleeve,
> My present words may be a constant proofe...
> For now' tis needfull that a while I race thee
> out of the comfort of my outward sight,
> That in thy hart I may lodge with delight....
> But what thou seest not with externall eyen [eyes],
> Thy inward hart shall feelingly perpend:
> My inward parly in thy inward eare,
> Will find sweet *Audience* thy soule to cheere.[85]

In a political context where the external practices of
Catholicism were no longer possible, Mary Magdalene
was thus infused with new meaning for English
Catholics. No longer available as the object of an external
cult, she was re-fashioned as a symbol of inward religion
and of faith in things unseen.

The Thoroughly Early Modern Mary

In the middle of the sixteenth century, the English theologian Bishop John Jewel (1522–1571) noticed something
different about artistic representations of Mary
Magdalene. She had been eroticized. In a sermon on
worship of images, Jewel questioned the value of religious
paintings that, rather than endorsing virtue, appeared to

---

[84] Robert Southwell, *Magdalens Funerall Teares* (London, 1592), pp. 77–78.

[85] Markham, *Mary Magdalens Lamentation for the Losse of Her Maister Jesus*, p. 24. Markham's *Mary Magdalens Lamentation* is a versification of Southwell's *Magdalens Funerall Teares*.

encourage its opposite. He condemned the trend 'wherein is set forth by the art of the painter an image with a nice and wanton apparel and countenance, more like to Venus or Flora than Mary Magdalene, or, if like to Mary Magdalene, it is when she played the harlot rather than when she wept for her sins'.[86]

This was an astute observation. For during the first decades of the sixteenth century, Mary Magdalene had been transformed in Italy into a Venus-like figure, a goddess of love. We might say that, where previously the emphasis on the 'repentant sinner' had been on her contrition, the stress was now on her seductive beauty. As Ingrid Maisch puts it, 'The medieval Magdalene was a (former) sinner, but that aspect of her legend was only important insofar as through it sinful people were brought to salvation. She was honoured because she had overcome sin. Now, however, she was interesting *precisely as* an exciting, seductively beautiful sinner'.[87]

We can map this shift in representations of Mary Magdalene by comparing two pictures of her eremitic life, the first by the Flemish artist Quentin Metsys (1466–1530), the second by the Italian painter Titian (c. 1488–1576). In the first of these (c. 1520s), Mary Magdalene appeared naked, her nudity covered by her long hair (see Plate 15). Mary is both sexless and innocent,

---

[86] John Griffins (ed.), *The Two Books of Homilies Appointed to Be Read in Churches* (Oxford: Oxford University Press, 1859), p. 266. On the attribution of this homily to Jewel, see pp. xxxi–xxxii.

[87] Ingrid Maisch, *Between Contempt and Veneration: Mary Magdalene, The Image of a Woman through the Centuries* (Collegeville, MN: The Liturgical Press, 1998), p. 65 (my italics).

her long penitence symbolized by her ascetically gaunt appearance. In stark contrast to this (from around the same time) is Titian's 'The Penitent Mary' (c. 1533) (see Plate 16). Here, Mary is again the naked woman of the eremitic life, although her hair no longer covers her breasts. She was presented as possessing most of the features of the ideal beauty of the Italian Renaissance – golden hair, white skin flushed with rosy cheeks, ruby lips, and dark eyes.[88] Breasts, reported Federico Luigini da Udine in his *Book of the Beautiful Woman* in 1554, were to be small and firm, 'and like two round and sweet apples'.[89]

Mary's obvious voluptuousness in the Titian work clashed with the supposed rigours of her *eremetica vita*. This was noticed at the time. The Florentine nobleman Baccio Valori (1535–1606) visited Venice as a young man. And there, he met Titian,

[A]lmost immobilised by age who, despite the fact that he was appreciated for painting from the life, showed me a very attractive Magdalen in the desert. Also I remember now that I told him she was too attractive, so fresh and dewy, for such penitence. Having understood that I meant that she should be gaunt through fasting, he answered laughing that he had painted her on the first day she had entered [her repentant state], before she began fasting, in order to be able to paint her as a penitent indeed, but also as lovely as he could, and that she certainly was.[90]

---

[88] See Mary Rogers, 'The Decorum of Women's Beauty: Trissino, Firenzuola, Luigini and the Representation of Women in Sixteenth-Century Painting', *Renaissance Studies* 2 (1988), pp. 47–88.
[89] Quoted by Haskins, *Mary Magdalen*, p. 246.
[90] Quoted by *Ibid*., p. 244.

This eroticisation of Mary was perhaps to reach its peak in a painting entitled 'The Penitent Mary Magdalen' by the Italian painter Francesco Furini (c. 1600–1646). Here the repentant Mary has transitioned to a pious soft porn (see Plate 17).

Titian's image of the penitent Magdalene with its 'tension between the convert and the coquette', as Margaret Arnold neatly has it, would remain a dominant feature of Mary Magdalene's visual identity well into the seventeenth century.[91] We find it echoed as late as the middle of the seventeenth century in the 'Penitent Magdalene' by the Dutch-English artist Peter Lely (1618–1680), principal painter to King Charles II (1630–1685), in which a sensual Mary Magdalene appeared in a cave contemplating a crucifix and a skull (see Plate 18).

If the Italian Early Modern Mary represented the sinner we should aspire *not* to be rather than the saint we should desire to become, the Northern European Early Modern Mary possessed a femininity, more sedate and controlled, regal and aristocratic, thoughtful, and even a little prim and proper. This was the courtly Mary Magdalene of Jacobus de Voragine's *The Golden Legend*, of 'noble station' and 'royal lineage', depicted wearing jewels, pearls, and sumptuous garments with book, alabaster jar, or musical instrument. The Italian/Flemish painter Ambrosius Benson's (c. 1495/1500–1550) 'The Magdalen Reading' was representative of the genre (see Plate 19). His was a Mary Magdalene both saintly and wealthy. And she offered a devotional model to the newly rich urban elite of a developing trade-based economy. As Annette

---

[91] See Arnold, *The Magdalene in the Reformation*, p. 118.

Lezotte writes, 'For the Early Modern worshipper grappling with the issue of how to practice *imitatio Christi* while acquiring riches, Mary Magdalene offered them a way to have their cake and eat it too'.[92]

The development of the genre of landscape painting also provided a new space in which to place Mary Magdalene. On the one hand, removed from her domestic surroundings, the courtly Mary could coalesce with the hermit Mary of the *Vita Eremitica*. Take, for example, the 'Mary Magdalene' of the Dutch painter Jan van Scorel (1495–1562) where a seductive Mary gazes towards the viewer, dressed in rich, pearl-encrusted garments holding the alabaster jar in a Northern European landscape (see Plate 20). On the other hand, the naked eremitic Mary Magdalene could also merge with a developing aesthetic interest in the female nude. The erotic could fruitfully join with the ascetic in a wilderness setting. Thus, for example, the Italian painter Orazio Gentileschi (1563–1638), at the time court painter to the English King Charles I (1600–1649), rendered 'The Repentant Magdalene' semi-naked with skull and opened book in a grotto landscape (see Plate 21).

A favourite saint, an erotic nude, and an attractive landscape – in the world of 'high' art, Mary was very marketable.[93] Without putting too fine a point on it,

---

[92] Annette Lezotte, 'Mary Magdalene and the Iconography of Domesticity' in Michelle Erhardt and Amy M. Morris (eds.), *Mary Magdalene: Iconographic Studies from the Middle Ages to the Baroque* (Leiden: Brill, 2012), p. 397.

[93] See Michelle Moseley-Christian, 'Marketing Mary Magdalene in Early Modern Northern European Prints and Paintings', in Michelle Erhardt and Amy M. Morris (eds.), *Mary Magdalene: Iconographic Studies from the Middle Ages to the Baroque* (Leiden: Brill, 2012), pp. 399–420.

Mary Magdalene was becoming 'secularised'. She was now a commodity in an art market more attuned to her being exhibited on the walls of a gallery, a stately home, or a Parisian salon than hung on those of the seminary, church, or cathedral. This was a trend to meet its peak in the second half of the nineteenth century.

5

Many Magdalenes

Redeemed and Redeeming

~

And a woman in the city, who was a sinner . . . stood behind him at his
feet, weeping, and began to bathe his feet with her tears and to dry
them with her hair.

Luke 7.37–8.

The Magdalenes

On Sunday morning, 7 October 1855, the renowned
Baptist preacher Charles Haddon Spurgeon (1834–1892)
delivered a sermon on conversion to his congregation at
New Park Street Chapel in Southwark, London. He
extolled the virtues of converting sinners and ensuring
their salvation. The principal means for saving sinners, he
declared, was through preaching. He went on, somewhat
melodramatically and not a little immodestly, to tell of the
effects of one of his sermons. It was a Sunday night, he
declared, not long ago, when

A poor harlot determined she would go and take her life on
Blackfriars Bridge. Passing by these doors one Sunday night,
she thought she would step in, and for the last time hear
something that might prepare her to stand before her Maker.
She forced herself into the aisle, and she could not escape until
I rose from the pulpit. The text was, 'Seest thou this woman?'
I dwelt upon Mary Magdalene and her sins; her washing the
Saviour's feet with her tears, and wiping them with the hair of

her head. There stood the woman, melted away with the thought that she should thus hear herself described, and her own life painted. Oh! to think of saving a poor harlot from death, to deliver such an one from going down to the grave, and then, as God pleased, to save her soul from going down to hell! ... When I thought of this text yesterday, I could only weep to think that God should have so favored me.[1]

The mid-Victorian period was very much preoccupied with prostitution. It had been for the better part of the past century. In the mid-eighteenth century, more practical measures to deal with prostitution than those of the Rev'd Sturgeon were taken. These went well beyond pious hopes that suicidal prostitutes might find themselves, in passing, drawn into churches to listen to sermons advocating their repentance.

In March of 1758, Robert Dingley (1710–1781), a prosperous London silk merchant and in the vanguard of a new wave of eighteenth-century public philanthropy, had put forward proposals 'for establishing a public place of reception for penitent prostitutes'. 'What act of benevolence then,' he asked, 'can be greater, than to give these real objects of compassion an opportunity to reclaim, and recover themselves from their otherwise lost state; an opportunity to become, of pests, useful members of society, as it is not doubted many of them may and will?'[2]

Dingley's proposal was supported by another philanthropic merchant, Jonas Hanway (1712–1786). The

---

[1]   C. H. Spurgeon, 'Conversion', in *Spurgeon's Sermons*, vol. 1, no. 45, 1855. Available at www.ccel.org/ccel/spurgeon/sermons01.xlii.html.
[2]   Quoted by William Dodd, *An Account of the Rise, Progress, and Present State of the Magdalen Hospital, for the Reception of Penitent Prostitutes ...* (London, 1770), p. 4.

commitment of Robert Dingley, Jonas Hanway, and a number of others led to the establishment in August 1758 of the first Magdalen-House. This was part of a more general movement at the time of the building of public institutions that was inspired by Christianity. Thus, in the introduction to the Magdalene rulebook, used by this first house, Hanway wrote,

There cannot be greater Objects of Compassion, than poor, young, thoughtless Females, plunged into ruin by those Temptations, to which their very youth, and personal advantages expose them, no less than those passions implanted by Nature, for wise, good, and great ends ... what virtue can be proof against such formidable Seducers, who offer too commonly, and too profusely promise, to transport the thoughtless Girls from Want, Confinement, and Restraint of Passions, to Luxury, Liberty, Gaiety, and Joy? And when once seduced, how soon their golden dreams vanish! Abandoned by the Seducer, deserted by their Friends, contemned by the World, they are left to struggle with Want, Despair, and Scorn, and even in their own defence to plunge deeper and deeper in sin, till Disease and Death conclude a miserable Being.[3]

We do not know who might have been the first to suggest the term 'Magdalen-House' as the 'brand name' for this venture in institution building. No doubt, to Hanway and his colleagues on the committee established to set up the Magdalen-House, it was an obvious choice. During the medieval period, sixty-three hospitals were

---

[3] [Jonas Hanway], *The Rules, Orders and Regulations, of the Magdalen House, for the Reception of Penitent Prostitutes* (London, 1760), pp. 3–4. Hanway's other great claim to fame was his use of an umbrella. In the 1750s, it was considered 'too French' to do so. He was roundly abused by hansom-cab drivers who saw the umbrella as diminishing their market on rainy days.

dedicated to Mary Magdalene in England. Many of these were devoted to the segregation and regulation of leprosy. As Mary of Bethany, Mary Magdalene was, of course, the brother of Lazarus whom Jesus had raised from the dead (John 11.38–44). For his part, Lazarus had become conflated with the leprous beggar called Lazarus who featured in Jesus's parable of the rich man and Lazarus (Luke 16.19–31). As a result, Lazarus was to become a patron saint of lepers. But Mary Magdalene, by virtue of her relation to Lazarus, also became a patron saint of lepers. In Italy, an alternative name for leper hospitals was *lazaretti*. In England, as Katherine Jansen notes, 'Maudlin-house' was virtually synonymous with leper hospital.[4] However, by the middle of the eighteenth century, leprosy had virtually disappeared from England. The leper hospitals, often named after Mary Magdalene, had become redundant. The term 'Magdalen-House' would now be reserved for repentant prostitutes.

Like lepers, prostitutes were also segregated and regulated in medieval society. Medieval houses for fallen women, like that planned by Hanway, provided both social assistance and social control. The connection between Mary Magdalene and the reformation of prostitutes began in the early twelfth century. One of the four houses of Robert of Arbrissels's (c. 1045–1116) Augustinian foundation, devoted to monks, nuns, lepers, and prostitutes, was dedicated to Mary Magdalene. Houses devoted to the reformation of prostitutes, most of them dedicated to Mary Magdalene, proliferated in France in the thirteenth and fourteenth centuries.

---

[4] Jansen, *The Making of the Magdalen*, p. 175.

In Germany, an order of repentant women, The Penitent Sisters of Blessed Mary Magdalene, appeared in the second quarter of the thirteenth century and spread throughout Germany, the Low Countries, Italy, France, Spain, and Portugal.[5]

Jonas Hanway was well aware of these Continental precursors to his plans. 'Motives of *policy*', he declared, 'as well as a sense of *moral* and *religious* obligation, have erected many institutions of this kind, which have been supported by some of the greatest, and noblest minded persons of both sexes, in *Italy, France, Spain*, and several other countries'.[6] The distinctiveness of his Magdalen-House, however, lay in its requiring that, unlike its previous Catholic forms, the women did not remain permanently but only temporarily. This was a Protestantized version of its Catholic predecessors: 'Here no *incense* will be offered, but the pure flames of devotion; nor will any *vows* be required .... When they return into the world, they will know how to shun temptation, and, however disguised under specious appearances, they will fly from it as from the teeth of a serpent'.[7]

That said, it is perhaps a matter for surprise that Jonas Hanway, in the Introductions to the first and the second editions of his rulebook for the Magdalen-House, made no mention of Mary Magdalene at all. There, perhaps, hangs a tale. His reluctance to do so was probably motivated by his becoming embroiled, at the time of the

---

[5] See *Ibid.*, pp. 177–184.
[6] Jonas Hanway, *Thoughts on a Plan for a Magdalen-House for Repentant Prostitutes* ... (London, 1758), p. 33.
[7] *Ibid.*, p. 37.

founding of the Magdalen-House, in what was an eighteenth-century English version of the early sixteenth-century 'The Quarrel of the Magdalene'. In a letter to Robert Dingley, shortly before the establishment of the first Magdalen-House in London, Hanway expressed the hope that their endeavour would lead to the reformation of many women. He looked to Christ's judgement of Mary Magdalene as the example for them to follow. 'What judgment', he asked, 'did the *Saviour of the world* pass on a harlot? What was the case of *Mary Magdalen?* Those who have erred most in this way, are frequently observed to have a peculiar mixture of such qualities as dispose the heart to repentance'.[8]

Hanway was a staunch member of the Church of England. Not unexpectedly, therefore, he accepted the Church's position that Mary Magdalene and the fallen woman of the Gospel of Luke were the same person. As we know, his judgement that she was a harlot was part of a long tradition. So he was surely surprised when an anonymous letter was published in October of 1758 that took him to task for having called his establishment 'a Magdalen-House' and for having called Mary Magdalen 'a harlot'. Its author gave no sign of being familiar with those who, in the early sixteenth century, had argued against the identification of Mary Magdalene with the sinner of the Gospel of Luke and Mary of Bethany. But his conclusion and the biblical arguments by which he came to it were essentially the same: *These*

---

[8] Jonas Hanway, *Letter V. to Robert Dingley, Esq; Being a Proposal for the Relief and Employment of Friendless Girls and Repentant Prostitutes* (London, 1758), p. 22.

were three different women and not one. This anonymous author's rather prissy summary of the case against Mary Magdalene being the sinful woman was that the wisdom, prudence, virtue, goodness, and compassion of Jesus counted against his admitting 'such a Person [as the sinful woman] into the Number of his Stated Attendants'.[9] Apparently Jesus came to save the sinners but not to fraternize (or sororize in this case) with them.

As for the character of Mary Magdalene, hers was one that could never be identified with a common prostitute. She was a woman of wealth and distinction, worthy of her position as a disciple of Jesus. 'I conceive of Her', the author declared, 'as a Woman of fine Understanding, and known Virtue and Discretion, with a Dignity of Behaviour, becoming her Age, her Wisdom and her high station. By all which She was a Credit to Him, whom she followed, as her Master and Benefactor'.[10] In short, we might say, she was the very model for the ideal wife of a highly respectable eighteenth-century clergyman.

The author of this book was exactly that – an eighteenth century clergyman. We know this only because a copy of this book found its way to the palace of Lambeth, the London residence of the Archbishop of Canterbury, where Archbishop Thomas Secker (1693–1768) wrote in his identifiable hand the name 'Nathaniel Lardner' on its title page. One of the most learned Christian scholars of

---

[9] Anon., *A Letter to Jonas Hanway Esq; in which Some Reasons Are Assigned Why Houses for the Reception of Penitent Women, Who Have Been Disorderly in Their Lives, Ought Not to Be Called Magdalen-Houses* (London, 1758), p. 13. The title page lists no author. The initials, 'A. B.' are given on the final page of the work.

[10] *Ibid.*, p. 14.

the eighteenth century, the Presbyterian Nathaniel Lardner (1684–1768) was on friendly terms with members of the Church of England, including the Archbishop of Canterbury. So it is likely that Secker was 'in the know' as to its authorship.[11]

Those who exhaustively (and exhaustingly) read the prolific Nathaniel Lardner might have noticed that, in the same year as his letter to Hanway, he had rejected by as early as 1742 the identity of Mary Magdalene and the fallen woman in a book on demoniacs in the New Testament. The opinion of their being the same, he there declared, 'so far as I am able to judge, is entirely without foundation in the Gospels. There is no reason at all to think, that *Marie Magdalen* and that woman are one and the same'.[12] This was, perhaps, the position we might have expected him to hold. As a Presbyterian, he would probably have accepted Calvin's opinion on this matter. He was also not a little embarrassed that a woman of such distinction should have been possessed by seven demons. In his anonymous letter to Hanway he rather cheekily (mis)quoted his own work on demoniacs to the effect that it was more likely that she was suffering from a 'distempered Frame of Mind, or Epilepsy, or somewhat else'. In any case, he was certain, it was 'some natural, not moral

---

[11] See H. F. B. Compston, *The Magdalen Hospital: The Story of a Great Charity* (London: Society for Promoting Christian Knowledge, 1917), p. 56. The authorship of Lardner was well known by the time of the publication of his eleven volume collected *Works* in 1788.

[12] Nathaniel Lardner, *The Case of the Demoniacs Mentioned in the New Testament: Four Discourses upon Mark 5.19* (London, 1758), p. 104. See also Nathaniel Lardner, *Sermons upon Various Subjects. Vol. II* (London, 1760), p. 316.

Distemper' that was intended.[13] As for the name
'Magdalen-House', he thought it was, in a Protestant
country, too redolent of popery for his comfort and he
suggested the name 'A Charity-House for penitent
Women' or 'A Charity-House for penitent Harlots'.[14]

By the time that Lardner was writing his letter to
Hanway, the philanthropist Hanway had already revised
his own opinion that Mary Magdalene was a harlot. By
then, he had moved from his identification of her with the
fallen woman towards a noble Mary Magdalene who was
miraculously cured of her ailment:

First, give me leave to take notice of the name of your charity. It
does not appear to me that Mary Magdalen was deficient in
point of chastity, as is vulgarly understood, I rather imagine she
was not. It is certain, she was a lady of distinction, and of a great
and noble mind. Her gratitude for the miraculous cure performed upon her, was so remarkable, that her story is related
with the greatest honor, and she will ever stand fair in the
records of fame.[15]

As to the name of the institution having the whiff of
popery, he later pointed out to Lardner that he thought
that no mischief would come of it, either to the reputation
of Mary Magdalene or to the repentance of the sinners
living there. Nor, he declared, 'do I think the interest of
the true *protestant evangelical faith* will suffer, more than

---

[13] Anon., *A Letter to Jonas Hanway Esq*, pp. 8–9. See also Lardner, *The Case of the Demoniacs Mentioned in the New Testament*, pp. 104–105.

[14] *Ibid.*, p. 27.

[15] Hanway, *Thoughts on a Plan for a Magdalen-House for Repentant Prostitutes ...*, p. 23. I have removed original italicizations from this passage.

the hospital for *Lunatics*, being dedicated to *St. Luke*, will occasion our posterity to consider this *Evangelist* as a madman'.[16] It is difficult in retrospect, granting Hanway's shift in opinion about Mary Magdalene, to know why he persisted in the name 'Magdalen-House'. It may have been that, regardless of her status, he wished to signal the continuity of his establishment with earlier Catholic versions of it. Hanway was, however, renowned for his stubbornness. This gentleman was not for turning. It may have been as simple as that.

The first Magdalen-House was situated on the site of the old London Hospital at 21 Prescott Street, Whitechapel. The first description we have of it was given by the writer Horace Walpole (1717–1797) who included Magdalen-House among his 'entertainments'. He wrote to his friend George Montagu of a visit with a number of his friends, including Prince Edward the brother of the future King George III, to the Magdalen-House on 27 January 1760. 'We were received by', he wrote, 'oh! A vast mob, for princes are not so common at that end of town as at this'. They were led straight into the chapel where, at the west end, over 130 of 'the sisterhood' of the 'new convent' were enclosed, 'all in grayish brown stuffs, broad handkerchiefs, and flat straw hats, with a blue riband, pulled quite over their faces'. As soon as they had taken their places, the Magdalens sang a hymn, 'you cannot imagine how well, and there wanted nothing but a little incense to drive away the devil – or to invite him'.

---

[16] Jonas Hanway, *Thoughts on a Plan for a Magdalen-House for Repentant Prostitutes ... The Second Edition* (London, 1759), postscript. St. Luke's Hospital for Lunatics was founded in London in 1751.

This was followed by psalms and a sermon by William Dodd (1729–1777), 'who contributed to the Popish idea one had imbibed, by haranguing totally in the French style, and very eloquently and touchingly'. Later they visited the refectory where 'all the nuns, without their hats, were ranged at long tables, ready for supper'. All of them, including two or three of twelve years of age, were 'recovered, and looking healthy'. Walpole and his entourage were shown their handiwork that was 'making linen, and bead-work'. Several of them 'swooned away with the confusion of being stared at'.[17]

A Woman Possessed?

We recall that Pope Gregory the Great had identified the seven demons that possessed Mary Magdalene with all the vices. Her demonic possession entailed her complete sinfulness. Nathaniel Lardner, by contrast, wanted to sanitize her of the tradition that she was morally depraved. Simply put, she was not bad but ill. In so arguing, Lardner was positioning himself on one side of an eighteenth-century debate about the status of demoniacs in the New Testament more generally. Thus, in his *The Case of the Demoniacs Mentioned in the New Testament*, a collection of four discourses on this topic that he first delivered in 1742, he outlined two current opinions. The first of these, 'the opinion of the vulgar' as he called it, was

[17] Horace Walpole, *The Letters of Horace Walpole* (London, 1759–1769), vol. 3, p. 37. The preacher on the occasion, William Dodd was renowned for his extravagant living. He was later to be hanged for forgery.

that the demoniacs of the time of Jesus *really* were demonically possessed. The second and less common opinion
was that these cases were to be explained *naturally* as
physical maladies 'which the human frame is subject to
in this state of mortality'.[18]

Although he recognized that, until recent times, the
first of these two opinions had been by far the most
common one, he rather contemptuously dismissed it.
'Possession by evil spirits', he declared, 'is a thing in itself
absurd and impossible, at the le[a]st unreasonable, and
improbable, and not to be supposed, unless there be clear
and full proof of it. Which, I think, there is not'.[19] As for
Jesus's apparent belief in demonic possession, this was
nothing more than his adapting 'his expressions to that
opinion, without countenancing or approving it'.[20]
Lardner's medical explanation was, quite simply, that
demoniacs suffered from epilepsy or 'falling sicknesse'.
That Jesus could cure sufferers from epilepsy was no less
a miracle, he suggested, than his capacity to cast out evil
spirits.

The eighteenth-century dispute about natural versus
supernatural explanations of demonic possession had been
raging since 1737.[21] It was a debate embedded within

---

[18] Lardner, *The Case of the Demoniacs Mentioned in the New Testament*,
p. 39.

[19] *Ibid.*, p. 76.   [20] *Ibid.*, p. 69. See also p. 91.

[21] On epilepsy, melancholy, and hysteria as medical 'explanations' of
demonic possession, see Brian P. Levack, *The Devil Within: Possession
& Exorcism in the Christian West* (New Haven, CT: Yale University
Press, 2013), pp. 115–129. For an excellent account of the debate, see
H. C. Erik Midelfort, 'The Gadarene Demoniac in the English
Enlightenment', in Scott K. Taylor, *A Linking of Heaven and Earth*
(London: Routledge, 2012), pp. 49–66.

eighteenth-century scepticism about demonology particularly and the possibility of miracles more generally.[22] This particular dispute was initiated by a work entitled *An Enquiry into the Meaning of Demoniacks in the New Testament*. This work was the immediate influence on Lardner's natural explanation of possession. The initials on the title page, T.P.A.P.O.A.B.I.T.C.O.S., stood for 'The precentor and prebendary of Alton Borealis in the Church of Salisbury'. Contemporary readers likely had little trouble identifying him. He was in fact the Anglican clergyman and general theological troublemaker Arthur Ashley Sykes (1684–1756).[23]

Sykes did not follow the path laid out by the liberal theologian Thomas Woolston (1688–1733). Woolston had denied the possibility of miracles in the Gospels altogether and had, as a result, been found guilty of blasphemy, fined, and imprisoned.[24] Sykes had no doubt that Christ was a miracle worker, whether he was exorcizing demons or healing the diseased. But he dismissed the notion of 'demonic possession' as a linguistic mistake in which diseases that were attributable to evil spirits were described in terms of possession by them.[25] Moreover, he

---

For the medicalization of possession as epilepsy, see Owsei Temkin, *The Falling Sickness: A History of Epilepsy from the Greeks to the Beginnings of Modern Neurology* (Baltimore: Johns Hopkins Press, 1971), p. 220ff.

[22] On miracles, see Jane Shaw, *Miracles in Enlightenment England* (New Haven, CT: Yale University Press, 2006).

[23] Arthur Ashley Sykes, *An Enquiry into the Meaning of Demoniacks in the New Testament* (London, 1737).

[24] See Thomas Woolston, *A Discourse on the Miracles of Our Saviour ...* (London, 1727).

[25] See Sykes, *An Enquiry into the Meaning of Demoniacks in the New Testament*, pp. 13–14.

argued, the so-called *daimonia* ('demons') of the Greek New Testament were not the *'diaboli'* ('devils') of the Latin version, but rather 'the departed *Souls of Dead Men*'.[26] All that said, his overall explanation of demonic possession was crystal clear. 'I know not', he declared, 'whether there is a single instance of a *Demoniack*, which may not fairly and justly be explained by Epilepsy, or Madness'.[27] As to the statement in the Gospels that Mary Magdalene had seven devils, 'The Meaning is, that she had affirmed in her *Melancholy*, that she had so many Devils in her, just as the [Gadarene] Madman said that he had a *Legion* of *Devils*' in him'.[28] In short, Mary's illness made her wrongly believe that she was demonically possessed.

Sykes's essay provoked more than twenty replies between 1737 and the end of the century.[29] For many, the denial of demonic possession was an interpretative bridge too far. Committed as they were to a literal reading of the Bible, Sykes's fellow biblical scholars remained, on the whole, unconvinced.[30] But he found a more receptive audience among medical professionals. Thus, for example, the English physician Richard Mead (1673–1754) in his posthumously published *Medica Sacra* in 1755, and taking Sykes as one of his two key

---

[26] *Ibid.*, p. 35.   [27] *Ibid.*, p. 53. See also p. 56.   [28] *Ibid.*, p. 57.

[29] I here count only those concerning demoniacs specifically and not those dealing with the more general issue of miracles.

[30] See, for example, on the genuine possession of Mary Magdalene, Thomas Church, *An Essay towards Vindicating the Literal Sense of the Demoniacks in the New Testament ...* (London, 1737), p. 77; Leonard Twells, *An Answer to the Enquiry into the Meaning of Demoniacks ...* (London, 1737), p. 55; William Worthington, *An Impartial Enquiry into the Case of the Gospel Demoniacks ...* (London, 1777), p. 83.

authorities, declared 'That the Daemoniacs ... mentioned in the gospels laboured under a disease really natural, tho' of an obstinate and difficult kind, appears to me very probable from the accounts given of them'.[31] By the 1770s, among biblical scholars, the tide was turning in favour of a less literal approach to the biblical texts. Thus, for example, in his *An Essay on the Demoniacs of the New Testament* in 1775, Hugh Farmer (1715–1787), an independent minister, took his lead from Sykes, Lardner, and Mead. So what, wrote Farmer, if Jesus and his disciples 'made use of the common popular language of the age and country in which they lived'.[32] It did not mean that they were thereby giving their endorsement to the opinion from which such language arose. In short, he suggested, we do not need to accommodate in the here and now the ignorance and superstition of previous ages. Thus, rather than being *literally* possessed by demons, the demoniacs in the New Testament were all either mad people or epileptics. 'Mary Magdalene,' he declared, 'out of whom went seven demons, and the man with a legion more especially, were stark mad'.[33]

All that said, Mary Magdalene was rather collateral damage in this dispute. The Gadarene demoniac was much more the focus of sceptical attention. He it was out of whom Jesus drove two thousand demons and sent them into a herd of swine who then promptly drowned themselves in the sea (Mark 5.1–17). And actually, much

---

[31] Richard Mead, *Medica Sacra; or, a Commentary on the Most Remarkable Diseases, Mentioned in the Holy Scriptures* (London, 1755), p. 73.

[32] Hugh Farmer, *An Essay on the Demoniacs of the New Testament* (London, 1775), p. 376

[33] *Ibid.*, p. 349.

deeper issues than demonic possession were in play. Was the worldview of the Bible to be taken at face value in the eighteenth century? How could the world of the Bible be brought into line with that of modern science? Was the Bible to be read as the inspired Word of God or as just another human document to be understood within the context of its own times? These questions continued to underpin the debate about demonic possession when it broke out in Germany in the mid-1770s. This too was embedded in issues about the literal truth of the Bible. As Erik Midelfort aptly put it, for the 'enlightened' biblical interpreters of the eighteenth century, 'demon possession provided the ideal topic with which to challenge tradition-alists to acknowledge that the gospels contained ridicu-lous stories'.[34]

The developing scepticism of the eighteenth century did no favours to Mary Magdalene the demoniac. Her demonic possession was in reality, at best epilepsy, at worst madness. The rational had supplanted the supernat-ural. And if the resurrection of Christ was little more than a fanciful story invented by the followers of Jesus, what was to be made of the role of Mary as its supposed first witness? For David Friedrich Strauss (1808–1874) in his *Das Leben Jesu, kritisch bearbeitet* (*The Life of Jesus, Critically Examined*), the supernatural elements of the life of Jesus – his birth, his miracles, his resurrection, and his ascension were all myths invented by the early church.[35] That the resurrection was a myth had severe implications

---

[34] Midelfort, 'The Gadarene Demoniac in the English Enlightenment,' p. 61.

[35] It was translated into English in 1846 by George Eliot (Marian Evans).

for the first witness to the resurrection and 'the apostle of the apostles'. Simply put, Mary, like the other disciples who imagined they had seen the resurrected Jesus, was deluded. She was of an 'impetuous temperament', Strauss declared, 'having been formerly a demoniac'.[36]

Strauss himself did not believe in the reality of demonic possession. He regarded the symptoms of the possessed as caused by diseases and not by demons. He cited the German biblical critic Johann Salomo Semler (1725–1791) as having been decisive in explaining the malady of the New Testament demoniacs in terms of natural causes and in ascribing the supposed supernatural sources to the prejudices of those days.[37] For his part, in his view of the natural causes of demonic possession, Semler had been particularly influenced by the eighteenth-century *English* debate and in particular by Arthur Ashley Sykes's *An Enquiry into the Meaning of Demoniacks in the New Testament*.[38] Boomerang-like, the debate about demonic possession had returned to England via Germany.

Like David Friedrich Strauss, the French orientalist Ernest Renan (1823–1892) rejected the traditional supernatural view of the New Testament. Renan's 1863 book

---

[36] D. F. Strauss, *The Life of Jesus, Critically Examined* (Cambridge: Cambridge University Press, 2010), vol. 3, p. 314. Haskins quotes Strauss as saying, Christianity had been founded on the 'ravings of a demented and love-lorn woman'. Haskins, *Mary Magdalen*, p. 330. I am unable to find this reference in Strauss.

[37] See H. C. Erik Midelfort, *Exorcism and Enlightenment: Johann Joseph Gassner and the Demons of Eighteenth-Century Germany* (New Haven, CT: Yale University Press, 2005).

[38] See Johann Salomo Semler, *Commentatio de Daemoniacis Quorum in N. T. Fit Mentio* (Halle: Hendel, 1769), p. 1, note 1.

Vie de Jesus (*Life of Jesus*) took a view of the resurrection of Jesus that was similarly sceptical. For Renan, the rise of Christianity was only the result of the vivid imagination of Mary Magdalene. On the Sunday morning, we read,

[T]he strangest rumours were spread in the Christian community. The cry, 'He is risen!' quickly spread amongst the disciples. Love caused it to find ready credence everywhere .... For the historian, the life of Jesus finishes with his last sigh. But such was the impression he had left in the heart of his disciples and of a few devoted women, that during some weeks more it was as if he were living and consoling them. Had his body been taken away, or did enthusiasm, always credulous, create afterward the group of narratives by which it was sought to establish faith in the resurrection?.. Let us say, however, that the strong imagination of Mary Magdalen played an important part in this circumstance. Divine power of love! Sacred moments in which the passion of one possessed gave to the world a resuscitated God.[39]

For Renan, Mary Magdalene suffered from inexplicable nervous maladies which Jesus was able to cure. As a result, after Jesus, it was Mary Magdalene who had done most for the foundation of Christianity. 'The glory of the resurrection belongs, then, to Mary of Magdala' he declared. 'The shadow created by the delicate sensibility of Magdalene', he continued, 'wanders still on the earth. Queen and patroness of idealists, Magdalene knew better than any one how to assert her dream, and impose on every one the vision of her passionate soul. Her great womanly affirmation: "He has risen", has been the basis

---

[39] Ernest Renan, *The Life of Jesus* (n.p.: A. L. Burt Company, 1863), pp. 374–375.

of the faith of humanity'.[40] Oscar Wilde (1854–1900), coincidentally a student of Magdalen College Oxford, drew upon these sentiments in a sonnet: 'And was thy Rising only dreamed by Her / Whose love of thee for all her sin atones?' As he remarked in a letter in 1876 to William Gladstone to whom he had sent the sonnet, 'Renan says somewhere that this was the divinest lie ever told'.[41]

Mary, Devoted and Domesticated

Despite its scepticism about the supernatural, the romantic style of Renan's *The Life of Jesus* appealed to a large number of readers. The journalist Richard Rolt Hutton (1826–1897) wrote of it, 'I have never read a professedly sceptical book that tended more powerfully to strengthen the faith it struggles to supplant'.[42] Renan's treatment of Mary Magdalene exemplified this paradox. She may have only *imagined* a risen Lord, but her belief in it was the consequence of the depth of her faith in Jesus, allied with her 'delicate sensibility' and 'passionate soul'. Renan's Mary Magdalene, like that of Strauss, was no longer the composite Mary made up of the demoniac Mary Magdalene, Mary of Bethany, and the sinful woman. Rather, it was the single Mary, the privileged woman who, having been healed of her illness, financially

[40] Ernest Renan, *The Apostles* (New York: Carleton, 1866), p. 61.
[41] Quoted by Richard Ellman, *Oscar Wilde* (New York: Alfred A. Knopf, 1988), p. 82.
[42] Quoted by Daniel L. Pals, *The Victorian Lives of Jesus* (San Antonio, TX: Trinity University Press, 1982), p. 39.

supported Jesus and his disciples and was the first witness of the resurrection.

Generally, her role in nineteenth century theology, literature, and art depended on whether she was perceived as the single or the composite Mary. As a consequence, her identity was infinitely malleable. As the Victorian art historian Anna Jameson (1794–1860) put it in 1848, 'Of all the personages who figure in history, in poetry, in art, Mary Magdalene is at once the most unreal and the most real: – the most *unreal*, if we attempt to fix her identity, which has been a subject of dispute for ages; the most *real*, if we consider her as having been, for ages, recognised and accepted in every Christian heart as the impersonation of the penitent sinner absolved through faith and love'.[43]

Jameson hesitated to affirm whether the demoniac Mary Magdalene, Mary of Bethany, and the sinful woman were three distinct persons or one and the same individual. But it was clearly Mary the repentant sinner whom Jameson most admired. She was 'the accepted and glorified penitent' who 'threw her mantle over all, and more especially over those of her own sex, who, having gone astray, were recalled from error and from shame, and laid down their wrongs, their sorrows, and their sins in trembling humility at the feet of the Redeemer'.[44] And it was the Mary Magdalene of the *Vita Apostolico-Eremetica* whose biography Jameson proceeded to tell. Jameson was the first art historian to connect the *Golden Legend* of Jacobus de Voragine with the history of Christian art.

---

[43] Anna Jameson, *Sacred and Legendary Art* (Cambridge: Cambridge University Press, 2012), vol. 1, p. 332.
[44] *Ibid.*, vol. 1, pp. 333–334.

So we might say that, with Jameson, there remained a vestigial nostalgia for the medieval tradition of the composite Mary who, after the ascension of Jesus, travelled to France and then retired to do penance in the desert. Even bereft of its traditional liturgical practices, the romantic composite Mary Magdalene of the *Golden Legend* resonated with many. As William Wordsworth (1770–1850) wrote,

> Angels and Saints, in every hamlet mourned!
> Ah! if the old idolatry be spurned,
> Let not your radiant Shapes desert the Land:
> ... and weeping Magdalene,
> Who in the penitential desert met
> Gales sweet as those that over Eden blew![45]

On the other hand, the single Mary, whether by design or by accident, was also often lined up alongside Mary of Bethany as two of the many women in the New Testament who, along with the mother of Jesus, were emblematic of the high regard in which Jesus held women. Thus, for example, for the popular evangelical non-conformist John Angell James (1785–1859) in his *Female Piety*, Jesus had exalted women to a height unknown before: 'He admitted them to his presence, conversed familiarly with them, and accepted the tokens of their gratitude, affection, and devotedness'.[46] It was to a woman, Mary Magdalene, he reminded his readers, 'that

---

45 William Wordsworth, 'Saints', in William Angus Knight (ed.), *The Poetical Works of William Wordsworth* (London: Macmillan & Co., 1896), vol. 7, p. 54.
46 John Angell James, *Female Piety: Or the Young Woman's Friend and Guide through Life to Immortality* (New York: Robert Carter & Brothers, 1853), p. 18.

the honour of the first manifestation of the risen Saviour was made; and thus a woman was preferred to apostles, and made the messenger of the blissful news to *them*'.[47] In this line-up, Mary the repentant prostitute had no place.

Thus, when she was severed from her identity as the sinful woman, Mary Magdalene was able to become one of the pious women of antiquity worthy of imitation. She was one of those to whom the popular Baptist writer Clara Lucas Balfour drew attention in her *The Women of Scripture* (1847). In this work, the women of Scripture embodied an array of virtues suitable for the nineteenth-century woman's own self-fashioning.[48] Mary and Martha represented the virtues of contemplation and action. The 'woman who was a sinner' modelled repentance. Mary Magdalene was the exemplar of fidelity.

Balfour explicitly distinguished the sinful woman from Mary Magdalene whose life, 'so far as the gospel narrative unfolds it, was pure and spotless'.[49] Her Mary Magdalene was a woman who, deeply bound to Jesus in gratitude for his removing her 'physical ills' – no mention of 'demonic possession' here – devoted herself and her property to the furtherance of Jesus's mission. Among the record of women's devotion, Mary Magdalene's was the most glori-ous. It was her presence at the death of Jesus that epitom-ized her fidelity. She remained 'throughout that awful tragedy: the retiring sun, the reeling earthquake, all the

---

[47] *Ibid.*, p. 11. I am indebted to Haskins, *Mary Magdalen* for drawing my attention to a number of sources in this section.

[48] See Rebecca Styler, *Literary Theology by Women Writers of the Nineteenth Century* (Farnham, Surrey: Ashgate, 2010), p. 78.

[49] Clara Lucas Balfour, *The Women of Scripture* (London: Houlston & Stoneman, 1847), p. 320.

dread phenomena of startled nature, failed to shake her steadfast soul from its firm resolve. She was present when the sacred body was taken down from the cross; she beheld its interment'.[50] Her reward for 'heroic fidelity' was to be the first witness of the resurrection: 'No higher honour, – no sweeter act of gracious, tender condescension could have been conferred, than that the risen Lord should first have manifested himself to Mary. She had "Waited latest at the cross, / Watched earliest at the grave". And she was rewarded by first beholding the august spectacle of a Saviour, who had burst the barriers of the tomb, conquered death and the grave, and risen triumphant over every foe'.[51]

Similarly, for Harriet Beecher Stowe (1811–1896), the abolitionist author of *Uncle Tom's Cabin*, Mary Magdalene was one of a number of female spiritual leaders within the pages of the Bible who could provide exemplary lives upon which modern women could fashion theirs – 'divinely approved, timeless models which they can follow in their own day'.[52] But unlike Balfour's, Stowe's Mary Magdalene was pre-eminently the sinful woman of the Gospel of Luke and not identical with Mary of Bethany, the sister of Martha. Her sins against chastity were not so much those of a woman as those of any person – sins not of gender but 'of a personal moral agency'.[53]

---

[50] *Ibid.*, pp. 323–324.   [51] *Ibid.*, pp. 328–329.

[52] Styler, *Literary Theology by Women Writers of the Nineteenth Century*, p. 76.

[53] Harriet Beecher Stowe, *Woman in Sacred History: A Series of Sketches Drawn from Scriptural, Historical, and Legendary Sources* (New York: J. B. Ford & Company, 1873), p. 298.

Perhaps this is why Stowe appears able to look past the erotic character of Pompeo Batoni's (1708–1787) portrait of Mary Magdalene reading in the wilderness that she included in her book (see Plate 22). According to her, Batoni sets before us one of the highest, noblest class of women – 'a creature so calm, so high, so pure, that we ask involuntarily, How could such a woman ever have fallen?'[54] To any particular 'fallen woman', her answer would have been an encouraging one. She wrote

There is a class of women who fall through what is highest in them, through the noblest capability of a human being, – utter self-sacrificing love . . . . Many women fall through the weakness of self-indulgent passion, many from love of luxury, many from vanity and pride, too many from the coercion of hard necessity; but among the sad, unblest crowd there is a class who are the victims of a power of self-forgetting love, which is one of the most angelic capabilities of our nature.[55]

Deceived, betrayed, and ruined by her own capacity for love, Mary drifted into the power of evil spirits, only to be rescued by the serene and healing purity of Jesus that 'calmed the throbbing fever of passion and gave the soul once more the image of its better self'.[56]

In post-civil war America, the temperance leader Stowe could also find in Mary's strong moral character a model for the sober, home-loving man preferring more to be at home with his virtuous devoted wife than getting drunk in the local bar. But that said, Stowe's Mary was the abandonment of the female self, once lost in lust, now self-surrendered in the love for another. Not perhaps a

---

[54] Stowe, *Woman in Sacred History*, p. 297.   [55] *Ibid.*, pp. 297–298.
[56] *Ibid.*, p. 302.

message to move the soul of a modern feminist. She wrote,

> We see in the manner in which Mary found her way to the feet of Jesus the directness and vehemence, the uncalculating self-sacrifice and self-abandon, of one of those natures which, when they move, move with a rush of undivided impulse; which, when they love, trust all, believe all, and are ready to sacrifice all. As once she had lost herself in this self-abandonment, so now at the feet of her God she gains all by the same power of self-surrender.[57]

Hers was a love that was later to find expression in preaching the Gospel. Her power to redeem others through her words, declared Stowe, was a consequence of the enormity of her own sins and the depths of her own redemption.

By the middle of the nineteenth century, within Protestant circles generally, the dominance of the composite Mary Magdalene was being eclipsed. On the one hand it was surpassed by the single Mary, on the other by a Mary identified either with Mary of Bethany or with the fallen woman of the Gospel of Luke. But the tradition of the composite Mary lingered on. Thus, for example, The Anglican clergyman Henry Stretton (c. 1814–1890), holder of the delightful title 'Perpetual Curate of Hixon, Diocese of Lichfield', preached a series of sermons from 1844 to 1848 on Mary Magdalene. Aware of the tradition of the composite Mary as having begun with Pope Gregory the Great, he devoted his first sermon to identifying Mary Magdalene with both the

---

[57] *Ibid.*

sinful woman and Mary of Bethany. 'What we loved well singly', he declared, 'we shall love better united; and we shall see in the combination of characteristics we have thought opposite, a variety of new beauties of which we had formed no conception while viewing them separately'.[58]

Stretton was constrained by the biblical story of Mary and Martha to endorse the contemplative Mary as having chosen the better part over the active Martha. His call however, Protestant that he was, was not to retreat from the world, 'to indulge in some fond conceit of an ill-regulated mind for a life of religious retirement'.[59] Rather, the life of Mary and that of Martha was to be an active one, imbued with devotion to God. Stretton's recommendation was for everyday life to be lived religiously: 'Let it not be supposed, however, that we are advocating a life in which nothing but religious worship is to be pursued as the higher way, or would represent Martha's part as one which comprehends in it nothing but active employment. What we commend so highly ... is that religious duties are made the *rule* of all other action'.[60] No one would have been in the least surprised were Stretton's sermon to be followed, as many sermons still were in my own Anglican childhood a century later, with one of the mid-Victorian period's favourite hymns. As I remember it,

[58] Henry Stretton, *The Acts of Saint Mary Magdalene Considered, in a Series of Discourses* ... (London: Joseph Masters, 1848), p. 3. Stretton gives an account of 'The Quarrel of the Magdalene' in the appendix, pp. 327–332.
[59] *Ibid.*, p. 84.   [60] *Ibid.*, p. 87.

Teach me my God and King,
In all things Thee to see;
And what I do in anything
To do it as for Thee . . .

A servant with this clause
Makes drudgery divine:
Who sweeps a room as for Thy laws,
Makes that and th' action fine.[61]

Stretton would happily have sung the second verse
above, although he would have applied it only to maidser-
vants. In Mary Magdalene being the first witness of the
resurrection and the apostle of the apostles, Stretton
believed that Jesus had announced to the world the equality of men and women. But in the case of women, it was
'restrained in its application' – women were equal but
different.[62] In the light of the favour shown to women
by Jesus, what then was the mission of women? The
domestic life of Mary and Martha, putting devotion to
God into daily practice in the home, was the model for all
Victorian women:

Her [woman's] great sphere is evidently in the retirements of
home. The secret of woman's power transpires in the dependent relation she stands in towards man. Her province consists
not in coming abroad to interfere with man in the direction of
affairs. It is not to be looked for in the contention with him for
political privileges, nor in any natural capacity for determining
questions of state policy or for arguing and making decrees
upon theological truths and tenets . . . . In the quiet and unob-
trusive, though secretly all-influential acts of a homelife consists

---

[61] The hymn was from a poem by George Herbert (1593–1633), 'The
Elixir'.
[62] Stretton, *The Acts of Saint Mary Magdalene Considered*, p. 284.

the blessed province of woman ... the mind of woman, by force of its commonly viewing things from an exactly opposite direction to that which is taken by man, is calculated to give steadiness and elevation to his judgment which would otherwise in its manifestations take a too worldly, not to say irreligious turn.[63]

Mary Magdalene, far now from the repentant sinner, has become an ideal of Victorian middle-class respectability – a pure, loving, and self-sacrificing helpmeet to her husband and a nurturer of her children, responsible for producing godly men. '[T]he lesson of the mother', Stretton declared, oft sinks deep into the sensitive intelligence of the child, and produces its fruits in the high-toned religion and morals of the man'.[64]

In 1848, the same year that the Perpetual Curate of Hixon published his sermons on Mary Magdalene, the American proto-feminist Elizabeth Cady Stanton (1815–1902) held the first American woman's rights convention in Seneca Falls, New York. Thirty years later, she was still involved in the struggle. 'We can make no impression on men', she declared, 'who accept the theological view of woman as the author of sin, and all that nonsense. The debris of the centuries must be cleared away before our arguments for equality can have the least significance to any of them'.[65] Having drafted a committee of women to work with her, she published the two volumes of the *Woman's Bible* In 1895 and 1898. These consisted of particular biblical passages that were relevant to women followed by commentaries prepared by her and

---

[63] *Ibid.*, p. 290.   [64] *Ibid.*, p. 291.
[65] Quoted by Kathi Kern, *Mrs Stanton's Bible* (Ithaca, NY: Cornell University Press, 2002), p. 1.

her co-workers. The books were condemned by men and at least some women as the work of Satan for they laid bare 'the contradictions that riddled Victorian conceptions of the ideal woman, an ideal that depended on the notion of woman's "natural" piety'.[66] That it was a work of the Devil was amusingly refuted by Stanton herself in the Preface to the second volume. 'His Satanic Majesty', she wrote, 'was not invited to join the Revising Committee, which consists of women alone'.[67] For her, the time had come when the Bible had to be read like all other books – 'accepting the good and rejecting the evil it teaches'.[68] Her *Woman's Bible* was certainly not a work that was going to win a lot of friends among her male, nor even among her female readers.

The Woman's Bible was having none of the self-sacrificing Mary Magdalene of Harriet Beecher Stowe and Henry Stretton. 'So a woman', Stanton declared, 'who spends all her time in churches, with priests, in charities, neglects to cultivate her own natural gifts, to make the most of herself as an individual in the scale of being, a responsible soul whose place no other can fill, is worse than an infidel. "Self-development is a higher duty than self-sacrifice", should be woman's motto henceforward'.[69] And she found little cause for praise in Mary having been the first witness of the resurrection. Where the male disciples of Jesus had seen nothing but cast-off clothes when they visited the tomb, Mary saw and talked

---

[66] *Ibid.*, p. 3.
[67] Elizabeth Cady Stanton et al., *The Woman's Bible* (New York: European Publishing Company, 1898), vol. 2, p. 7.
[68] *Ibid.*, vol. 2, p. 8.   [69] *Ibid.*, vol. 2, p. 131.

with angels and with Jesus. 'As usual', we read, 'the woman is always most ready to believe miracles and fables, however extravagant and though beyond all human comprehension'.[70] That said, one of her contributors nonetheless found that 'Mary Magdalene is, in many respects, the tenderest and most loving character in the New Testament'.[71] Her love for Christ knew no bounds, even in the shadow of the cross. She it was who waited at the sepulchre, who hastened in the early morning to his tomb. 'And yet', we are told, 'the only comfort Christ gave to this true and loving soul lies in these strangely cold and heartless words: "Touch me not"'.[72]

A Woman of Distinction?

If Mary was playing a significant role in the nineteenth century in debates around gender and the role of women, she was also featuring in questions around class. In the 1820s, the German Prince Pückler-Muskau was shocked by the multitude of prostitutes in England. 'It is most strange', he declared, 'that in no country on earth is this afflicting and humiliating spectacle so openly exhibited as in the religious and decorous England. The evil goes to such an extent, that in the theatres it is often difficult to keep off these repulsive beings, especially if they are drunk, which is not seldom the case'.[73]

The prostitutes of nineteenth-century England were not the children of the aristocracy. They were the daughters of the poor. By the middle of the nineteenth

[70] *Ibid.*, vol. 2, p. 143.   [71] *Ibid.*, vol. 2, p. 144.   [72] *Ibid*
[73] Quoted by Haskins, *Mary Magdalen*, p. 322.

century, it was recognized that poverty was the chief cause of prostitution. Thus, for example, the English essayist William R. Greg (1809–1881) rejected the belief that the prostitute revels in 'the *enjoyment* of licentious pleasures; lost and dead to all sense of remorse and shame; wallowing in mire because she loves it'.[74] While he recognized that vanity, greed, and deception were on occasion the causes of prostitution, it was grinding poverty that was 'the most prolific source of prostitution, in this and in all other countries'.[75] For their incapacity to turn away from their lives of vice, 'harsh, savage, unjust, unchristian public opinion' was to blame. Jesus's treatment of Mary Magdalene had been overlooked:

Forgetting our Master's precepts – forgetting our human frailty – forgetting our own heavy portion in the common guilt – we turn contemptuously aside from the kneeling and weeping Magdalen, coldly bid her to despair, and leave her *alone with the irreparable*. Instead of helping her up, we thrust her down when endeavouring to rise; we choose to regard her, not as frail, but as depraved .... She is driven into prostitution by the weight of all society pressing down upon her.[76]

Sympathetic voices like William Greg's were few in number. And, despite the Magdalen houses of which there were fifty in 1856 and 308 fifty years later, the opportunities for reformed prostitutes to re-enter society were few. In Wilkie Collins's (1824–1889) novel *The New Magdalen* (1873), for example, the heroine Mercy

---

[74] W. R. Greg, 'Prostitution', *The Westminster Review* 53 (1850), p. 451.
[75] *Ibid.*, p. 460. [76] *Ibid.*, p. 471.

Merrick, a former prostitute who has finally become a nurse after being rejected for any other return into society, asked a new acquaintance whose identity she was soon to assume, 'Have you ever read of your unhappy fellow-creatures (the starving outcasts of the population) whom Want has betrayed to Sin? ... Have you heard – when those starving and sinning fellow-creatures happen to be women – of Refuges established to protect and reclaim them? ... *I* was once one of those women'.[77]

While in the Magdalen House, her despair was lessened by a sermon on the joy in heaven over the sinner that repents (Luke 15.7): 'the weary round of my life showed its nobler side again while he spoke'.[78] Like her biblical counterpart, she became the penitent fallen woman who was redeemed by her nursing of wounded soldiers. As a nurse, she was gentle, compassionate, and kind – and of a noble bearing: 'Pale and sad, her expression and her manner both eloquently suggestive of suppressed suffering and sorrow, there was an innate nobility in the carriage of this woman's head, an innate grandeur in the gaze of her large grey eyes, and in the lines of her finely-proportioned face, which made her irresistibly striking and beautiful, seen under any circumstances and clad in any dress'.[79] She was, at the end of the day, 'one of the noblest of God's creatures'.[80] In spite of Mercy's nobility of character, she was able to re-enter society, not only because she had assumed a false identity, but also because she was of 'high birth'. At the end of the

---

[77] Wilkie Collins, *The New Magdalen* (New York: Charles Scribner's Sons, 1908), p. 13.
[78] *Ibid.*, p. 17.   [79] *Ibid.*, p. 6.   [80] *Ibid.*, p. 272.

work, she reveals herself to be the illegitimate child of a beautiful gentlewoman deserted by her father, 'a man of high rank; proud of his position, and well known in the society of that time'.[81] The redeemed Magdalene was, after all, a woman of class, brought low through no fault of her own and redeemed in the end by the nobility of her character.

Collins's image of Mary Magdalene as a working-class prostitute who makes good, albeit of unknown noble birth, was not one that resonated in Victorian England. Many preferred to think of her, not as a repentant prostitute, but rather as a woman of the upper classes. Thus, for example, the Anglican Prebendary of York, the Reverend George Wray (1782–1878) began his *A Vindication of the Character of Mary Magdalene* (1870) by attempting to identify just who she was. For him Mary Magdalene was neither the fallen woman nor Mary of Bethany. Mary Magdalene was the single Mary who, along with Joanna and Susanna, ministered to Jesus from their wealth (Luke 8.2–3). The company she kept, he declared, suggests a woman of class and negates the idea of her being a woman of ill repute. All these women, he declared, 'seem to have been persons of superior condition of life, for they ministered unto Jesus *of their substance*'.[82]

---

[81] *Ibid.*, p. 298.

[82] George Wray, *A Vindication of the Character of Mary Magdalene* (London: Rivingtons, 1870), p. 5. For this and the sources that follow, I am grateful to Patricia S. Kruppa, '"More Sweet and Liquid than any other": Victorian Images of Mary Magdalene', in R. W. Davis and R. J. Helmstadter, *Religion and Irreligion in Victorian Society* (London: Routledge, 1992), pp. 117–132.

Rossetti's Merrymaking Mary

The wealthy young woman of Jacobus de Voragine's *The Golden Legend*, 'born of parents who were of noble station' and 'of royal lineage', who nonetheless fell into sin also provided a source for Mary's having been a 'better sort of woman'. This was the 'party-girl' Mary Magdalene of the Pre-Raphaelite English painter Dante Gabriel Rossetti (1826–1882) in his 'Mary Magdalen at the Door of Simon the Pharisee', right at the moment she is about to enter the house where Jesus was dining (see Plate 23).[83] It was a moment in time that Rossetti put into verse:

> Oh loose me! Seest thou not my Bridegroom's face
> That draws me to Him? For His feet my kiss,
> My hair, my tears He craves today: – and oh!
> What words can tell what other day and place
> Shall see me clasp these blood-stained feet of His?
> He needs, calls me, loves me: let me go![84]

Among Rossetti's friends was the American abolition-ist minister (and friend of Elizabeth Stanton) Moncure Conway (1832–1907). In 1867, Rossetti had given Conway a full-size photograph of this work that remained for him 'a source of happiness'.[85] In his autobiography, he described the drawing thus:

A large company of merrymakers is passing along the narrow street with music, all in rich costumes and garlands, led by the

---

[83] On this work, see Haskins, *Mary Magdalen*, pp. 348–350.

[84] Quoted by Virginia Surtees, *The Painting and Drawings of Dante Gabriel Rossetti (1828–1882)* (Oxford: Clarendon Press, 1971), p. 62.

[85] Moncure Daniel Conway, *Autobiography: Memories and Experiences of Moncure Daniel Conway* (Cambridge: Cambridge University Press, 2012), vol. 2, p. 113.

fairest of them – Mary Magdalene. But as they pass Mary sees at an open window a face that makes her pause; the eyes of Jesus have met hers. She is seen ascending the few steps that lead to the door, not heeding the youths trying to restrain her, tearing off her garlands; her long wavy hair floats back, and the pathetically beautiful face is stretched forward, for ever turned away from her gay companions who stand stricken with wonder, to the one face. From her girdle hangs the antique round flagon of spikenard.[86]

This was a picture, Conway went on to say, which started him on a new quest for Mary Magdalene.

When in 1867 Rossetti gave Conway the photograph of Mary at the door of Simon the Pharisee, Conway like Rossetti was a supporter of the composite Mary Magdalene. But by 1897, he had clearly rethought his position. On Wednesday 14 April of that year, he had noticed in the Westminster Gazette the report of a sermon preached by the Bishop of London, Mandell Creighton (1843–1901) on that day. In the history of the death and resurrection of Jesus, the Bishop had said, every person mentioned exhibited every sort of character. Thus, the three Marys at the crucifixion (John 19.25) represented three permanent types of women. Mary the mother of Jesus stood for 'the purest, noblest, and most dignified of her sex'; Mary the wife of Clopas for 'the religious housewife', and Mary Magdalene for 'the penitent'.[87] A letter to the editor by Moncure Conway was published two days later. He objected to the description

---

[86] *Ibid.*, vol. 2, p. 114.
[87] Anon., 'Bishop Creighton in the City To-day', in *The Westminster Gazette*, Wednesday 14 April 1897.

of Mary Magdalene as 'the penitent'. '[T]here is no intimation whatever in the Bible', he declared, 'that Mary Magdalene was at any time other than a pure woman of perfectly correct life. Is this not substituting for the New Testament the "traditions of men"?'[88] The Bishop, whether reluctantly or otherwise is unknown, agreed with Conway that there was no New Testament authority for the identity of Mary Magdalene and the penitent woman of the Gospel of Luke.

The result of Conway's quest appeared in 1903 in an article entitled 'Mary Magdalene'. It amounted to a vehement rejection of the tradition of the composite Mary. 'There is not another instance in history', he wrote, 'of a woman's name having become proverbial through thirteen centuries as representative of a certain type of character without the slightest historical foundation for it'.[89] That said, he believed that the legend of her immoral life had been perpetuated by admiration for her. And he remarked that most of his readers 'will feel irritated at the thought of parting with the romance which poets and artists have found so fascinating'.[90]

The composite Mary, he declared, was the result of the combination of two or three distinct incidents in the New Testament – 'a combination formed by human nature and quickened in all its development by the emotions and aspirations of the human heart'.[91] Conway had found the historical Mary Magdalene within the pages of the

[88] Moncure D. Conway, 'A Calumniated Lady', in *The Westminster Gazette*, Friday 16 April 1897.
[89] Moncure D. Conway, 'Mary Magdalene', *The Critic* 42 (1903), p. 212.
[90] *Ibid.*   [91] *Ibid.*, p. 214.

New Testament Gospels. And yet, still, it was Rossetti's composite Mary that moved him deeply. When Mary tears off her garlands when she meets the eye of Jesus, 'she is drawn to the feet of a king whose domain is not of this world, her own Rabboni, and her splendid raiment becomes the livery of a vanishing world'.[92]

The Victorian Mary Magdalene was not only a woman of distinction, but she was also young and lovely. In his *Mary Magdalen: A Chronicle* (1891), the American writer Edgar Saltus (1855–1921) has Mary as a first century *bon vivant* – an heiress with a castle in Magdala inherited from her father or perhaps from an older lover. She was the 'toast of the tetrarchy' in Judea. Her ambition was to go to Rome where 'Tiberius will give me a palace. I shall sleep on the down the Teutons bring. I shall drink pearls dissolved in falernian. I shall sup on peacocks' tongues'.[93] To see her was to acquire a new conception of beauty. Her life was nothing but sensual delight:

To her, youth had been a chalice of aromatic wine. She had drained it and found no dregs. Day had been interwoven with splendors, and night with the rays of the sun. Where she passed she conquered; when she smiled there were slaves ready-made. There had been hot brawls where she trod, the gleam of white knives. Men had killed each other because of her eyes, and women had wept themselves to death. For her a priest had gone mad, and a betrothed had hid herself in the sea.[94]

[92] *Ibid.*, p. 215.
[93] Edgar Saltus, *Mary Magdalen: A Chronicle* (New York: Brentano's, 1919), p. 37.
[94] *Ibid.*, pp. 80–81.

It was this 'young and lovely' Mary Magdalene, or at least Victorian imaginings of how young and lovely women ought to look, that featured in Victorian art. Thus, for example, the Victorian art critic John Ruskin (1819–1900) despised Titian's Mary Magdalene (see Plate 16). She was 'markedly and entirely belonging to the lowest class, a stout, redfaced woman, dull, and coarse of feature'.[95] That said, he did give Titian credit for daring to doubt the romantic fable of Mary Magdalene and rejecting the sentimental faith surrounding it. Titian saw that 'it was possible for plain women to love no less than beautiful ones; and for stout persons to repent as well as those more delicately made ... the Magdalene would have received her pardon not the less quickly because her wit was none of the readiest; and would not have been regarded with less compassion by her Master because her eyes were swollen, or her dress disordered'.[96]

This was why, Ruskin declared, he found the picture so painful. Little wonder that he so much preferred Rossetti's 'Mary Magdalen at the Door of Simon the Pharisee'. He liked this drawing, he wrote in a letter to Rossetti in 1854, 'because I have naturally a great dread of subjects altogether painful, and I can be happy in thinking of Mary Magdalene'.[97] In a later letter to Rossetti, he remarked, 'That "Magdalene" is magnificent to my mind, in every possible way: it stays by me'.[98]

---

[95] Edward Tyas Cook and Alexander Wedderburn (eds.), *The Works of John Ruskin* (Cambridge: Cambridge University Press, 2010), vol. 5, p. 227.
[96] *Ibid.*, vol. 5.   [97] *Ibid.*, vol. 36, p. 168.   [98] *Ibid.*, vol. 36, p. 272.

Rossetti's Mary Magdalene was the composite Mary Magdalene of Catholic tradition. Although an agnostic by inclination, he was nonetheless personally attracted to Catholicism and to the Anglo-Catholicism of the Oxford Movement that aimed to bring Catholic ritual practices into the Church of England – Latin hymns, elaborate vestments, the adoration of the saints, and 'bells and smells'. And there is a symmetry between the Pre-Raphaelite image of Mary Magdalene and the vision of her in a sermon in 1841 by John Henry Newman (1801–1890), leading Anglo-Catholic, later Catholic churchman, and (as of 2019) Catholic saint. Mary Magdalene came to the house of Simon the Pharisee, declared Newman, 'young and beautiful, and "rejoicing in her youth"'.[99] Along with saints Peter and Paul, she was a saint of love, ardent and impetuous – the distinguishing marks of those who were sinners before they were saints. Newman's Mary Magdalene was not, however, Rossetti's wealthy young 'socialite'. Rather, according to Newman, she was there at the feast as part of the hired help. She had come, he said, as 'a necessary embellishment of the entertainment', to honour the feast 'with her sweet odours and cool unguents for the forehead and hair of the guests'.[100] But 'lo, a wondrous sight', declared Newman,

[T]hat poor, many-coloured child of guilt approaches to crown with her sweet ointment the head of Him to whom the feast was given . . . . He is looking at her: it is the Shepherd looking at the lost sheep, and the lost sheep surrenders herself to Him . . . .

---

[99] John Henry Cardinal Newman, *Discourses Addressed to Mixed Congregations* (London: Longmans, Green, & Co., 1897), p. 75.
[100] *Ibid.*

Those wanton hands, those polluted lips, have touched, have kissed the feet of the Eternal, and He shrank not from the homage. And as she hung over them, and as she moistened them from her full eyes, how did the love for One so great, yet so gentle, wax vehement within her, lighting up a flame which never was to die from that moment even for ever! ... Henceforth, my brethren, love was to her, as to St. Augustine and to St. Ignatius Loyola afterwards, as a wound in the soul, so full of desire as to become anguish.[101]

Newman's Mary was only a servant but, like Rossetti's, she was young, beautiful, and sensual. We do not know what Newman thought of Rossetti's Mary Magdalene. Other clergymen were decidedly nervous of her. In July of 1883, Rossetti's mother and sister had commissioned the British artist Frederic Shields (1833–1911) to design a memorial window for the church of All Saints, Birchington on sea, in the graveyard of which Rossetti had been buried in the previous year. One of the two designs that Shields submitted to the vicar, John Alcock, was based on Rossetti's 'Mary Magdalen at the Door of Simon the Pharisee'. Much to Shields's dismay, he received a letter from Alcock rejecting the proposed design. 'I do not think', the vicar wrote, 'this picture is likely to inspire devotional thoughts and feelings, and fear that in some cases it might rather do the reverse'.[102] Shields replied that 'Mrs. and Miss Rossetti could not have anticipated, even in dreams, such an objection arising, for they have been accustomed to regard the

---

[101] *Ibid.*, pp. 76–78.
[102] Ernestine Mills (ed.), *The Life and Letters of Frederic Shields* (London: Longmans, 1912), p. 280.

design as directly opponent to evil'.[103] Alcock was unmoved, perhaps not surprisingly, by Shields saying that the vicar was a victim of the 'dead, unhelpful conventionality common to religious art'.[104] While the vicar did not think it likely that the ladies of the parish would cast aside their hats and dresses as Mary had her garlands, he remained adamant that the design would be more degrading than elevating.[105]

John Alcock (and John Henry Newman for that matter) would undoubtedly have been further taken aback by some other contemporary depictions of Mary. Thus, for example, the Mary Magdalene of the Pre-Raphaelite Frederick Sandys (1829–1904) was more *femme fatale* than fallen woman (see Plate 24), as was 'The Magdalen' of William Etty (1787–1849) (see Plate 25). The Mary Magdalene of the Belgian painter Alfred Stevens (1823–1906), for which the actor Sarah Bernhardt was the model, was more seductress than penitent (see Plate 26). The French artist Jules Lefebvre's (1836–1911) stunning 'Mary Magdalene in the Cave' references the tradition of the eremitic Mary with an audience both passionate and pious in mind (see Plate 27).

Without doubt, and perhaps for obvious reasons, Mary Magdalene as 'the fallen woman' interested the market for fine art far more than the Mary Magdalene who witnessed the resurrection of Jesus or the Mary of Bethany who sat at his feet while her sister Martha toiled

---

[103] *Ibid.*, p. 282.   [104] *Ibid.*
[105] For a full account of the Rossetti memorials, see Karen Dielman, 'Sacramental Memorializing: Upon the Death of Dante Gabriel Rossetti', *Nineteenth-Century Contexts*, 37 (2015), pp. 215–231.

in the kitchen. At the end of the nineteenth century, Mary remained sacred, saintly, and ascetic. But she had also become profane, sensual, and erotic. Hers was now a *persona* that allowed for the creation of new and alternative lives of Mary Magdalene as both the lover and wife of Jesus.

6

Mary Magdalene
Lover and Wife

≈

I am my beloved's,
And his desire is for me.
Come my beloved,
Let us go forth into the fields and lodge in the villages . . .
There I will give you my love.

Song of Solomon, 7.10–12

Mary and *The Da Vinci Code*

Alongside the 'traditional' lives of Mary Magdalene that
we have been exploring in this book thus far, there is an
array of 'alternative' lives of Mary Magdalene. These are
contained within the Western 'esoteric' tradition.[1] They
are essentially attempts to make dominant the 'true' life of
Mary Magdalene that, according to the esoteric tradition,
has been obscured, even repressed, by the patriarchal
church. According to the supporters of the esoteric
Mary Magdalene, her 'true' life has been known, preserved, and transmitted by a few wise men (and some
women) who often belonged to secret societies. Like the
traditional lives of Mary Magdalene, these alternative lives
built on the life of Mary Magdalene after the crucifixion

---

[1] See Wouter J. Hanegraaf, *Western Esotericism: A Guide for the Perplexed*
(London: Bloomsbury, 2013). On secret societies within the esoteric
tradition, see pp. 33–36.

of Jesus. But there were two crucial differences between the traditional and these alternative lives. First, Mary Magdalene was the wife or lover of Jesus. Second, Jesus and Mary had children, thus creating a 'bloodline' descending from Jesus and Mary to the present. The most successful of these alternative lives is undoubtedly *The Da Vinci Code* (2003) by Dan Brown (1964–). With over 80 million copies sold, *The Da Vinci Code* gave Mary Magdalene both a new life and a new afterlife in modern Western culture. It synthesized a number of earlier alternative lives and, in its turn, provided the impetus for a growing industry of alternative lives of Mary.[2]

The Mary Magdalene of *The Da Vinci Code* is not the composite Mary of the Western traditions. The book strongly rejects the identification of Mary Magdalene with the sinful woman of the Gospel of Luke. To the cryptologist Sophie Neveu's suggestion that Mary Magdalene was a prostitute, the Grail expert Sir Leigh Teabing declared that 'Magdalene was no such thing. That unfortunate misconception was the legacy of a smear campaign launched by the early Church' in order to cover up her true role.[3] In addition, as Teabing told Sophie later, it was in

[2] Although a bit of a potboiler, *The Da Vinci Code* is a surprisingly good read. For those who haven't read it and do not wish to, the following summary notes will contextualize our discussion: 'The Da Vinci Code', Plot Overview.'

Located at www.sparknotes.com/lit/davincicode/summary/. For the better part of this discussion, I have eschewed 'fact-checking' *The Da Vinci Code*. In spite of the inclination of many readers to read it as a work of history (or, at least, as reflective of 'real history'), it is after all only a work of fiction. For readers inclined to 'fact-checking', see Carl E. Olson and Sandra Miesel, *The Da Vinci Hoax: Exposing the Errors in* The Da Vinci Code (San Francisco: Ignatius Press, 2004).

[3] Dan Brown, *The Da Vinci Code* (London: Corgi, 2004), p. 325.

order to hide her powerful family ties that 'Magdalene was later recast as a whore'.[4] The book is silent as to when this occurred. But the film version of the book clearly alludes to Pope Gregory the Great as the smearer-in-chief. Mary was 'smeared by the church in 591 anno domini', declared Teabing. The identification of Mary Magdalene with the fallen woman enabled the Church to hide the fact that it was to Mary Magdalene that Jesus had assigned the task of founding the church. 'Jesus was the original feminist', we read.[5] But this identification also allowed the Church to repress the knowledge of Jesus's marriage to her and the possibility of their having had children. 'The Church', we read, 'in order to defend itself against the Magdalene's power, perpetuated her image as a whore and buried evidence of Christ's marriage to her, thereby defusing any potential claims that Christ had a surviving bloodline and was a mortal prophet [and not a divine being]'.[6]

Be that as it may, it is difficult to line up the Mary of *The Da Vinci Code* with the Mary Magdalene of the Gospel stories. There is no mention in the book of Mary as a healed demoniac, of her supporting of Jesus and the disciples out of her own wealth, or of her presence at the crucifixion and the resurrection. There is no mention either of Mary, the sister of Martha and Lazarus, who washed the feet of Jesus with her tears and wiped them with her hair. Nor does the *Da Vinci* Mary align with the Western traditions of her life after the death of Jesus – except for one crucial detail. After the crucifixion, we are told, 'Mary Magdalene travelled to France'.[7]

---

[4] *Ibid.*, p. 332.   [5] *Ibid.*, p. 330.   [6] *Ibid.*, p. 337.   [7] *Ibid.*, p. 339.

Nevertheless, we can construct a life of Mary Magdalene from various passages within *Da Vinci* that gradually let us into her imagined hidden life. Crucially, she was of a royal bloodline that descended from the tribe of Benjamin, one of the twelve tribes of Israel, and from Benjamin himself, the youngest son of Jacob and his wife Rachel. Saul, the first Israelite king, was a descendant of Benjamin, hence the *Da Vinci* claim that Mary Magdalene 'was of royal descent'.[8] As Mary had a bloodline reaching back to King Saul, so Jesus had a bloodline that went back to King Solomon and to his father King David (Matthew 1.6–7). These two royal bloodlines came together when Jesus married Mary Magdalene. 'By marrying into the powerful house of Benjamin', Teabing informs us, 'Jesus fused two royal bloodlines, creating a potent political union with the potential of making a legitimate claim to the throne and restoring the line of kings as it was under Solomon'.[9]

Within the New Testament, there is no hint of any marriage between Jesus and Mary nor, for that matter, is there any suggestion of a sexual relationship. Nevertheless, *Da Vinci* finds evidence for their marriage, both indirect and direct. The indirect evidence looks to the general assumption that marriage was the norm for men of the age of Jesus and of his times and that therefore he was most likely married. 'If Jesus were not married', Robert Langdon, Professor of Religious Symbology at Harvard University and *Da Vinci*'s 'academic as hero', declared, 'at least one of the Bible's gospels would have

---

[8] *Ibid.*, p. 332.   [9] *Ibid.*

mentioned it and offered some explanation for His unnatural state of bachelorhood'.[10] It is not clear whence Dan Brown derived this idea. But he may well have been influenced by Schalom Ben-Chorin's *Brother Jesus: The Nazarene through Jewish Eyes* (2001) for whom an unmarried Rabbi would have been 'hardly imaginable' in the time of Jesus.[11] The direct evidence was derived from the so-called Gnostic Gospels, and the two key passages are those from *The Gospel of Philip* and the *Gospel of Mary* that we have already looked at in Chapter 1.[12] In the former of these, we read that 'Christ loved her more than all the disciples and used to kiss her often on the mouth'; in the second, Levi said that Jesus 'loved her more than us'.[13] As we will see later, Brown will make larger claims than these upon which to build his case.

Within the New Testament, there is no suggestion that Mary Magdalene was present at Jesus's Last Supper. Although there is in *Da Vinci* itself no *explicit* suggestion that Mary Magdalene was present at the Last Supper, we can assume, from his account of Leonardo da Vinci's (1452–1519) painting of 'The Last Supper' that Leonardo so believed and *Da Vinci* wishes us to think so too (see Plate 28). This is a reading of Leonardo's work that is derived in the main from the book *The Templar Revelation* (1997), one of the works held in Sir Leigh Teabring's library which *Da Vinci* conveniently points us

---

[10] *Ibid.*, p. 327.
[11] See Schalom Ben-Chorin, *Brother Jesus: The Nazarene through Jewish Eyes* (Athens: University of Georgia Press, 2001), p. 101.
[12] See 'The Gnostic Mary', Chapter 1.
[13] Brown, *The Da Vinci Code*, pp. 328, 330.

towards.[14] Central to the story of *Da Vinci* is the claim that the figure on the right hand side of Jesus is Mary Magdalene. Traditionally, this figure has been identified as the disciple John 'whom Jesus loved' (John 20.2). But for *Da Vinci*, it is a matter of 'historical record' that Mary and Jesus were married and 'Da Vinci was certainly aware of the fact. *The Last Supper* practically shouts at the viewer that Jesus and Magdalene were a pair'.[15] Whispering so quietly that no one has heard might be more to the point.

Cheap shots aside, *Da Vinci* nonetheless makes some fun moves. First, in Leonardo's painting, Jesus and Mary were clothed as mirror images of each other, Jesus in a red robe and blue cloak, Mary in the reverse (yin and yang). Second, Mary and Jesus seem to be joined at the hip and leaning away from each other as if to create a negative space between them – a space that has the shape of a chalice and the female womb. Third, when Jesus and Mary are considered as compositional elements, the shape of the letter 'M' could be seen, perhaps standing for 'Matrimonio' or 'Mary Magdalene'. Finally, 'The Last Supper' has Peter, to Mary's right, leaning menacingly towards her 'and slicing his blade-like hand across her neck'. *Da Vinci* would incline us to take this as emblematic of the conflict between Peter and Mary in the early church evidenced in the Gnostic Gospels. In the context of the book as a whole, we are expected to take it as reflective of the larger conflict between a patriarchal and

---

[14] See *Ibid.*, p. 336. See also Lynn Picknett and Clive Prince, *The Templar Revelation* (London: Corgi Books, 2007).

[15] Brown, *The Da Vinci Code*, p. 326.

a matriarchal Christianity only resolved within Christianity, according to *Da Vinci*, by the emperor Constantine at the Council of Nicea in 325 CE.[16] Between Christianity and paganism, Constantine 'could see that Christianity was on the rise, and he simply backed the winning horse'.[17]

As we will see later, other alternative lives of Mary have her and Jesus marrying after a crucifixion that Jesus survives. *Da Vinci*, however, has them married before the crucifixion and, presumably, the death of Jesus. For Mary Magdalene, we are told, was pregnant at the time of the crucifixion. Within a short time after the death of Jesus, for the safety of her unborn child, Mary fled the Holy Land and secretly travelled to France. Where in the traditional lives Mary continued her career of preaching the Gospel in France, the *Da Vinci* Mary found refuge in the Jewish community there and gave birth to a daughter whose name was Sarah. 'Magdalene's and Sarah's lives', Leigh Teabing informed Sophie Neveu, 'were scrupulously chronicled by their Jewish protectors. Remember that Magdalene's child belonged to the lineage of Jewish kings – David and Solomon. For this reason, the Jews in France considered Magdalene sacred royalty and revered her as the progenitor of the royal line of kings'.[18] Scholars of that era, we are told, further chronicled Mary Magdalene's days in France, including the birth of Sarah and the subsequent family tree. These chronicles included a manuscript called *The Magdalene Diaries* – Mary's own account of her relationship with Christ, his crucifixion, and her time in France. These were included in the

---

[16] *Ibid.*, p. 331.   [17] *Ibid.*, p. 311.   [18] *Ibid.*, p. 339.

so-called Sangreal documents that were eventually buried under the ruins of Solomon's temple in Jerusalem. In spite of these documents, *Da Vinci* is silent about the life of Mary Magdalene after the birth of her daughter. The film version enigmatically says only, 'Mary Magdalene lived out her days in hiding'. Neither the book nor the film tells us where or when she died.

Holy Blood, Holy Grail

According to all four New Testament Gospels, it was Joseph of Arimathea who took responsibility for the burial of Jesus (Mark 15.42–46, Matthew 27.57–60, Luke 23.50–53, John 19.38–42). But, apart from that, he has no other role in the New Testament. In the traditional versions of Mary Magdalene's journey to France after the death of Jesus, Joseph of Arimathea also had no part. Nevertheless, from the late twelfth century, Joseph began to be connected with the Arthurian legends as the first keeper of the Holy Grail – the chalice that was used by Jesus in the Last Supper. Joseph of Arimathea was introduced into the Arthurian legends by the French poet Robert de Boron in his *Joseph of Arimathea* (c. 1200).[19] Robert took the idea of the Grail from earlier romances, identified it with the chalice used at the Last Supper, and linked it to Joseph of Arimathea.

According to Robert, 'the Grail', with which Christ performed his sacrament at the Last Supper, was taken from the supper by a Jew. In turn, it was given to Pontius Pilate who put it in safekeeping until he was informed that

[19] This was the first of a trilogy, followed by *Merlin* and *Perceval*.

Jesus had been executed. Pilate, not wanting to possess anything that might connect him with the death of Jesus, gave it to Joseph who had come to Pilate seeking permission to have the body of Jesus for burial. As Joseph was washing the body of Jesus, bright red blood was still flowing out of his wounds. Joseph at once set the Grail to collect the blood of Jesus: 'He thought the drops of blood that were falling would be better in the vessel than elsewhere'.[20] When Joseph was later imprisoned, the risen Christ brought the Grail to him, entrusting it to him and his descendants.

This brief excursion into the complex world of Arthurian legend allows us to cast light on the only reference to Joseph of Arimathea in *Da Vinci*. For it is with the help of Joseph of Arimathea, we read, that 'Mary Magdalene secretly travelled to France'.[21] In short, Joseph of Arimathea provides the crucial narrative link between the Grail and Mary Magdalene and enables the *Da Vinci* Mary to be embedded within the Arthurian legends of the Grail. As Robert Langdon had discerned through his historical research and as Leigh Teabing revealed to Sophie Neveu, the chalice was not a physical object used at the Last Supper. Thus, when Sophie is asked how many wine glasses are on the table in

---

[20] Nigel Bryant (trans.), *Merlin and the Grail, Joseph of Arimathea, Merlin, Perceval: The Trilogy of Prose Romances attributed to Robert de Boron* (Cambridge: D. S. Brewer, 2001), p. 19. See also, Richard Barber, *The Holy Grail: Imagination and Belief* (Cambridge, MA: Harvard University Press, 2004), ch. 3. For an accessible account of the Grail traditions, see Juliette Wood, *The Holy Grail: History and Legend* (Cardiff: University of Wales Press, 2012).

[21] Brown, *The Da Vinci Code*, p. 339.

Leonardo's painting, she comes to the realization that everyone at the table had a glass of wine: 'Thirteen cups... tiny, stemless, and made of glass. There was no chalice in the painting. No Holy Grail'.[22] Leonardo's fresco, Teabing goes on to tell Sophie, is the entire key to the mystery of the Holy Grail: 'Sophie scanned the work eagerly. "Does this fresco tell us *what* the Grail really is?" "Not what it is," Teabing whispered, "But rather *who* it is. The Holy Grail is not a thing. It is in fact,... a *person*"'.[23] As we have already surmised, and as Sophie soon realizes, it is the woman sitting on the right of Jesus, namely, Mary Magdalene.[24]

Within the broader context of *Da Vinci*, the Holy Grail has an array of meanings that enable the story to maintain a narrative arc of which the identification of Mary with the Grail in Leonardo's *The Last Supper* is its peak. The Holy Grail is not only Mary's person but it was so by virtue of her womb. As Joseph of Arimathea's vessel carried the blood of Jesus, so did the womb of Mary Magdalene carry Jesus's royal bloodline: 'Mary Magdalene was the Holy Vessel. She was the chalice that bore the royal bloodline of Jesus Christ. She was the womb that bore the lineage and the vine from which the sacred fruit sprang forth'.[25] To go with this claim, a further neat if etymologically spurious move. The documents within which the truth of Jesus and Mary's

---

[22] *Ibid.*, p. 316. The film version makes no mention of thirteen cups (not least because they are 'invisible' in Leonardo's work), saying only 'not a single cup. No chalice'. Both book and film are on firmer ground in the claim that 'there was no chalice in the painting. No Holy Grail'.

[23] *Ibid.*, p. 316.   [24] See *Ibid.*, p. 325.   [25] *Ibid.*, p. 333.

bloodline was contained were called the Sangreal documents. The word 'Sangreal', we are told, derives from San Greal – Holy Grail. But in its most ancient form it was 'Sang Real' – Royal Blood.[26] This slick move was not original to *Da Vinci*. In the fourteenth century, the English chronicler John Harding (1378–1465) translated 'sangreal' as 'royal blood'. This reading was to find its way into the book *Holy Blood Holy Grail* in 1982 (of which more anon), thence into *Da Vinci*.

The Holy Grail is not only the person of Mary Magdalene and the Holy Blood, but it is also her sarcophagus and the bones within it. 'The quest for the Holy Grail,' declared Teabing, 'is literally the quest to kneel before the bones of Mary Magdalene. A journey to pray at the feet of the outcast one, the lost sacred feminine'.[27] Thus, the quest for the Holy Grail is a quest for a tomb that contains the remains of Mary Magdalene.

It also contains the so-called Sangreal documents that give evidence of the bloodline of Christ. According to the alternative history of *Da Vinci*, the bloodline grew quietly under cover in France until the fifth century when 'it intermarried with royal blood and created a dynasty known as the Merovingian bloodline' that ruled France from the middle of the fifth century until 751.[28] According to this alternative history, The Merovingian dynasty was almost exterminated by the Catholic church. But the lineage continued through to a Godefroi de Bouillon who founded the secret brotherhood known as the Priory of Sion in Jerusalem in 1099 to keep alive the

---

[26] *Ibid.*, p. 333.   [27] *Ibid.*, p. 340.   [28] *Ibid.*, p. 342.

secret of his bloodline.[29] During their time in Jerusalem, the Priory learned of a hidden cache of documents buried beneath the ruins of Herod's temple that had been built on top of the temple of Solomon. In order to retrieve the documents, the Priory of Sion created a military arm called the Order of the Poor Knights of Christ and the Temple of Solomon, more commonly known as the Knights Templar. The Priory of Sion, dedicated to protecting these documents and the Holy Grail continued until the present, including among its members Botticelli, Isaac Newton, Victor Hugo, and, of course, Leonardo Da Vinci. All that said, we are at the point now where we can lay out the main plot of *The Da Vinci Code*.

The Priory of Sion, with the tacit approval of the Church, has kept the truth of the Holy Grail and the documents that support it secret. Nevertheless, the Priory has always intended to unveil the secret, 'shouting the true story of Jesus Christ from the rooftops'.[30] And it plans to make it public soon after the millennial year 2000. Astrologically this time signals the end of the 2,000 year-long Age of Pisces (the fish and the symbol of Jesus) and the dawning (as all aging hippies will know) of the Age of Aquarius. Theologically, it marks the End of Days, that period of time that will end with the return of Jesus and the beginning of a new millennial period. In order to keep the *real truth* about Christianity becoming public, the Vatican, or at least its own conservative

[29] The French Nobleman Godefroi of Bouillon (1060–1100) was one of the leaders of the first Crusade and King of Jerusalem from 1099 to 1100.
[30] Brown, *The Da Vinci Code*, p. 355.

secretive society Opus Dei, has to murder all those who know the secret (the Grand Master and the four guardians of the Priory of Sion). It has then to find the sepulchre of Mary Magdalene and destroy the documents within it, along with the remains of Mary. Hence the book begins with the murder of Jacques Saunière, Grand Master of the Priory of Sion, curator at the Louvre, and grandfather of Sophie Neveu. It nears its end with the recognition of Sophie as one of the descendants of Mary and Jesus. As Langdon says to Sophie in the film version, 'You are the secret'. For Dan Brown, this is the greatest story ever told rather than the standard Christian story that is the greatest ever sold.[31]

As we noted above, of Mary's life after the birth of her daughter, *Da Vinci* remains silent, although we can assume that she remained in France. But in keeping with the Arthurian tradition that the Holy Grail was located in Britain, *Da Vinci* also locates the tomb of Mary Magdalene there, specifically, beneath the Rosslyn Chapel south of Edinburgh. For *Da Vinci*, this chapel provides the link between the Grail, the Priory of Sion, and the Templars. For the Templars had designed Rosslyn Chapel as a replica of Solomon's Temple with a subterranean vault that held the Grail echoing 'the Grail's original hiding place' in Jerusalem.[32] However, by the time that Robert Langdon and Sophie Neveu arrive at Rosslyn, Mary Magdalene has been long gone. As the curator of Rosslyn Chapel Marie Chauvel informs them,

---

[31] See *Ibid.*, p. 354.

[32] *Ibid.*, p. 564. The connection of the Templars, Rosslyn Chapel, and the Grail goes back no further than the 1980s.

'One of the Priory's most ancient charges was one day to return the Grail to her homeland of France where she could rest for eternity. For centuries she was dragged across the countryside to keep her safe. Most undignified. Jacques's [Saunière] charge when he became Grand Master was to restore her honour by returning her to France and building her a resting place fit for a queen'.[33] Mary is back in France, but she is to be found, not in Provencal nor in Vézelay as the Western traditions have it, but in Paris – beneath the inverted pyramid of the Louvre, the key to her location having been inscribed in a poem on a piece of papyrus.

According to Sir Leigh Teabing, the royal bloodline of Jesus had been chronicled in scores of historical works. Among the several dozen in his library on this topic, he declared *Holy Blood, Holy Grail* (1982) as 'perhaps the best known tome'.[34] Certainly, it was Dan Brown's key resource for *The Da Vinci Code*. The most significant difference between the Mary Magdalene of *Da Vinci* and of *Holy Blood* lies in the rejection of the composite Mary in the case of the former and her endorsement in the latter. Thus, Mary Magdalene is the fallen woman of Luke. That she is 'fallen' is not the consequence of her being a prostitute – a later blackening of her name, but a result of her membership of a pagan cult. She is also Mary of Bethany, the sister of Martha and Lazarus. Were Jesus not married, it is argued, this would have been sufficiently unusual for a man of his time for it to have been commented upon in the Gospels. But, of course, there was one wedding which, according to *Holy Blood*, may well have

---

[33] *Ibid.*, p. 581.   [34] *Ibid.*, p. 337.

been that of Jesus, namely the wedding in Cana in Galilee in which Jesus turned the water into wine (John 2.1–11).[35] Who then did Jesus marry? The two most likely candidates were Mary Magdalene and Mary of Bethany. But if they are one and the same person, the problem is solved. 'If Jesus was indeed married,' *Holy Blood* concludes, 'there would thus seem to be only one candidate for the wife – one woman who recurs repeatedly in the Gospels under different names and in different roles'.[36] As for the tradition we examined earlier that it was John the disciple 'whom Jesus loved' (John 20.2) who was the groom at this wedding, *Holy Blood* identifies John with Lazarus (who could not, of course, have been marrying his own sister).

Unlike *Da Vinci* which appears to have Jesus die on the cross, *Holy Blood* has him surviving the crucifixion, although it remains uncertain about his life afterwards. He may have died in Kashmir, in Egypt, or in Judea, but likely not in France. In a key sense, it matters little: '[W]hat happened to Jesus was of less importance than what happened to the holy family – and especially to his brother-in-law [Lazarus], his wife and his children'.[37] Not only did Jesus not rise from the dead, but neither did Lazarus, his apparent death and resurrection being nothing but his initiation into a 'mystery' religion. Lazarus's life after his 'resurrection' is clearer than that of Jesus after his (non-) resurrection. For *Holy Blood* follows both

---

[35] See Michael Baigent, Richard Leigh, and Henry Lincoln, *Holy Blood, Holy Grail* (New York: Bantam Dell, 2004), pp. 332–333. In contrast to *Da Vinci*, this work claims to be a work of non-fiction. As with *Da Vinci*, I have in the main eschewed 'fact-checking' *Holy Blood*. That would necessitate a volume of its own.

[36] *Ibid.*, pp. 337–338.   [37] *Ibid.*, p. 359.

Jacobus de Voragine's and pseudo-Rabanus's accounts of Mary's journey to France. Thus, Lazarus, as we recall, accompanied Martha and Mary to France.[38]

To those who traditionally travelled with Mary, *Holy Blood* adds Joseph of Arimathea, thus providing the link between Joseph and the 'Holy Grail'. Joseph, Lazarus, and Maximin were put ashore at Marseilles along with Mary Magdalene 'who, as tradition subsequently maintains, was carrying with her the Holy Grail, the "blood royal"' of the house of David and of the house of Benjamin.[39] Mary Magdalene, we are told, remained in France with Lazarus, eventually dying at either Aix-en-Provence or Saint Baume, where presumably, no suggestions to the contrary being offered, she remained.[40] So, unlike *Da Vinci*, there is no interest in *Holy Blood* in the search for her remains or the adoration of them. Nevertheless, as we might expect by now, *Mary Magdalene is the Holy Grail*: 'the Holy Grail would have been quite literally, the receptacle or vessel that received and contained Jesus's blood. In other words, it would have been the womb of the Magdalen – and by extension the Magdalen herself'.[41] But the Grail is also Jesus's bloodline and his descendants – 'the "Sang Real", the "Real" or "Royal" blood of which the Templars, created by the

---

[38] See *Ibid.*, p. 472, n. 16.

[39] *Ibid.*, p. 344. There is, of course, no 'tradition' that maintains this. According to *Holy Blood*, Mary arrived in France also with other children fathered by Jesus.

[40] Joseph of Arimathea is said to have left Mary and Lazarus in France and travelled to England where he established a church in Glastonbury. Hence, there is no suggestion of his taking the Grail to England nor of its ever ending up there.

[41] *Ibid.*, p. 400.

Prieuré de Sion, were appointed guardians'.[42] For its part, the Catholic Church tried to kill the bloodline descendants and their guardians (the Cathars and the Templars) to ensure the supremacy of the Roman episcopacy descended from Peter, without fear of its being taken over by a false 'pope' from the succession of Mary Magdalene.

Mary the Goddess

In *The Da Vinci Code*, alongside the conspiracy theory of the Catholic suppression of Mary Magdalene as the Holy Grail, there is another. This is to the effect that the Catholic Church tried to erase the idea of Mary Magdalene as a goddess. From the time of Constantine in the fourth century, *Da Vinci's* key villain in the piece, the world was converted from matriarchal paganism to patriarchal Christianity by demonising the 'sacred feminine'. This early matriarchal religion, *Da Vinci's* Harvard religionist Robert Langdon informs us, 'was based on the divine order of Nature. The goddess Venus and the planet Venus were one and the same. The goddess had a place in the night-time sky and was known by many names – Venus, the Eastern Star, Ishtar, Astarte – all of them powerful female concepts with ties to Nature and Mother Earth'.[43] The medieval cult of Mary Magdalene was, on this account, the remains of the pre-Christian religion of the goddess. Its key ritual celebrating the reproductive power of the female – the Hieros Gamos (Sacred Marriage) – was perpetuated within the Priory of Sion.[44]

[42] *Ibid.*, p. 400. [43] Brown, *The Da Vinci Code*, p. 57.
[44] See *ibid.*, p. 407.

For its part, the Church perpetrated the myth of Jesus as a god while trying to suppress the goddess tradition exemplified in Mary Magdalene. Thus, *Da Vinci* follows in the footsteps of Margaret Murray's account of the European witch hunts. Those 'deemed "witches" by the Church included all female scholars, priestesses, gypsies, mystics, nature lovers, herb gatherers and any women "suspiciously attuned to the natural world"'.[45] According to *Da Vinci*, it led to the deaths of 5 million women.[46] It was the restraining of this religion of the goddess that had let men run rampant for 2,000 years, leaving human life out of balance. 'Women', we are informed, 'once celebrated as an essential half of spiritual enlightenment, had been banished from the temples of the world ... an unstable situation marked by testosterone-fuelled wars, a plethora of misogynistic societies and a growing disrespect for mother earth'.[47]

Da Vinci's inspiration for goddess religion (and the 'soft' feminist agenda within *Da Vinci* more generally) was two other works that were held in Sir Leigh Teabing's library – Margaret Starbird's *The Goddess in the Gospels* (1998) and her *The Woman with the Alabaster Jar* (1993). With Starbird, we are now on pretty familiar 'sacred ground'. Although she set out as a Catholic woman to reject *Holy Blood* as blasphemy, Starbird was

---

[45] *Ibid.*, p. 170. See also Margaret Murray, *The Witch-Cult in Western Europe* (Oxford: Clarendon Press, 1921). Murray's thesis is no longer accepted by specialists in the European witch hunts.

[46] The film version of the book changes the number to the far more historically likely 50,000.

[47] *Ibid.*, p. 171.

converted to its central premise, namely, that Jesus and Mary Magdalene were married. Like *Holy Blood*, but unlike *Da Vinci*, the Mary Magdalene of *The Alabaster Jar* is the composite Mary. She cites Gregory the Great's identification of Mary Magdalene with both Mary of Bethany and the fallen woman. But she rejects the notion of Mary as a prostitute. Rather, she was a sacred priestess in one of the goddess cults of the Roman Empire. Thus, 'the anointing by the woman [of Jesus] in the gospels is reminiscent of . . . the rites of the "Sacred Marriage" celebrating the union of a local god and goddess'.[48] The 'Sacred Marriage', she claims in her *Goddess in the Gospels*, was a part of Jesus's teaching, later suppressed by the Church.[49]

At some point, Jesus had a secret dynastic marriage with Mary thus linking the houses of David and Benjamin. After the crucifixion, Mary fled to Egypt with the aid of Joseph of Arimathea, the custodian of the 'Sangraal'. We recall that, in *Da Vinci*, Mary had a daughter named Sarah who was born after her arrival in France. In *The Alabaster Jar*, however, the birth of Sarah took place in Egypt and, twelve or so years later (c. 42), Mary left Alexandria with Sarah (and probably with Joseph of Arimathea) seeking a safer haven on the coast of France.

The origins of Sarah in *The Alabaster Jar* can be found in a version of the medieval story of the sea-borne Marys.

---

[48] Margaret Starbird, *The Woman with the Alabaster Jar: Mary Magdalen and the Holy Grail* (Rochester, VT: Bear & Company, 1993), Kindle edition, p. 31.

[49] See Margaret Starbird, *The Goddess in the Gospels: Reclaiming the Sacred Feminine* (Rochester, VT: Bear & Company, 1998), pp. 157–158.

As we noted in Chapter 2, in one of the versions of this story, the Marys are accompanied on their journey from the Holy Land to France by the Egyptian Sarah and by Joseph of Arimathea. In the medieval tradition, Sarah was a servant of one of the Marys – usually, Mary the mother of James the younger. *The Alabaster Jar*, however, gives an original late-twentieth-century spin to this story by declaring that this Egyptian maid was really Sarah, the daughter of Jesus and Mary. The medieval tradition that she was a servant of one of the Marys, claims *The Alabaster Jar*, was the result of a mistake made by the inhabitants of Saintes-Maries-de-la-Mer, the town where the three Marys landed. The people of the town, we read, wrongly assumed that she 'must have been the servant of the family from Bethany' whereas she was in fact the 'child of Jesus, born after Mary's flight to Alexandria'.[50] In addition, the story of the sea-borne Marys gave a medieval origin to the central role that Joseph of Arimathea, as one of those who accompanied Mary to France, plays in modern alternative lives of Mary Magdalene as the Holy Grail.

Ironically, the imagining of Mary Magdalene as part of a mystery religion or a religion of nature within *Holy Blood* and *The Alabaster Jar* reinforces the connection of Mary Magdalene to the fallen woman of Luke. So central has the image of Mary Magdalene as the repentant prostitute been within Western Christianity that her redemption within the modern world requires the radical revising of her image as the repentant whore. In the case of the

[50] Starbird, *The Woman with the Alabaster Jar*, p. 61.

alternative lives of Mary, it amounts to the belief that
'a fallen woman' was nothing but a description of her by
those who opposed and repressed the religion of nature to
which she belonged. Thus, for Starbird, Mary Magdalene
was the Holy Grail. Within *The Alabaster Jar*, the bloodline of Jesus eventually connected to the Merovingian
dynasty, the Priory of Sion, Knights Templar, and so
on. Nevertheless, for *The Alabaster Jar* the bloodline issue
was finally irrelevant. For Starbird, a feminist theme
remains dominant. What mattered was the *resurrected
feminine consciousness* that 'will continue to move toward
equal partnership [with the male consciousness] in spite of
the myth of the dominant male that has been perpetrated
for millennia'.[51]

Unlike *Holy Grail*, Starbird saw no virtue in those
hidden societies that knew the secret of the Holy Grail.
Neither her 'hidden Church of Love' nor the Catholic
Church was able, in the end, to transcend their bitter
power struggles. It is Starbird's hope – a very forlorn
one I suspect – that the Catholic Church will finally
discover the truth of the sacred feminine. Then 'it will
decide it is time to receive the Bride in joyful
thanksgiving . . . to announce her safe return and to wel-
come her home!'[52] In the meantime, Mary Magdalene, as
symbolic of the sacred feminine, continues to resonate in
modern spiritualities outside of the Church – New Age
spiritualities that focus on the sacred feminine within the
self, Goddess spiritualities that focus on the feminine
side of the divine nature, and neo-pagan and Wiccan

---

[51] *Ibid.*, p. 178.   [52] *Ibid.*, p. 180.

spiritualities that look to the divine feminine within the natural world and its rhythms.[53]

The feminist movement in the late twentieth century has played a significant role in shaping the alternative lives of Mary Magdalene. But within feminist readings of Mary reliant upon historical criticism of the Bible, her image as a fallen woman has provided the context for her redemption from a patriarchal Christianity that illegitimately imposed that construction upon her. Thus, for example, Catholic theologian Elisabeth Schüssler Fiorenza reads Mary's apostolic status as an example not only for women, but 'for all those who belong to Jesus's very own familial community'.[54] Feminist literary critic and Roman Catholic Jane Schaberg has Mary providing a model for a new radicalized 'Magdalene Christianity' that stands for the oppressed, one that is focused on the experiences of racism, sexism, poverty, classism, and colonialism. Mary Magdalene, she declares, 'is the one who stands by the dying, wrongfully accused, executed; she fails to anoint at an empty tomb of the disappeared. Simply there, she becomes the place, the location, not just the symbol of the God who is thought to abandon, but does not abandon .... Each of us wishes for one like the Magdalene to go down with us into death, to stay with us to the end'.[55]

---

[53] See James S. Mastaler, 'The Magdalene of Internet: New Age, Goddess, and Nature Spiritualities', in Lupieri (ed.), *Mary Magdalene from the New Testament to the New Age and Beyond*, pp. 337–363.

[54] Quoted by Teresa J. Calpino, 'The Magdalene of Contemporary Biblical Scholarship', in Lupieri (ed.), *Mary Magdalene from the New Testament to the New Age and Beyond*, p. 306.

[55] Schaberg, *The Resurrection of Mary Magdalene*, p.15.

For Susan Haskins, as modern scholarship in general has freed Mary Magdalene from the image of the repentant whore, there has come the opportunity for Mary to provide a different model for women inside the Church. 'If the "victimization" of Mary Magdalen', she writes, 'can stand as a metaphor for the historically subordinate position of women in Christianity, now that the woman so long regarded as a penitent sinner has been shown in her true light, then it may be that Christianity's view of woman in history itself requires some kind of radical revision'.[56] Modern women, she declares, are better served by Mary Magdalene 'as a figure of independence, courage, action, faith and love' than by her legendary mythical persona as the fallen woman.[57]

The Cathar Connection

On 22 July 1209, the heretical group the Cathars (otherwise known as the Albigensians) were massacred in the first battle of the Crusade called against them by Pope Innocent III (c. 1160–1216) in the French city of Béziers. The city was destroyed and its residents, both Cathars and Catholics, were killed, in spite of their taking sanctuary in the cathedral, and in the churches of Saint Jude and Saint Mary Magdalene. As the Cistercian monk Peter of Vaux-de-Cernay pointed out in his *The History of the Albigensian Crusade*, 'The city was taken on the Feast Day of the Blessed Mary Magdalene. What a splendid example of divine justice and

---

[56] Haskins, *Mary Magdalene*, p. 392.   [57] *Ibid*., p. 400.

Providence!'[58] According to Peter, some 7,000 of the citizens of Béziers were killed in the church dedicated to Mary.

The Cathars were distinguished by their commitment to dualism. The core of their theology was the belief that the world, and all that was in it, had been created not by God but by the Devil. In its more moderate form, Catharism held that the Devil was subordinate to God. In its more radical form, it asserted that Satan was (or was the son of or commander-in-chief of) a principle of evil independent of God.[59] It was the resultant tendency of Catharism towards a world-denying and world-transcending asceticism that saw Mary Magdalene and her post-repentance life of penitence held up as a model for female Cathars.[60]

Next to the Templars, the Cathars are the most favoured source for the claim within the alternative lives of Mary Magdalene that Jesus and Mary were married and had children. Thus, for example, Lynn Picknett and Clive Prince in their *The Templar Revelation* (1997) see a sexual relationship between Jesus and Mary as part of the Cathar tradition of southern France.[61] According to Margaret Starbird, the purpose of the crusade against the Cathars was to obliterate 'the belief that Jesus and

[58] W. A. Sibley and M. D. Sibley, *Peter of Vaux-de-Cernay: The History of the Albigensian Crusade* (Woodbridge, Suffolk: Boydell), p. 51.

[59] See Malcolm Barber, *The Cathars* (Edinburgh: Longman, 2000).

[60] See Jansen, *The Making of the Magdalen*, p. 242. See also Antonio Sennis (ed.), *Cathars in Question* (Rochester, NY: Boydell & Brewer, 2016), pp. 177–184.

[61] See Lynn Picknett and Clive Prince, *The Templar Revelation*, pp. 121–123.

Mary Magdalene were beloveds' who were the parents of a child.[62]

Granting their disdain for physical sexuality and their commitment to celibacy, it is unlikely that the medieval Cathars would have endorsed a physical sexual relationship between Jesus and Mary. However, among the heresy hunters, it *was* claimed that the Cathars believed that Jesus and Mary were lovers. And it is from the accounts of hostile heretic hunters that the story of the sexual connection between Mary and Jesus has been developed within the esoteric Mary tradition.

The earliest of claims of the heresy hunters comes around the first decade of the thirteenth century in a document entitled 'An Exposure of the Albigensian and Waldensian Heresies', a work attributed to Ermengaud of Béziers. The Albigensians (Cathars) of Southern France, he noted, spoke slightingly of the marriage of the flesh. Nevertheless, he declared, 'they teach in their secret meetings that Mary Magdalen was the wife of Christ. She was the Samaritan woman to whom He said, "Call thy husband". She was the woman taken in adultery, whom Christ set free lest the Jews stone her, and she was with Him in three places, in the temple, at the well, and in the garden'.[63] This was a composite Mary, but not

---

[62] Quoted by Mary Ann Beavis, 'The Cathar Mary Magdalene and the Sacred Feminine: Pop Culture Legend vs. Medieval Doctrine', *Journal of Religion and Popular Culture* 24 (2012), p. 420. This article provides an excellent account of the relation between the esoteric Mary and the Cathars.

[63] Walter L. Wakefield and Austin P. Evans (eds.), *Heresies of the High Middle Ages: Selected Sources Translated and Annotated* (New York: Columbia University Press, 1969), p. 234.

the one with which we are familiar. It connected Mary Magdalene not with the fallen woman of Luke nor with Mary of Bethany but with two other women in the Gospel of John. One was the woman who was taken in adultery whom Jesus told to 'go and sin no more' (John 8.1–11). The other was the Samaritan woman at the well who declared that she had no husband before Jesus replied, 'You are right in saying "I have no husband"; for you have had five husbands and the one you have now is not your husband' (John 4.18).

The second account was probably derived from that of Ermengaud, although it was rhetorically much more 'over the top' than its predecessor. It can be dated to 1213 and was contained in Peter of Vaux de Cernay's *History of the Albigensian Crusade* mentioned above. According to Peter,

The heretics even affirmed in their secret assemblies that the Christ who was born in terrestrial and visible Bethlehem and crucified in Jerusalem was evil, and that Mary Magdalen was his concubine and the very woman taken in adultery of whom we read in the Gospel; for the good Christ, they said, never ate nor drank nor took on real flesh, and was never of this world, except in a spiritual sense in the body of Paul. That is why we said 'born in terrestrial and visible Bethlehem', because the heretics professed to believe that there is another new and invisible land, in which, according to certain of them, the good Christ was born and was crucified. The heretics also taught that the good God had two wives, Oola and Ooliba [*sic*], upon whom He begat sons and daughters.[64]

---

[64] *Ibid.*, p. 238.

The idea of the two wives of God was derived from the Old Testament book of Ezekiel (23. 1–49). In that book, Oholah and Oholibah, were, metaphorically at least, two sisters who became the adulterous wives of God and bore him both sons and daughters.

In this account too, Mary Magdalene was identified, not with Mary of Bethany nor with the fallen woman of Luke, but again with the woman taken in adultery. Thus, if the Cathars did identify Mary Magdalene with the woman taken in adultery, they were continuing the Western tradition of Mary Magdalene as a promiscuous woman. That said, there is a significant difference in the two accounts above. In the first, Mary Magdalene was said to be *the wife* of Christ. But, in this second account, she was *the concubine* of Christ rather than his wife. Moreover, she was the sexual partner of an earthly evil Jesus over against an ethereal good Jesus who had heavenly wives and children. This was a teaching about Christ that reflected the theological dualism within radical Catharism. As there were good and evil Gods, so too were there good and evil Christs.

The third account of Cathar belief comes from an anonymous document that seems to draw upon the first two accounts above. But it has a good God who also commits adultery with the wife of the evil God. The Cathars say, we read,

that the good God had two wives, Collam and Hoolibam [*sic*], from whom he engendered sons and daughters in human fashion. They say that he had to do with the wife of the malign god, and the malign god, enraged thereby, sent his son into the court of the good God, whom he deceived, and took from thence gold and silver, human and animal souls. And sent them forth and dispersed them among his seven realms.

Then the text turns to Mary Magdalene: 'They also declare that the Christ was the husband of Mary Magdalen. To show this, they explain that he was alone with her three times: in the temple, in the garden, and at the well'.[65]

With the Cathars, or at least the beliefs attributed to them, we are a long way from the romantic, sexual relationship of Mary and Jesus in the alternative lives of Mary. As Mary Ann Beavis neatly puts it, 'Contrary to pop cultural assertions, whatever the Cathars meant by representing Jesus and Mary as a couple, it is unlikely that they meant to portray them as a wholesome paradigm of human marriage, to portray loving sexuality as an earthly manifestation of the divine as both male and female, or to demonstrate the full humanity of Jesus'.[66] Similarly, 'the Cathar doctrine that the good and evil deities had mysterious and sometimes adulterous, celestial wives is a far cry from the call for restoration of the sacred feminine' heralded by the supporters of the esoteric Mary.[67] Moreover, although the Cathars may have believed that the good God had children by his heavenly wives, there is no mention at all of any children of Christ and Mary Magdalene – so much for Holy Blood, Holy Grails, the sacred feminine, and royal bloodlines descending from Jesus and Mary.

[65] *Ibid.*, p. 719, n. 35.
[66] Beavis, 'The Cathar Mary Magdalene and the Sacred Feminine', p. 426.
[67] *Ibid.*, p. 426.

Jesus, Mary, and the Essenes

The constructors of the alternative lives of Mary Magdalene claim a long pedigree that goes back to the time of Jesus and Mary. To illuminate their lives, explain the authors of *The Templar Revelation*, 'we had to pause and examine many groups and secret organisations with a totally new and objective eye: the Freemasons, the Knights Templar, the Cathars, the Priory of Sion, the Essenes and the cult of Isis and Osiris'.[68] Generally, within the Western esoteric tradition, Jesus was an Essene, came out of, or was strongly influenced by the Essene tradition.

The Essenes were a Jewish religious sect that existed from the second century BCE to the end of the first century CE. Very little is known about them. But the so-called Dead Sea Scrolls that were discovered in Israel at Qumran in 1946/7 probably originated from an Essene community. Certainly, the Essenes saw themselves as God's chosen people. They were the 'sons of light' over against 'the sons of darkness' Separated from what they saw as the corrupt religion of Israel, they were strict adherents of the Jewish law with a strong emphasis on ritual purity. They believed that the end of the world was at hand, at which time there would be a resurrection of the dead and God's final judgement on the good and the wicked.

They lived in expectation of a messiah from the tribe of Judah, a new king, and the prophet or Teacher of Righteousness. That said, sufficiently little is known about

---

[68] Picknett and Prince, *The Templar Revelation*, p. 15.

them to provide ample scope for the esoteric tradition imaginatively to fill in the gaps. They were perceived as an ancient 'other' over against the mainstream of Judaism and Christianity. Generally, within twentieth-century esotericism, the Essenes provided a conduit by means of which the ancient wisdom of Atlantis and Egypt was preserved, thence into the teaching of Jesus and thence into the Western tradition. As Simon Joseph puts it, the Essenes 'continue to haunt the ruined remains of an ancient past long forgotten, a lost people who survive now only in the imaginations of their modern interpreters, a "missing link" in the study of early Christian origins'.[69]

The most imaginative account in the late twentieth century of the relation between Jesus, Mary Magdalene, and the Essenes is contained in a popular work entitled *Jesus the Man: A New Interpretation from the Dead Sea Scrolls* (1992), by an Australian Protestant and feminist scholar, Barbara Thiering (1930–2015). Translated into nine languages, it became an international bestseller. Undoubtedly, it was the claim that Jesus was married to Mary Magdalene that created global headlines. It was, we might say, *The Da Vinci Code* for the 1990s. However, although this work stands clearly in the tradition of the esoteric lives of Mary, it sits outside of the tradition of *Da Vinci* and its predecessors. In order to take advantage of the *Da Vinci* craze, her book was renamed *Jesus the Man: Decoding the Real Story of Jesus and Mary* in a 2006 edition. But in the year before that, Thiering rejected any

---

[69] Simon J. Joseph, *Jesus, the Essenes, and Christian Origins* (Waco, TX: Baylor University Press, 2018), p. 7.

relationship between her work and the *Da Vinci* texts describing them as 'fraudulent books on the Holy Grail'.[70] There is no indication (perhaps surprisingly) that Thiering had any influence on the *Da Vinci* tradition.[71] Certainly, Thiering's overall account of the life of Jesus and Mary has the virtue, if it be that, of genuine originality.

Central to Thiering's account of the life of Jesus was the claim that he was of the royal line of King David, was initiated as an Essene, and was eventually the leader of a breakaway faction of the Essenes called 'the twelve apostles'.[72] The belief that Jesus was an Essene was not original to Thiering. It has an intellectual heritage that reaches back to the eighteenth century. Thus, for example, as early as 1717, the English scholar Humphrey Prideaux (1648–1724) criticized 'infidel

---

[70] See Barbara Thiering, 'The Marriage of Jesus'. Available at www.peshertechnique.infinitesoulutions.com/index_Marriage_of_Jesus.html.

[71] As far as I can see, while *Da Vinci* mentions the Dead Sea Scrolls, wrongly describing them as Christian texts (p. 314), it makes no mention of the Essenes. They do appear in *Holy Blood* and in *The Templar Revelation*. This latter text rejects the identification of Jesus as an Essene (p. 303, 329) along with the identification of the Dead Sea Scrolls as arising from an Essene group. On the other hand, *Holy Blood* remarks that Jesus was 'well versed in Essene thought' (p. 373). It also suggests that the figures in white who appeared in the resurrection accounts were Essenes. The same interpretative move is made by Thiering. This reading of the 'angels' at the resurrection within the esoteric tradition as Essenes originated with Bahrdt and Venturini. See note 74. For the Essenes in the Western Tradition generally, see Reender Kranenborg, 'The Presentation of the Essenes in Western Esotericism', *Journal of Contemporary Religion* 13 (1998), pp. 245–256.

[72] Barbara Thiering, *Jesus the Man: A New Interpretation from the Dead Sea Scrolls* (Sydney: Doubleday, 1992), p. 400.

Deists' for declaring that 'Christ and his followers were no other than a sect branched out from that of the Essenes'.[73]

Within the eighteenth-century Enlightenment, the Essenes became ancient models of rational religion. Thus, for example, the German Protestant theologian Karl Friedrich Bahrdt (1741–1792) imagined Jesus as an Essene teacher of a religion of reason who, with the help of the Essenes, faked his miracles, including his death and resurrection. We find a similarly naturalistic account of the miracles of an Essene Jesus and of his resurrection in the German theologian Karl Heinrich Venturini (1768–1849). We cannot tell if Thiering's similar reduction of the supernatural within the New Testament Gospels was directly derived from these theologians. Their names do not appear in any of her works. It is likely, however, that she has indirectly absorbed the eighteenth-century 'naturalistic' Essene Jesus via the accounts given of Bahrdt and Venturini in Albert Schweitzer's *The Quest of the Historical Jesus* (1906) with which work she was familiar.[74] As she points out, her account of Jesus the man was one that was able to interpret the apparently supernatural miracle stories,

---

[73] Joseph, *Jesus, the Essenes, and Christian Origins*, p. 2.

[74] Schweitzer's work does not appear in Thiering's bibliography. But see *Jesus the Man*, p. 73, where she quotes Schweitzer. See also, Albert Schweitzer, *The Quest of the Historical Jesus: A Critical Study of Its Progress from Reimarus to Wrede* (London: Adam & Charles Black, 1954), pp. 38–47. The key works are Bahrdt's *Briefe über die Bibel im Volkston* (1782) and *Ausführung des Plan und Zwecks Jesu* (1784–), and Venturini's *Natürliche Geschichte des großen Propheten von Nazareth* (1800–1802).

including that of the resurrection, in completely natural terms.[75]

However all that may be, the originality of Barbara Thiering lies in her understanding of the relationship between 'the *pesher* technique' and the New Testament. Along with other scholars, Thiering argued that the community that wrote the Dead Sea Scrolls believed that, beneath the surface of the prophetic texts in the Hebrew Bible, was a secret revelation to which they now held the key. Thus, they could read a book of prophecy and give it a new '*pesher*' (Hebrew for 'interpretation') relevant to their own time and their new community. In short, they were able to decode the hidden meaning behind the surface of the Hebrew texts. Thiering's next two moves were the crucial ones. First, she argued, if a group that held such a view of Scripture had set out to write its own scripture, 'they would have set it up as being capable of a *pesher*. It would be a "mystery", a kind of puzzle, capable of a solution by those with special knowledge'.[76]

Second, since the Gospels and the Acts of the Apostles within the New Testament were the product of a Christian community derived from the Essenes, these books also, she argued, have been written in a code decipherable through the use of the pesher technique. Thus, 'The results of the application of the *pesher* technique to the gospels and Acts, drawing upon a number of contemporary sources for the information needed, give a whole history of Jesus, and also of the community that preceded him and from which he and his disciples broke

---

[75] Thiering, *Jesus the Man*, p. 23   [76] See *Ibid.*, p. 22.

away'.[77] And, we might add, a whole new 'fabulous' (in all senses of the word) history of Mary Magdalene – one that was focused on her marriage to Jesus and one that we can reconstruct from the often confused and unclear hints in the text.[78]

The Mary Magdalene of Barbara Thiering was the most composite Mary in the history of Christian thought. As with the traditional composite Mary, she was Mary of Bethany and the fallen woman. But she was also the daughter of Jairus whom Jesus raised from the dead (Mark 5.21–24, 35–43). For Thiering, the real meaning of this story was that it was Mary's first initiation into the Qumran community. It was an initiation that Thiering believes took place in the year 17 when Mary was fourteen years of age and Jesus twenty-three. Mary was also identified with the maid called Rhoda in the Acts of the Apostles (12.13–15). This identification enabled Thiering to have Mary thrown out of Christianity in the year 44. It was Mary/Rhoda who announced to the disciples that it was the apostle Peter at the door after his release from prison. The disciples told her that she was 'raving' – meaning that 'she belonged to one of the ecstatic orders, with associated zealotry and the way of life of the "seekers-after-smooth-things"', as a result of which she 'could no longer be counted with Christians'.[79]

---

[77] *Ibid.*, p. 25.

[78] I avoid 'fact-checking' Thiering in this account. For a thorough critique, see N. T. Wright, *Who Was Jesus?* (Grand Rapids, MI: William B. Eerdmans, 1992). 'Of all of the books I have ever read about Jesus', he writes, 'Barbara Thiering's is one of the strangest' (p. 19).

[79] Thiering, *Jesus the Man*, p. 146.

According to Thiering, the Essenes believed that the holiest life was one that rejected sex and marriage. Nevertheless, they instituted a second order, one that allowed marriage for the sake of having sons. Thus, although members of this second order lived monastic-ally, they left temporarily in order to be married, prefer-ably with a young woman in her teens. As Thiering explained it, a first wedding permitted a couple to live together for a trial, then when the girl was three months pregnant, a second wedding followed from which there could be no divorce. The man returned to the monastery after the birth, to come back to his wife only after inter-vals of years for further conceptions.[80]

Thus, Mary Magdalene was the bride of Jesus. Their first wedding was in September in the year 30, when she was twenty-seven years of age and Jesus thirty-six. That she was much older at the time of her marriage than other women of the Essenes was the result, Thiering suggested, that she had been married once before and was perhaps a widow. Mary did not conceive her first child until December 32 CE. In March 33 CE, shortly before the crucifixion of Jesus, the second wedding took place with Mary three months pregnant. In its Gospel form, this was the story in which Mary 'is the woman with the alabaster jar of ointment, who carried out a wedding ritual dating back to the Song of Solomon, kissing the bridegroom's feet and anointing them with ointment as a symbol of sexual union'.[81] In September of that same year, Mary

[80] See Barbara Thiering, *Jesus of the Apocalypse: The Life of Jesus after the Crucifixion* (Sydney: Doubleday, 1995), p. 26.
[81] *Ibid.*, pp. 26–27.

Magdalene gave birth to a daughter called Tamar. This child, under the names of Damaris and Phoebe (Acts 17.34, Romans 16.1–2) married Paul the apostle. In June 37 CE, Mary and Jesus had their first son named Jesus Justus. He was identified by Thiering with the Jesus Justus who was with Paul in Rome, whose greetings Paul sent to the Colossians (Colossians 4.11). In March 44 CE, a further son was born. Thiering's inventiveness seems to have deserted her at this point and no name was given for this child.

In keeping with the Gospels, Thiering has Mary Magdalene present at the crucifixion of Jesus and at his tomb, although she has him crucified, not alongside two anonymous bandits (Mark 15.27) but with Simon Magus (Acts 8.9–24) and Judas Iscariot, both political militants who had led an insurrection against the Romans. It was Judas Iscariot, of course, who betrayed Jesus. But Simon Magus's only appearance in the New Testament is in the Acts of the Apostles (8.9–24). There, he tried to buy from the apostles Peter and John the power to bring the Holy Spirit upon converts. It was this Simon whom Thiering 'backwrites' as an Essene and, next to Jesus, the most important player in the Gospels. For he was also identified with Lazarus, the brother of Mary of Bethany and hence, on Thiering's account, the brother of Mary Magdalene.

Unlike in the Gospel accounts, however, Thiering's Jesus neither dies on the cross nor rises from the dead. Rather, after six hours on the cross, he was offered snake poison that rendered him unconscious. Within the tomb, he was administered an antidote by Simon and recovered from the effects of the poison. Thiering's elaboration of the resurrection accounts is elaborate and obtuse in the extreme.[82] Suffice it to say, therefore, that Mary encountered her husband: 'In the dim light [of the cave] she saw Jesus standing, but, assuming him to be lying down, she thought it was someone else . . . . The man standing spoke to her one word: "Mary". She then knew it was Jesus, and went to touch him. He said, "Do not touch me"; he was not yet cleansed from the effects of his illness'.[83] Thiering has an explanation for the *belief* that Jesus rose from the dead. Later, we read, Mary was told by 'a young man, dressed in a white robe' (Simon Magus, according to Thiering) that 'He is risen' (Mark 16.5–6). Mary, along with the other women who visited the tomb, knew that Jesus had not risen from the dead. Nevertheless, the formula that was used by Simon was passed on to others, who could choose to believe in a resurrection if it helped their faith.[84]

We can recall that Mary Magdalene had been dispossessed of seven demons (Luke 8.2, Mark 16.9). According to Thiering, the event behind this occurred in June of 32 CE. The seventh of these demons was Judas Iscariot. He was a member of the militant Zealots. In 29 and 30 CE, he had proposed an alliance with the faction for peace in 'the twelve apostles', but was rejected by Jesus. Mary was a member of Judas's faction. But she was also under the authority of Judas who, in his role as chief of the Scribes, had authority over celibate women before and after marriage. Thus, the dispossession of Mary's demons was in reality her removal by Jesus from the authority of Judas.

---

[82] See Thiering, *Jesus the Man*, pp. 122–125, 242–246.
[83] *Ibid.*, p. 124. [84] See *Ibid.*

After the 'resurrection', Mary and Jesus travelled throughout the lands around the Mediterranean. But the marriage of Jesus and Mary was not long to survive the birth of their second son in March 44 CE. In Cyprus in September of that year, Simon and Jesus finally parted ways. Mary's sympathies lay with Simon and, disappointed in Jesus's pacifist approach, she thus decided to leave Jesus and, as we noted in the story of Mary/Rhoda above, she was expelled from the Christian community. In 50 CE, Jesus remarried, this time to Lydia, a female bishop from Thyatira. Jesus arrived in Rome with Paul in 61 CE and probably died there, after the persecutions of the emperor Nero, in 64 AD at the age of seventy.[85] But Thiering also surmises in *Jesus the Man* that he may have found refuge in the south of France 'beginning the many legends found in France and England, such as that of the Holy Grail'.[86] She suggests too that the family of Jesus, including his two sons 'may be presumed to have travelled north, to the Herodian estates in southern France'.[87] That all said, Thiering shows no special interest in the 'secret' lineage of Jesus in the manner of the Holy Grail writers.[88]

---

[85] In Thiering, *Jesus of the Apocalypse*, p. 449, he is said to have died in 70 CE at the age of 76. Elsewhere, on an internet site, Thiering has Jesus dying in Rome, on Tiber Island, at the age of 78 in 72 CE. See Barbara Thiering, 'The Descendants of Jesus ... ' Available at THE PESHER TECHNIQUE: Dr. Barbara Thiering's Writings (infinitesoulutions.com). This site also contains information on Jesus Justus, based around a '*pesher*' reading of the book of Revelation.

[86] Thiering, *Jesus the Man*, p. 160.   [87] *Ibid.*, p. 404.

[88] That said, in her *Jesus of the Apocalypse*, Thiering gives quite extensive accounts of the son of Jesus – Jesus Justus, along with his grandson Jesus III and his great grandson Jesus IV.

Thiering's account of the life of Mary Magdalene after her divorce from Jesus is unclear. In an internet posting in 2007, Thiering suggested that she remained with Simon Magus and travelled with him to Rome and that she died before 58 CE. Thiering holds that female ascetic communities in the tradition of Simon Magus were established in the south of France towards the end of the first century. Mary Magdalene was looked to as the titular head of these communities. That explained, Thiering declared, the persistence of the traditions about Mary in those regions. As for the esoteric tradition that Mary had gone to France 'as recent writers exploiting their version of the hidden history have claimed', her answer was 'No'.[89]

'The Gospel of Jesus's Wife'

To those interested in exploring the role of women within the early Christian church, the Gnostic Gospels were a key source. They seemed to offer early Christian resources to those opposed to a modern patriarchal Christianity intent on keeping women in a subordinate role both within the Church and within society more generally. And to those, esotericists or otherwise, concerned with exploring the possibilities of a physical intimacy, or even a marriage between Jesus and Mary Magdalene, *The Gospel of Philip* (late second-early third century) was crucial. The relevant passage reads as follows: 'As for the Wisdom who is called "the barren",

---

[89] Barbara Thiering, 'Mary Magdalene.' Available at THE PESHERTECHNIQUE: Dr. Barbara Thiering's Writings (infinitesoulutions.com).

she is the mother [of the] angels. And the companion of the [Savior is] Mary Magdalene. [But Christ loved her] more than [all] the disciples, [and used to] kiss her [often] on her [mouth]'.[90]

Among the esotericists, this passage was absolutely decisive. Thus, in *Da Vinci*, when Sophie Neveu remarked that the above text said nothing of marriage, Sir Leigh Teabing pointed out to Sophie Neveu, '*Au contraire* ... As any Aramaic scholar will tell you, the word companion, in those days, literally meant spouse'.[91] Well, actually, as any Aramaic scholar would tell you, *The Gospel of Philip* was written in Coptic, not in Aramaic. But, leaving that aside, of the same passage in *The Gospel of Philip* Margaret Starbird declared, 'she was the close companion or "consort" of the Lord, who often kissed her on the mouth'.[92] Similarly, having quoted the passage from *The Gospel of Philip*, Barbara Thiering wrote, 'This was not a purely spiritual relationship, but a real marriage'.[93]

Those who were arguing that Jesus was married were pushing against the tide of Christian tradition. The celibate status of Jesus had been the accepted position within Christianity since the late second century when the Greek theologian Clement of Alexandria (c. 150–c. 215) criticized those who were arguing for Christian celibacy on the grounds of the example of Christ. Clement was in favour of marriage not least because, in having children, men were following God's creative fatherhood. But he did

---

[90] Isenberg, *The Gospel of Philip*, p. 138. See Chapter 1 for more on this passage.

[91] Brown, *The Da Vinci Code*, p. 328.

[92] Starbird, *The Woman with the Alabaster Jar*, p. 53.

[93] Thiering, *Jesus the Man*, p. 88.

admit that Jesus himself had remained celibate and he gave three reasons for this. First, he had his own bride – the church. Second, he was not a common man and was not therefore in need of a physical partner. And third, since he was God's son and had eternal life, he was under no obligation to produce children.[94]

That said, by the last decade of the twentieth century, and before the work of Barbara Thiering and the *Da Vinci* texts were having their public impact, the notion that Mary and Jesus were husband and wife was working its way into more mainstream Christian and academic circles. The esoteric and mainstream accounts of the relationship of Jesus and Mary were beginning to align.[95] This connection began with the 'Jesus Seminar'. The inaugural meeting was held on 21 March 1985. Thirty senior religion scholars attended. By careful scrutiny of the New Testament Gospels, the seminar aimed to establish which of the words of Jesus could be said to be authentic and which were the invention of the Gospel writers. To the New Testament, they added the apocryphal Gospel, *The Gospel of Thomas*.

In 1993, the group published its findings up to that point in a book entitled *The Five Gospels: What Did Jesus Really Say?* The founder of the Jesus Seminar, Robert W. Funk (1926–2005) expected to cause public outrage. And he did just that. This was because the outcome of the seminar was that most of the words attributed to Jesus in

---

[94] See John Ferguson (trans.), *Stromateis, Books 1–3* (Washington, DC: The Catholic University of America Press, 1991), Book 3, Chapter 49, p. 286.

[95] Barbara Thiering was a member of the Jesus Seminar.

these writings were rejected as his authentic sayings. As a result, the Jesus that emerged was multicultural, inclusive, politically correct, pro-women, and not embarrassingly divine.[96] Actually, then, pretty much like the members of the Jesus Seminar. Moreover, they declared, Jesus was not the author of the Christian celibate tradition. 'Jesus did not advocate celibacy', they declared. Further, 'A majority of the Fellows [of the Seminar] doubted, in fact, that Jesus himself was celibate. They regarded it as probable that he had a special relationship with at least one woman, Mary of Magdala'.[97] Working the boundary between radical and liberal approaches to the Gospel records, this was as far as the Jesus Seminar felt that it could go, although it was far further than the Christian tradition generally had.

The same boundary riding occurred in the Seminar's account of the resurrection. Thus, in *The Acts of Jesus* (1998), they believed that Mary Magdalene was among the early witnesses to the resurrection. That said, it is difficult to know just what this means since 'the stories in Matthew and John about the appearance to her are fictional' and 'The body of Jesus probably decayed as do all corpses. The resurrection of Jesus was not an event that could have been captured by a video camera'.[98] Surprisingly, the Jesus Seminar had no problem with Mary having been possessed by demons and freed from

[96] See Olsen and Miesel, *The Da Vinci Hoax*, p. 127.

[97] Robert W. Funk, Roy W. Hoover, and the Jesus Seminar, *The Five Gospels: The Search for the Authentic Words of Jesus* (San Francisco: Harper, 1993), pp. 220–221.

[98] Robert W. Funk and the Jesus Seminar, *The Acts of Jesus* (San Francisco: Harper, 1998), p. 533.

them by Jesus, although it rejected the notion that these were demons of sexuality and that she was a prostitute. That all granted, the Mary of the Jesus Seminar was the single Mary who had 'suffered for many centuries from that one ill-deserved connection', that is, the identification of Mary Magdalene with the fallen woman of the gospel of Luke.

One of the founding members of the Jesus Seminar was the Harvard-based feminist historian Karen King (1954–).[99] On 18 September 2012, Rome played host to the quadrennial conference of the International Congress of Coptic Studies. On the evening of that day, Karen King delivered a paper bearing the seemingly harmless title 'A New Coptic Fragment'. She announced the discovery of a fragment of papyrus, only about the size of a credit card, which would bring into question the Christian tradition that Jesus was unmarried (see Plate 29). It came, she believed, from the fourth century. Moreover, this fragment was part of a larger lost Gospel. 'I dubbed it', she said, '– just simply for reference purposes – "The Gospel of Jesus's Wife"'.[100] According to King, the woman referred to as the wife of Jesus was Mary Magdalene. The fragment read as follows:

"not [to] me. My mother gave me life … "
"The disciples said to Jesus, " …
… deny. Mary is (not?) worthy of it …
… " Jesus said to them, "My wife …
… she is able to be my disciple …

99 For this discussion on Karen L. King, I am indebted to Ariel Sabar, *Veritas: A Harvard Professor, A Con Man, and the Gospel of Jesus's Wife* (Melbourne: Scribe, 2020).
100 Quoted by Sabar, *Veritas*, p. ix.

... Let wicked people swell up ...
... As for me, I am with her in order to ...
... an image ...[101]

If this tiny piece of papyrus was authentic, it contained, King believed, the only known textual evidence from the early Christian world to depict a married Jesus. This was really the 'Holy Grail' (metaphorically, anyway) of early Christian studies. Feminist historians and theologians committed to the enhancement of the role of women in the church rejoiced – a little prematurely, as we will see.

On that same day, 18 September 2012, *The New York Times* announced King's discovery. Although she was listed as a consultant in the credits of the film version of *The Da Vinci Code*, King indicated in 2012 that she wanted nothing to do with the book or its author. Nevertheless, the fragment did suggest, she said, that 'some early Christians had a tradition that Jesus was married'.[102] King repeatedly cautioned, it was reported, that the fragment should not be taken as proof that Jesus was *actually* married. On that day also, 18 September 2012, King posted the first version of a paper entitled '"Jesus said to them, 'My wife...'": A New Coptic Gospel Papyrus' on the Harvard Divinity School website. In that paper, she declared, 'what can be said securely is that our fragment contains the first known statement that explicitly claims

---

[101] Karen L. King, '"Jesus said to them, 'My wife...'": A New Coptic Papyrus Fragment', *Harvard Theological Review* 107 (2014), p. 133. For ease of reading, I have removed the orthographical marks '[' and ']' from the text at the beginning and end of lines. There are two legible words on the reverse side of the papyrus– 'my mother' and 'forth'.

[102] Laurie Goldstein, 'A Faded Piece of Papyrus Refers to Jesus' Wife.' Available at www.nytimes.com/2012/09/19/us/historian-says-piece-of-papyrus-refers-to-jesus-wife.html.

that Jesus had [a] wife'.[103] And she went on to say that it was 'highly likely that this Mary would have been understood to be Mary of Magdala, given the existence of early Christian traditions which identified a close relationship between Jesus and Mary'.[104] Thus, she concluded, '*The Gospel of Jesus's Wife* makes it possible to speak with certainty of the existence of a tradition affirming that Jesus was married (probably to Mary Magdalene), and it is highly probable that this tradition dated back to the second half of the second century'.[105] It was not until April 2014 that a much revised version of this article entitled '"Jesus said to them, 'My wife...'": A New Coptic Papyrus Fragment' was finally published in the prestigious *Harvard Theological Review*.[106] To those that had first heard her presentation in Rome, two questions remained foremost. First, was the fragment really suggesting that a group of early Christians believed that Mary Magdalene was the wife of Jesus? And second, was the fragment authentic?[107] King's article in 2014 set out to answer these questions.

In her interpretation of the papyrus fragment in this 2014 article, it is clear that King was reneging on her

---

[103] Karen L. King, with contributions by AnneMarie Luijendijk, '"Jesus said to them, 'My wife...'": A New Coptic Gospel Papyrus', p. 45. Available at

web.archive.org/web/20120921154949/http://news.hds.harvard .edu/files/King_JesusSaidToThem_draft_0917.pdf. I am grateful to Ariel Sabar for making this available to me.

[104] *Ibid.*, p. 29.   [105] *Ibid.*, p. 47.

[106] Karen L. King, '"Jesus said to them, 'My wife...'": A New Coptic Papyrus Fragment', *Harvard Theological Review* 107 (2014), pp. 131–159.

[107] See Sabar, *Veritas*, pp. 89–97. Sabar was the only reporter present at King's presentation.

earlier claims about its significance. The sub-title, for example, has pulled back from the suggestion that the papyrus fragment was part of a gospel: 'A New Coptic Gospel Papyrus' in 2012 became 'A New Coptic Papyrus Fragment' in 2014. In this 2014 version, King was no longer certain that the Mary of the fragment was Mary Magdalene. It could be Jesus's mother, Mary Magdalene, or some other Mary.[108] In addition, the marriage referred to, she wrote, 'might be carnal, celibate, metaphorical, and/or symbolic-paradigmatic'.[109] No longer was there any suggestion that the papyrus was evidence of a tradition within early Christianity that Jesus was married. The main point of the fragment turned out to be a completely non-controversial one. It is 'simply to affirm', she declared, 'that women who are wives and mothers can be Jesus's disciples'.[110] This is a point, we might say, that the New Testament had already made clear and was never a matter for dispute.[111] This claim that the text was *only* about whether wives and mothers could be disciples of Christ enabled King to take the heat away from the claims that the fragment was a forgery intended to play into modern debates about the married status of Jesus in popular media, fiction, and (alleged) modern hoaxes. 'If the fragment concerns the discipleship of wives and mothers, however', she declared, 'these are mostly irrelevant as well as unsubstantiated'.[112]

More importantly, the claim of the first version of this article, namely, that the fragment contains the first known

---

[108] See King, 'Jesus said to them, "My wife…"', p. 152.   [109] *Ibid.*
[110] *Ibid.*, p. 158.   [111] See Luke 8.3, Matthew 27.56.
[112] King, 'Jesus said to them, "My wife…"', p. 157.

text explicitly to claim that Jesus had a wife, has now disappeared. That role seems to have now been taken by *The Gospel of Philip*. This *Gospel*, she now claimed, 'does portray Mary Magdalene as the spousal partner of the fleshly (incarnate) Jesus'.[113] Indeed, a year earlier, in 2013, King was already then moving the emphasis on the early tradition that Jesus was married away from 'The Gospel of Jesus's Wife' and towards *The Gospel of Philip*. Thus, in an article devoted to the question of the marital status of Jesus in *The Gospel of Philip* in 2013, she argued that it was plausible to read the term 'companion' ['koinônos'] in the passage 'And the companion of the [Savior is] Mary Magdalene' as meaning 'his spouse' and 'the one he is joined with in marriage'.[114] For her, this was a new interpretation of *The Gospel of Philip*. It was quite different from her earlier interpretation of it. It was, moreover, a reading of *The Gospel of Philip* that was going against the general scholarly consensus on this passage. And it was one that, coincidentally, was aligning itself with the *Da Vinci* interpretation of it.

In short, whereas, in the first version of her article on 'The Gospel of Jesus's Wife' in 2012, it was unequivocal that the papyrus fragment was the only ancient text explicitly to portray Jesus as married, that has now become quite uncertain. And it now appeared that it was *The Gospel of Philip* and not the papyrus fragment she had originally called 'The Gospel of Jesus's Wife' that had

---

[113] *Ibid.*, p. 150.

[114] Karen L. King, 'The Place of the Gospel of Philip in the Context of Early Christian Claims about Jesus's Marital Status', *New Testament Studies* 59 (2013), p. 577.

this distinction. This was perhaps a sign that King was starting to lose confidence in her fragment and was moving elsewhere the debate about the question of any early traditions that Jesus was married.[115] In short, not only did the papyrus fragment have nothing to say about whether Jesus and Mary Magdalene were married, it no longer had anything of interest to say even about whether there was *a tradition in the early church* that Jesus was married to Mary Magdalene.

But was the papyrus fragment authentic or a modern forgery? Well, in the light of her new interpretation of its contents, it now hardly mattered. And in 2014 King now agreed, on the basis of a radiocarbon testing of the material, that the papyrus fragment was not from the fourth century but rather had a mean date of 741 CE.[116] Still, the *Harvard Theological Review* was backing her in with five articles devoted to the science of the fragment. It also gave her the opportunity to respond to an analysis of the contents of the fragment that had concluded, without the slightest doubt, 'that the document is a forgery, and not a very good one at that'.[117]

In the end, the scientific evidence was compatible with its being both authentic and a fake. King stuck to her guns. On its being a modern fake, she wrote,

[T]he gravest difficulty for me lies in explaining how a forger incompetent in Coptic language with poor scribal skills (perhaps

---

[115] As Ariel Sabar suggests. See Sabar, *Veritas*, p. 333.

[116] See King, 'Jesus said to them, "My wife…"', p. 159.

[117] Leo Depuydt, 'The Alleged *Gospel of Jesus's Wife*: Assessment and Evaluation of Authenticity', *Harvard Theological Review* 107 (2014), p. 172.

even anachronistically using a brush) was yet so highly skilled as to secure ancient papyrus, make ink with an ancient technique, leave no ink traces out of place at the microscopic level, achieve patterns of differential aging, fabricate a paper trail of modern supporting documents, and provide a good fit for an ancient historical context – one that no serious scholar considers to be evidence of the historical Jesus's marital status. In my judgment such a combination of bumbling and sophistication seems extremely unlikely.[118]

Yet, 'a combination of bumbling and sophistication' was exactly what it was. Such a combination, investigative reporter Ariel Sabar wrote, 'could well be the epitaph of many of history's most infamous forgers'.[119] It was the tracing of the chain of ownership of the fragment and its accompanying documents by Sabar that inescapably led to the conclusion that the fragment was a modern forgery. And it finally led Karen King to the admission that the fragment was probably a fake.[120]

According to Sabar, 'The Gospel of Jesus's Wife' was the product of a frustrated German Egyptologist with limited Coptic skills by the name of Walter Fritz. He had obtained a fragment of centuries-old papyrus, had made ink from ancient recipes, had written a text upon it in passable Coptic, had created background documents, had offered it to Karen King in July 2010, and had delivered it to her in December 2011. What were his

---

[118] King, 'Jesus said to them, "My wife…"', pp. 157–158.
[119] Ariel Sabar, 'The Unbelievable Tale of Jesus's Wife', *Atlantic* 318 (2016), p. 70.
[120] See Ariel Sabar, 'Karen King Responds to "The Unbelievable Tale of Jesus's Wife"', *The Atlantic* (web only), 16 June 2016. Available at www.theatlantic.com/politics/archive/2016/06/karen-king-responds-to-the-unbelievable-tale-of-jesus-wife/487484/.

motives? Sabar suggests that it was the thwarting of his dreams of being an Egyptologist: 'He might well have nursed a grudge against the elite scholars who had failed to appreciate his intellectual gifts – who told him he was mediocre at Coptic and short of original ideas'.[121] But why did Fritz forge a fragment that suggested that Jesus and Mary were husband and wife? Perhaps, as Sabar suggests, *The Da Vinci Code* was the Rosetta Stone of Fritz's motives. 'To turn a *Da Vinci Code* fantasy into reality', he writes, 'all you needed was material proof of Jesus's marriage, and a real-life Robert Langdon. In the book, Langdon – a Harvard professor of "religious symbology" – finds the modern descendants of Jesus and Mary Magdalene's daughter thanks to a cryptic message on a scrap of papyrus. Perhaps Fritz and his wife had found their Langdon in Karen King'.[122]

The Last Temptation

The overwhelming modern scholarly consensus is that there is no decisive evidence of an early Christian tradition that Jesus and Mary Magdalene were married. Karen King's experience will probably ensure that, in the immediate future at least, this is a pathway down which no modern scholars will want to go. Ironically, the period from 1960 to the present was the golden age of the Western belief that Jesus had a sexual relationship with Mary Magdalene. This very modern tradition began with the novel of Nikos Kazantzakis entitled *The Last*

---

[121] Sabar, *Veritas*, p. 187. See also pp. 233, 252–253, 256–259.
[122] Sabar, 'The Unbelievable Tale of Jesus's Wife', p. 74.

Temptation of Christ in its English translation in 1960.[123]
Da Vinci was influenced by it. Sophie Neveu remembered
from her childhood hearing that the film version of *The
Last Temptation* (1988) 'was about Jesus having sex with a
lady called Mary Magdalene'.[124] The Mary Magdalene of
The Last Temptation is the fallen woman of the Gospel of
Luke *and* the woman taken in adultery (John 7.53–8.11)
but not Mary of Bethany. In short, the Greek Orthodox
Kazantzakis's Mary was poised halfway between Eastern
and Western understandings of her identity.

In Jesus's ongoing battle between flesh and spirit,
Mary represented the flesh. She was the cousin of Jesus
who, when Jesus was not inclined to marry her, became a
prostitute and moved to Magdala. Mary was open for
business on the Sabbath, a breach that led the Zealot
Barabbas to organize an attempt to have her stoned.
Jesus intervened to save her and a repentant Mary
became his constant companion. Sensing that the death
of Jesus was close, she anointed Jesus's feet with expensive perfume and dried them with her hair. In the dream
sequence at the end of the book, the Devil persuaded
Jesus, who was on the point of death, to come down
from the cross. He led Jesus to taste the pleasures of sex
and marriage that he had denied himself. Mary
Magdalene led him to a lemon grove where they made
love. Deeply moved by the experience, Jesus wanted to
call their son Paraclete – the Greek name for the
Holy Spirit.

---

[123] The original Greek version was published in 1955.
[124] Brown, *The Da Vinci Code*, p. 329. The film version of *The Last
   Temptation* was directed by Martin Scorsese.

Allowing Jesus to sleep, Mary was way laid by Saul (later Paul) who allowed her to be stoned to death. Jesus then married Mary of Bethany and her sister Martha, with both of whom he has many children. Jesus's domestic happiness was shattered when he was visited by his former disciples. Judas Iscariot denounced Jesus for not having fulfilled his mission and for having pursued the easier option of marriage and family. The crucified Jesus returned to consciousness and rejoiced that he had not succumbed to this last temptation. He cried out triumphantly, 'It is accomplished' although, writes Kazantzakis, it was as though he had said, 'Everything has begun'.[125] What *had* begun, as we have seen, was a tradition in both fiction and non-fiction that Mary was both Jesus's wife and lover.

This new tradition does not tell us anything about Mary Magdalene. But it does tell us something about our own moment in time. It tells us that, for both believers and non-believers, the question of whether Jesus and Mary were lovers or were married still matters. At its broadest, it tells us that the Christian orthodox tradition that Jesus was unmarried or non-sexual is narrow and confining. It also speaks to a general cultural predilection for hidden histories – for the presence of 'truths' beneath the accepted histories and for the conspiracy theories that go along with them.

In addition to this, it reflects the desire that has arisen out of the feminist movement for women to have played a greater than heretofore accepted role in the life of Jesus

---

[125] Nikos Kazantzakis, *The Last Temptation of Christ* (New York: Simon & Schuster, 2015), p. 496.

and in the history of the Christian church. Theologically, it reflects the modern need for a Jesus who is fully human, one who entered into the deepest of human relationships – that between a man and a woman. Barbara Thiering's title *Jesus the Man* bears witness to this. Ironically, as it reflects a Jesus more fully human, it resonates in New Age Goddess and nature spiritualities to the desire to find a woman who is fully divine – an earthly and heavenly Mary to balance an earthly and heavenly Jesus.

Finally, the beginnings of this tradition align with the Western sexual revolution. As in *Jesus Christ Superstar* (1970), Mary Magdalene assumes the role of the sexually liberated woman, in love with Jesus and thus unsure of how, as a prostitute, to love him. The new tradition of Mary as both the wife and lover of Jesus was an assertion of the virtue of female sexuality. It was, at the same time, a declaration of the value of human sexuality against a religion that, in its exaltation of chastity and celibacy, had been traditionally unsympathetic to it.

The feast day of Mary Magdalene has traditionally been 22 July. Within the Latin Mass, the Gospel reading for that day had been the story of the fallen woman in the Gospel of Luke. The composite Mary Magdalene was at the heart of Catholic practice, as much in the twentieth century as the seventh. In 1969, however, there was a subtle liturgical change, probably unnoticed by most. The Gospel reading for the day was changed from the fallen woman in the Gospel of Luke to the passage from the Gospel of John in which Mary was the first witness of the resurrection. With minimum fanfare, the Catholic Church was quietly confessing that it had been wrong about the identity of Mary Magdalene for the past

1,400 years, ever since Gregory the Great had identified Mary Magdalene with the fallen woman of Luke. But it was only on 2 February 2021 that Pope Francis decreed that Mary of Bethany would be joining Martha and Lazarus on *their* feast day on 29 July. With this decree, Mary Magdalene was officially separated from Mary of Bethany. No longer identified with the fallen woman of Luke nor with Mary of Bethany, 22 July has now become the feast day of the single Mary. With this papal decree, the composite Mary Magdalene of the Western church is no more.

EPILOGUE

On Myth and History

~

Myth narrates a sacred history; it relates an event that took place in primordial Time, the fabled time of the 'beginnings'.

Mircea Eliade, *Myth and Reality*

For the better part of the last 200 years, the purpose of the writing of history has been to determine what really happened. As a matter of principle, it excluded sacred stories that involved the supernatural world from its consideration. These were relegated to the realm of myth, to be explained as the imaginary product of other more terrestrial concerns – social, political, psychological, or economic.

On this understanding of the division between history and myth, what can be said about the historical Mary Magdalene? Assuming that the New Testament Gospels are the sort of texts that *can* be sifted for historical evidence, the answer is – not much. As we have seen, we can say that Mary Magdalene was a disciple of Jesus from a town called Magdala, that she was one of a number of women sufficiently wealthy to provide for Jesus and his close followers from their own means, and that she was present at the crucifixion. In keeping with the rejection of the supernatural, most modern historians would reject the possibility of her possession by demons, although some might re-interpret it as suggestive of some mental or physical infirmity. Most would also reject the possibility of her having encountered a man who had risen from the dead, although some might re-interpret it as a delusion produced by the trauma of Christ's death or more positively as a mythological affirmation of the continuing centrality of Jesus in her life.

On this kind of distinction between myth and history, the lives of Mary Magdalene that we have been exploring in this book, those that elaborate her life with Christ both before and after his death, are religious myths. On the one hand, this is because of the overwhelming presence of the supernatural and the miraculous within them. On the other hand, it is the result of their having been written at least some 750 years after the events that they report on. This is a temporal gap that, in the absence of any other evidence, is too large for the historian to bridge.

That said, and granting the interweaving of the lives of Mary Magdalene with her afterlives, we might ask whether the relics of Mary could provide evidence for the veracity of any of the lives, or any part of them? Again, perhaps unfortunately, the short answer is no. As we have seen, the problems, then and now, that surround establishing the authenticity of any of the many relics are sufficient for us to rule them out as capable of establishing the truth of the lives or any part of them. Moreover, within the context of the cult of Mary Magdalene, it is much more the case that the lives served to verify the authenticity of the relics rather than the relics to validate the lives.

In sum, the lives of Mary Magdalene are pious fictions. But this does not diminish their historical value. They cannot be understood as records of what happened in the first century. But they can be interpreted as stories that reflect the religious lives of those who created them and of those who, whether for otherworldly or more this worldly reasons, engaged with them. They do give us intimate insights into medieval and early modern religious life. It is worthwhile reiterating the remarks of Paul Ricoeur on poetry and fiction that we quoted at the beginning of this book: 'new possibilities of being-in-the-world are opened up within everyday reality . . . . And in this way everyday reality is metamorphosed by means of what we would call the imaginative variations that literature works on the real'.[1]

However, the lives of Mary Magdalene are also myths in a quite different sense. First, the creators of these lives gave them an historical pedigree. They located them in the first century. As such, the lives *were presented as* history – as accounts of what happened then. Second, and as a consequence, far from displaying a *fiction*, they revealed *truth par excellence*. For their creators and their readers, the lives of Mary Magdalene revealed transcendent truths and ultimate realities.

They were revelatory in this sense because they told stories about a sacred time in the past when heaven and earth were close together and the sacred entered the profane. It was the time when God became man and walked upon the earth and Mary Magdalene was his companion. In this sense, the lives of Mary Magdalene were myths with an origin within historical time rather than, like many myths of origins, before or outside of time. So they linked the historical present with the sacred time and the sacred places of the past.

---

[1] Paul Ricoeur, *Figuring the Sacred: Religion, Narrative, and Imagination*, p. 43.

More importantly, they enabled that sacred time and those sacred spaces to be appropriated *within the present*. They did so by enabling the transcendent to reveal itself in the present through ritual practices in new sacred places – Ephesus, Saint Maximin, Vézelay – that were focused on the bodily remains of Mary Magdalene. These were places where heaven and earth were closest to each other and where the saint, through her relics, was present in body and spirit. Each space was, in effect, an *axis mundi* – a cosmic centre that enabled communication between the earthly and heavenly realms.

This study has tried to bridge the gap between the myth and history of Mary Magdalene. For the most part, we have been engaged in a history of the myths of Mary Magdalene and an exploration of how and when they arose within particular cultural and intellectual contexts. We have traced Mary Magdalene from her beginnings in the New Testament to Gregory the Great's identification of her with Mary of Bethany and the fallen woman. From there, we have followed the development of her lives from pseudo-Odo's first biography of her to her eremitic, apostolic, and subsequently apostolic-eremitic lives. As we have seen, these struck deep into the everyday life of Christendom as the myths around her life gradually emerged and the cult around her afterlives expanded. The new possibilities of being-in-the-world that were created by the traditional lives of Mary Magdalene continue to the present day. New alternative lives have appeared that have opened up new possibilities – the priesthood of women, the divine goddess, the divine in nature, the key to the legend of the Holy Grail, a beacon of hope for the modern sex worker. In short, the lives of Mary Magdalene were myths that mattered – and still are.

It is fashionable in some contemporary writing of history to blur the distinction between the factual and the fictional, to suggest that *all* history writing is myth-making and that the two are indistinguishable. This work has proceeded from the belief that, in the writing of history, both are necessary and that it is possible to do justice to the writing of history as myth-making *and* as fact-finding. On the one hand, doing history entails an ethical commitment to write accounts in the present that do justice to the documentary evidence of the past. The narrative has to respect the facts. On the other hand, in so far as the purpose of writing history is not merely to determine what happened but also to discern the meaning of it in the past and for the present, it is an activity in the creation of myths – myths of meaning if not of events. This is the creative tension between history and myth that I have attempted to illustrate and exemplify in this book.

BIBLIOGRAPHY

ANF: Roberts, Alexander and James Donaldson (eds.), revised by A. Cleveland Coxe, *Ante-Nicene Fathers* (Peabody, MA: Hendrickson Publishers, 2004).

BHG: Bibliotheca Hagiographica Graeca.

BHL: Bibliotheca Hagiographica Latina.

KJV: King James Version

NPNF (first series): Schaff, Philip (ed.), *Nicene and Post-Nicene Fathers, first series* (Peabody, MA: Hendrickson Publishers, 2012).

NPNF (second series): Schaff Philip and Henry Wace (eds.), *Nicene and Post-Nicene Fathers, second series* (Peabody, MA: Hendrickson Publishers, 2012).

PG: Migne, Jacques Paul (ed.), Patrologiae Cursus Completus, Graeca.

PL: Migne, Jacques Paul (ed.), Patrologiae Cursus Completus, Latina.

Albanès, J.–H., 'Inventaire des Objets Précieux conserves au Couvent de Saint-Maximin, en Provence, en 1504', *Revue des Sociétés Savantes*, ser. 6, vol. 5 (1877), pp. 289–311.

Almond, Philip C., *Afterlife: A History of Life after Death* (London: I. B. Tauris, 2016).

Andrea, Alfred J. (ed.), *Contemporary Sources for the Fourth Crusade* (Leiden: Brill, 2008).

Andrewes, Lancelot, *XCVI Sermons by the Right Honourable and Reverend Father in God, Lancelot Andrewes, late Lord Bishop of Winchester* (London, 1629).

Anon., 'Bishop Creighton in the City To-day', in *The Westminster Gazette*, Wednesday, 14 April 1897.

A Letter to Jonas Hanway Esq; in which Some Reasons are assigned why Houses for the Reception of Penitent Women, who have been disorderly in their Lives, ought not to be called Magdalen-Houses (London, 1758).

'The Itinerary of St. Willibald', in Rev. Canon Brownlow (trans.), *The Hodoeporicon of Saint Willibald* (London: Palestine Pilgrims' Text Society, 1891).

Arnold, Margaret, *The Magdalene in the Reformation* (Cambridge, MA: Belknap Press, 2018).

Bachrach, Bernard S., et al., *Deeds of the Bishop of Cambrai, Translation and Commentary* (Abingdon: Routledge, 2018).

Baedeker, K. (ed.), *Palestine and Syria: Handbook for Travellers* (Leipsic: Karl Baedeker, 1876).

Baert, Barbara, '"Who Touched Me and My Clothes?" The Healing of the Woman with the Haemorrhage (Mark 5: 24b–34parr) in Early Mediaeval Visual Culture', in *Annual of the Antwerp Royal Museum*, 2009, pp. 9–51.

Baigent, Michael, Richard Leigh, and Henry Lincoln, *Holy Blood, Holy Grail* (New York: Bantam Dell, 2004).

Balfour, Clara Lucas, *The Women of Scripture* (London: Houlston & Stoneman, 1847).

Barber, Malcolm, *The Cathars* (Edinburgh: Longman, 2000).

Barber, Richard, *The Holy Grail: Imagination and Belief* (Cambridge, MA: Harvard University Press, 2004).

Beavis, Mary Ann, 'The Cathar Mary Magdalene and the Sacred Feminine: Pop Culture Legend vs. Medieval Doctrine', *Journal of Religion and Popular Culture* 24 (2012), pp. 419–431.

Bedouelle, Guy, 'Jacques Lefèvre D'Étaples', in Carter Lindberg (ed.), *The Reformation Theologians* (Oxford: Blackwell, 2002), pp. 19–33.

Ben-Chorin, Schalom, *Brother Jesus: The Nazarene through Jewish Eyes* (Athens: University of Georgia Press, 2001).

Birkbeck, George, Norman Hill, and L. F. Powell (eds.), *Boswell's Life of Johnson, Vol. 1: The Life (1709–1765)* (Oxford: Oxford University Press, 1934).

Bishop, John, *Beautifull Blossomes, gathered by John Byshop, from the Best Trees of All Kyndes...* (London, 1577).

Borgnet, Auguste (ed.), *Opera Omnia* (Paris: Vivè, 1890–1899).

Brown, Dan, *The Da Vinci Code* (London: Corgi, 2004).

Brown, Peter, *The Cult of the Saints: Its Rise and Function in Latin Christianity* (Chicago: University of Chicago Press, 1981).

Bryant, Nigel (trans.), *Merlin and the Grail, Joseph of Arimathea, Merlin, Perceval: The Trilogy of Prose Romances Attributed to Robert de Boron* (Cambridge: D. S. Brewer, 2001).

Budge, E. A. Wallis *Coptic Apocrypha in the Dialect of Upper Egypt* (London: Longmans & Co. et alia, 1913).

Budge, E. A. Wallis, *Miscellaneous Coptic Texts in the Dialect of Upper Egypt* (London: Longmans & Co., et alia, 1915).

Bynum, Caroline Walker, *Fragmentation and Redemption: Essays on Gender and the Human Body in Medieval Religion* (New York: Zone Books, 2012).

  The Resurrection of the Body in Western Christianity, 200–1336 (New York: Columbia University Press, 2017).

Cai, P. Raphaelis O. P., Thomas Aquinas, *Super Evangelium S. Ioannis Lectura* (Rome: Marietti, 1952).

Calpino, Teresa J., 'The Magdalene of Contemporary Biblical Scholarship', in Edmondo F. Lupieri (ed.), *Mary Magdalene from the New Testament to the New Age and Beyond* (Leiden: Brill, 2020), pp. 298–317.

Calvin, John, *A Treatise on Relics* (Edinburgh: Johnstone, Hunter & Co., 1870).

Cerrato, J. A., *Hippolytus between East and West: The Commentaries and the Provenance of the Corpus* (Oxford: Oxford University Press, 2002).

Church, Thomas, *An Essay towards Vindicating the Literal Sense of the Demoniacks in the New Testament* ... (London, 1737).

Ciggaar, Krijnie N., 'Une Description de Constantinople Tradite par un Pèlerin Anglais', *Revue des Études Byzantines* 34 (1976), pp. 211–267.

Clemens, Neal Raymond Jr., 'The Establishment of the Cult of Mary Magdalen in France, 1279–1543,' PhD thesis, Columbia University, 1997.

Collins, Wilkie, *The New Magdalen* (New York: Charles Scribner's Sons, 1908).

Compston, H. F. B., *The Magdalen Hospital: The Story of a Great Charity* (London: Society for Promoting Christian Knowledge, 1917).

Connor, Patrick W., *Anglo-Saxon Exeter: A Tenth-Century Cultural History* (Woodbridge: Boydell, 1993).

Conway, Moncure Daniel, *Autobiography: Memories and Experiences of Moncure Daniel Conway* (Cambridge: Cambridge University Press, 2012).

'A Calumniated Lady', in *The Westminster Gazette*, Friday 16 April, 1897.

'Mary Magdalene', *The Critic* 42 (1903), pp. 212–216.

Cook, Edward Tyas, and Alexander Wedderburn (eds.), *The Works of John Ruskin* (Cambridge: Cambridge University Press, 2010).

Corley, Kathleen E., *Private Women, Public Meals: Social Conflict in the Synoptic Tradition* (Peabody, MA: Hendrickson Publishers, 1993).

Coulton, G. G., *From St. Francis to Dante: Translations from the Chronicle of the Franciscan Salimbene, 1221–1288* (Philadelphia: University of Pennsylvania Press, 1972).

(ed.), *Life in the Middle Ages* (Cambridge: Cambridge University Press, 1928).

Cross, J. E., 'Mary Magdalen in the *Old English Martyrology*: The Earliest Extant "Narrat Josephus" Variant of her Legend', *Speculum* 53 (1978), pp. 16–25.

Delehaye, Hippolyte (ed.), *Synaxarion Ecclesiae Constantinopolitanum e codice Sirmondiano nunc Berolinensi*. Available at https://archive.org/details/Delehaye SynaxariumConstantinopolitanum/page/n3/mode/2up.

Depuydt, Leo, 'The Alleged *Gospel of Jesus's Wife*: Assessment and Evaluation of Authenticity', *Harvard Theological Review* 107 (2014), pp. 172–189.

Dielman, Karen, 'Sacramental Memorializing: Upon the Death of Dante Gabriel Rossetti', *Nineteenth-Century Contexts*, 37 (2015), pp. 215–231.

Dodd, William, *An Account of the Rise, Progress, and Present State of the Magdalen Hospital, for the Reception of Penitent Prostitutes* ... (London, 1770).

Dudden, F. Homes, *Gregory the Great: His Place in History and Thought* (London: Longmans, Green, & Co., 1905).

Duffy, Eamon, *The Stripping of the Altars: Traditional Religion in England c.1400–c.1580* (New Haven, CT: Yale University Press, 2005).

Elliott, J. K., *The Apocryphal New Testament* (Oxford: Clarendon, 1993).

Ellman, Richard, *Oscar Wilde* (New York: Alfred A. Knopf, 1988).

Farmer, Hugh, *An Essay on the Demoniacs of the New Testament* (London, 1775).

Ferguson, John (trans.), *Stromateis, Books 1–3* (Washington, DC: The Catholic University of America Press, 1991).

Foot, Sarah, *Æthelstan: The First King of England* (New Haven, CT: Yale University Press, 2011).

Foskolou, Vassilikia A., 'Mary Magdalene between East and West: Cult and Image, Relics and Politics in the Late Thirteenth-Century Eastern Mediterranean', *Dumbarton Oaks Papers* 65/66 (2011–2012), pp. 271–296.

Foss, Clive, *Ephesus after Antiquity: A Late Antique, Byzantine and Turkish City* (Cambridge: Cambridge University Press, 1979).

Fox, George, *The Woman Learning in Silence* ... (London, 1656).

Fox, Margaret Askew Fell, *Womens Speaking Justified, Proved and Allowed of by the Scriptures* ... (London, 1656).

'Fourth Lateran Council: 1215,' *Papal Encyclicals Online*. Available at www.papalencyclicals.net/councils/ecum12-2.htm#62.

France, John (ed. and trans.), *Rodvlfi Glabri: Historiarvm Libri Qvinqve* (Oxford: Clarendon Press, 1989).

Frank, Georgia, 'From Antioch to Arles: Lay Devotion in Context,' in Augustine Casiday and Frederick W. Norris (eds.), *The Cambridge History of Christianity: Constantine to c.600* (Cambridge: Cambridge University Press, 2014), pp. 531–547.

Funk, Robert W. and the Jesus Seminar, *The Acts of Jesus* (San Francisco: Harper, 1998).

Funk, Robert W., Roy W. Hoover, and the Jesus Seminar, *The Five Gospels: The Search for the Authentic Words of Jesus* (San Francisco: Harper, 1993).

Geary, Patrick J., *Furta Sacra: Thefts of Relics in the Central Middle Ages* (Princeton, NJ: Princeton University Press, 2011).

Goldstein, Laurie 'A Faded Piece of Papyrus Refers to Jesus' Wife.' Available at www.nytimes.com/2012/09/19/us/historian-says-piece-of-papyrus-refers-to-jesus-wife.html.

Greg, W. R., 'Prostitution', *The Westminster Review* 53 (1850), pp. 448–506.

Griffins, John (ed.), *The Two Books of Homilies Appointed to Be Read in Churches* (Oxford: Oxford University Press, 1859).

Halm, Philipp Maria, and Rudolf Berliner (eds.), *Das Hallische Heiltum* (Berlin: Deutscher Verein für Kunstwissenschaft, 1931).

Hanegraaf, Wouter J., *Western Esotericism: A Guide for the Perplexed* (London: Bloomsbury, 2013).

Hanway, Jonas, *Letter V. to Robert Dingley, Esq; Being a Proposal for the Relief and Employment of Friendless Girls and Repentant Prostitutes* (London, 1758).

The Rules, Orders and Regulations, of the Magdalen House, for the Reception of Penitent Prostitutes (London, 1760).

Thoughts on a Plan for a Magdalen-House for Repentant Prostitutes ... (London, 1758).

Thoughts on a Plan for a Magdalen-House for Repentant Prostitutes ... The Second Edition (London, 1759).

Haskins, Susan, *Mary Magdalen: Myth and Metaphor* (London: Harper Collins, 1994).

Hawtrey, Valentina (trans.), *The Life of Saint Mary Magdalen Translated from the Italian of an Unknown Fourteenth Century Writer* (London: John Lane, The Bodley Head).

Hazlitt, William (ed. and trans.), *The Table Talk of Martin Luther* (London: Bell & Daldy, 1872).

Head, Thomas (ed.), *Medieval Hagiography: An Anthology* (London: Routledge, 2000).

Hillerbrand, Hans J. (ed.), *The Reformation: A Narrative History Related by Contemporary Observers and Participants* (Grand Rapids, MI: Baker Book House, 1978).

Holzmeister, Urban, 'Die Magdalenfrage in der kirchlichen Überlieferung', *Zeitschrift für katholische Theologie* 46 (1922), pp. 402–422.

Hooper, John, *Certeine Comfortable Expositions of the Constant Martyr of Christ, M. John Hooper, Bishop of Gloucester and Worcester* ... (London, 1580).

Howell, A. G. Ferrers (trans.), *The Lives of S. Francis of Assisi by Brother Thomas of Celano* (London: Methuen & Co., 1855).

Hufstader, Anselm, 'Lefèvre D'Étaples and the Magdalen', *Studies in the Renaissance* 16 (1969), pp. 31–60.

Hurter H., *Sanctorum Patrum Opuscula Selecta* (Oeniponte: Libraria Academica Wagneriana, 1892).

Hutchings, W. H. (ed. and trans.), *The Life of Christ by S. Bonaventure* (London: Rivingtons, 1888).

Ilan, Tal, 'Notes on the Distribution of Jewish Women's Names in Palestine in the Second Temple and Mishnaic Periods', *Journal of Jewish Studies* 40 (1989), pp. 186–200.

Iogna-Prat, Dominique, 'La Madelaine du Sermo in Veneratione Sanctae Mariae Magdalenae attribué à Odon de Cluny, Mélanges de l'École Française de Rome', *Moyen Age* 104 (1992), pp. 37–90.

James, John Angell, *Female Piety: Or the Young Woman's Friend and Guide through Life to Immortality* (New York: Robert Carter & Brothers, 1853).

Jameson, Anna, *Sacred and Legendary Art* (Cambridge: Cambridge University Press, 2012).

Jansen, Katherine Ludwig, *The Making of the Magdalen: Preaching and Popular Devotion in the Later Middle Ages* (Princeton, NJ: Princeton University Press, 2000).

Johnston, Barbara Jean, 'Sacred Kingship and Royal Patronage in the Vie de la Magdalene: Pilgrimage, Politics, Passion Plays, and the Life of Louise of Savoy,' PhD thesis, Florida State University, 2007.

Joseph, Simon J., *Jesus, the Essenes, and Christian Origins* (Waco, TX: Baylor University Press, 2018).

Karant-Nunn, Susan C. *Reformation of Feeling: Shaping the Religious Emotions in Early Modern Germany* (Oxford: Oxford University Press, 2010).

Karant-Nunn, Susan C., and Merry E. Wiesner-Hanks, *Luther on Women: A Sourcebook* (Cambridge: Cambridge University Press, 2003).

Kazantzakis, Nikos, *The Last Temptation of Christ* (New York: Simon & Schuster, 2015).

Kern, Kathi, *Mrs Stanton's Bible* (Ithaca, NY: Cornell University Press, 2002).

King, Karen L., '"Jesus Said to Them, 'My Wife...'": A New Coptic Papyrus Fragment', *Harvard Theological Review* 107 (2014), pp. 131–159.

'The Gospel of Mary,' in E. Schüssler Fiorenza, *Searching the Scriptures. Volume 2: A Feminist Commentary* (London: SCM Press, 1997), pp. 601–634.

'The Place of the Gospel of Philip in the Context of Early Christian Claims about Jesus's Marital Status', *New Testament Studies* 59 (2013), pp. 565–587.

King, Karen L., with contributions by AnneMarie Luijendijk, '"Jesus Said to Them, 'My Wife...'": A New Coptic Gospel Papyrus.' Available at https://web.archive.org/web/20120921154949/http://news.hds.harvard.edu/files/King_JesusSaidToThem_draft_0917.pdf.

Klein, Holger A., 'Eastern Objects and Western Desires: Relics and Reliquaries between Byzantium and the West', *Dumbarton Oaks Papers* 58 (2004), pp. 283–314.

Klepper, Deeana Copeland, 'Theories of Interpretation: The Quadriga and Its Successors,' in Euan Cameron (ed.), *The New Cambridge History of the Bible, Volume 3: From*

1450–1750 (Cambridge: Cambridge University Press, 2016), pp. 418–438.

Kranenborg, Reender, 'The Presentation of the Essenes in Western Esotericism', *Journal of Contemporary Religion* 13 (1998), pp. 245–256.

Krueger, Derek, 'The Religion of Relics in Late Antiquity and Byzantium,' in Martina Bagnoli et al. (eds.), *Treasures of Heaven: Saints, Relics, and Devotion in Medieval Europe* (London: British Museum Press, 2011), pp. 5–17.

Kruppa, Patricia S. '"More Sweet and Liquid Than Any Other": Victorian Images of Mary Magdalene,' in R. W. Davis and R. J. Helmstadter, *Religion and Irreligion in Victorian Society* (London: Routledge, 1992), pp. 117–132.

Kunder, Amanda, 'The Patristic Magdalene: Symbol for the Church and Witness to the Resurrection,' in Edmondo F. (ed.), *Mary Magdalene from the New Testament to the New Age and Beyond* (Leiden: Brill, 2020), pp. 105–127.

Lardner, Nathaniel, *Sermons upon various Subjects. Vol. II* (London, 1760).

The Case of the Demoniacs Mentioned in the New Testament: Four Discourses upon Mark 5.19 (London, 1758).

Lenker, John Nicholas (ed.), *Martin Luther: Sermons*, vol. 2. Available at http://sermons.martinluther.us/Luther_Lenker_Vol_2.pdf.

Levack, Brian P., *The Devil Within: Possession & Exorcism in the Christian West* (New Haven, CT: Yale University Press, 2013).

Lezotte, Annette, 'Mary Magdalene and the Iconography of Domesticity' in Michelle Erhardt and Amy M. Morris (eds.), *Mary Magdalene: Iconographic Studies from the Middle Ages to the Baroque* (Leiden: Brill, 2012), pp. 383–397.

Lupieri Edmondo F. (ed.), *Mary Magdalene from the New Testament to the New Age and Beyond* (Leiden: Brill, 2020).

Luther, Martin, *Martin Luthers Werke: Kritische Gesamtsausgabe [Weimarer Ausgabe]* (Weimar: Hermann Böhlau, 1883–).

Three Treatises (Philadelphia: Fortress Press, 1970).

Maddox, Donald,'Du Déclin au Renouveau: Vézelay, Girart de Rousillon, et l'Inventio des Reliques de la Madeleine,' in Emmanuelle Baumgartner and Laurence Harf-Lancner (eds.), *Progrès, Réaction, Décadence dans l'Occident Médiéval* (Geneva: Droz, 2003), pp. 95–109.

Maisch, Ingrid, *Between Contempt and Veneration: Mary Magdalene, the Image of a Woman through the Centuries* (Collegeville, MN: The Liturgical Press, 1998).

Malvern, Marjorie J., *Venus in Sackcloth: The Magdalen's Origins and Metamorphoses* (Carbondale: Southern Illinois University Press, 1975).

Marjanen, Antti, *The Woman Jesus Loved: Mary Magdalene in the Nag Hammadi Library and Related Documents* (Leiden: Brill, 1996).

Markham, Gervase, *Mary Magdalens Lamentation for the Losse of Her Maister Jesus* (London, 1604).

Mastaler, James S., "The Magdalene of Internet: New Age, Goddess, and Nature Spiritualities,' in Edmondo F. Lupieri (ed.), *Mary Magdalene from the New Testament to the New Age and Beyond* (Leiden: Brill, 2020), pp. 337–363.

McClain, Lisa, '"They Have Taken Away My Lord": Mary Magdalene, Christ's Missing Body, and the Mass in Reformation England', *Sixteenth Century Journal* 38 (2007), pp. 77–96.

McConvery, Brendan, 'Hippolytus' *Commentary on the Song of Songs* and John 20: Intertextual Reading in Early Christianity', *Irish Theological Quarterly* 71 (2006), pp. 211–222.

McCormick, Michael, *Origins of the European Economy* (Cambridge: Cambridge University Press, 2002).

McNeill, John T., *Calvin: Institutes of the Christian Religion* (Louisville, KY: Westminster John Knox Press, 2006).

Mead, Richard, *Medica Sacra; or, a Commentary on the Most Remarkable Diseases, Mentioned in the Holy Scriptures* (London, 1755).

Midelfort, H. C. Erik, *Exorcism and Enlightenment: Johann Joseph Gassner and the Demons of Eighteenth-Century Germany* (New Haven, CT: Yale University Press, 2005).
'The Gadarene Demoniac in the English Enlightenment,' in Scott K. Taylor, *A Linking of Heaven and Earth* (London: Routledge, 2012), pp. 49–66.

Miller, Susan, *Women in Mark's Gospel* (London: T & T Clark, 2004).

Mills Ernestine (ed.), *The Life and Letters of Frederic Shields* (London: Longmans, 1912).

Morris, Colin, 'A Critique of Popular Religion: Guibert of Nogent on "The Relics of the Saints",' in G. J. Cuming and Derek Baker (eds.), *Popular Belief and Practice* (Cambridge: Cambridge University Press, 1972), pp. 55–60.

Moseley-Christian, Michelle, 'Marketing Mary Magdalene in Early Modern Northern European Prints and Paintings,' in Michelle Erhardt and Amy M. Morris (eds.), *Mary Magdalene: Iconographic Studies from the Middle Ages to the Baroque* (Leiden: Brill, 2012), pp. 399–420.

Murray, Margaret, *The Witch-Cult in Western Europe* (Oxford: Clarendon Press, 1921).

Murray, Robert, *Symbols of Church and Kingdom: A Study in Early Syriac Tradition* (London: T & T Clark, 2006).

Mycoff, David A., *A Critical Edition of the Legend of Mary Magdalena from Caxton's Golden Legende of 1483* (Salzburg: Institut für Anglistik und Amerikanistik, Universität Salzburg, 1985).

Mycoff, David (trans.), *The Life of Saint Mary Magdalene and of Her Sister Saint Martha* (Athens, OH: Cistercian Publications, 1989).

Newman, John Henry Cardinal, *Discourses Addressed to Mixed Congregations* (London: Longmans, Green, & Co., 1897).

Olson, Carl E., and Sandra Miesel, *The Da Vinci Hoax: Exposing the Errors in The Da Vinci Code* (San Francisco: Ignatius Press, 2004).

Otto, Rudolf, *The Idea of the Holy* (Oxford: Oxford University Press, 1958).

Pagels, Elaine, *The Gnostic Gospels* (London: Phoenix, 2006).

Palardy, William B. (trans.), *St. Peter Chrysologus: Selected Sermons Volume 3* (Washington, DC: The Catholic University Press of America, 2005).

Pals, Daniel L., *The Victorian Lives of Jesus* (San Antonio, TX: Trinity University Press, 1982).

Parrott, Douglas M. (ed.), George W. MacRae, and R. McL. Wilson (trans.), *The Gospel of Mary (BG 8502, 1)*, in James M. Robinson (ed.), *The Nag Hammadi Library in English* (Leiden: Brill, 1977).

(trans.), *The Sophia of Jesus Christ*, in James M. Robinson (ed.), *The Nag Hammadi Library*. Available at http:// khazarzar.skeptik.net/books/nhl.pdf.

Peacock, Edward (ed.), *Instructions for Parish Priests by John Myrc* (London: Trübner & Co, 1868).

Pelikan, Jaroslav (ed.), *Luther's Works* (St. Louis, MO: Concordia Publishing House, 1955-86).

Pendrill, Charles, *Old Parish Life in London* (London: Oxford University Press, 1937).

Picknett, Lynn and Clive Prince, *The Templar Revelation* (London: Corgi Books, 2007).

Porrer, Sheila M. (ed. and trans.), *Jacques Lefèvre D'Étaples and the Three Maries Debates* (Geneva: Librairie Droz, 2009).

Pringle, Denys, *Pilgrimage to Jerusalem and the Holy Land, 1187–1291* (London: Routledge, 2012).

Pringle, William (trans.), *Commentary on the Gospel According to John* (Edinburgh: Calvin Translation Society, 1847).

Rauer, Christine (ed.), *The Old English Martyrology: Edition, Translation and Commentary* (Cambridge: D. S. Brewer, 2013).

Renan, Ernest, *The Apostles* (New York: Carleton, 1866).

The Life of Jesus (A.L. Burt Company, 1863).

Rettig, John W. (trans.), *St. Augustine: Tractates on the Gospel of John 1–10* (Washington, DC: The Catholic University of America Press, 1988).

Tractates on the Gospel of John 112–24; Tractates on the First Epistle of John (Washington, DC: The Catholic University Press of America, 1995).

Tractates on the Gospel of John 28–54 (Washington, DC: Catholic University Press of America, 2010).

Ricoeur, Paul, *Figuring the Sacred: Religion, Narrative, and Imagination* (Minneapolis, MN: Fortress Press, 1995).

Robinson, James M. (ed.), *The Nag Hammadi Library in English* (Leiden: Brill, 1977).

Rock, Hugh, 'Quakerism Understood in Relation to Calvinism: The Theology of George Fox', *Scottish Journal of Theology* 70 (2017), pp. 333–347.

Rogers, Mary, 'The Decorum of Women's Beauty: Trissino, Firenzuola, Luigini and the Representation of Women in Sixteenth-century Painting', *Renaissance Studies* 2 (1988), pp. 47–88.

Rogers, Trent A., 'The Apocryphal Magdalene: Expanding and Limiting Her Importance,' in Edmondo F. Lupieri (ed.), *Mary Magdalene from the New Testament to the New Age and Beyond* (Leiden: Brill, 2020), pp. 26–49.

Roper, Lyndal, 'Luther Relics,' in Jennifer Spinks and Dagmar Eichberger, *Religion, the Supernatural and Visual Culture in Early Modern Europe* (Leiden: Brill, 2015), pp. 330–53.

Rubenstein, Jay, *Guibert of Nogent: Portrait of a Medieval Mind* (New York: Routledge, 2016).

Ryan, William Granger and Helmut Ripperger (trans.), *The Golden Legend of Jacobus de Voragine* (New York: Arno Press, 1969).

Ryan, William Granger (trans.), *The Golden Legend: Readings from the Saints* (Princeton, NJ: Princeton University Press, 2012).

Sabar, Ariel, 'Karen King Responds to "The Unbelievable Tale of Jesus's Wife",' *The Atlantic* (web only), 16 June, 2016. Available at www.theatlantic.com/politics/archive/2016/06/karen-king-responds-to-the-unbelievable-tale-of-jesus-wife/487484/.

'The Unbelievable Tale of Jesus's Wife', *Atlantic* 318 (2016),
pp. 64–78.

*Veritas: A Harvard Professor, a Con Man, and the Gospel of
Jesus's Wife* (Melbourne: Scribe, 2020). *Saints in Rome and
Beyond*, Available at www.saintsinrome.com/2013/08/st-
mary-magdalene_3.html.

Saltus, Edgar, *Mary Magdalen: A Chronicle* (New York:
Brentano's, 1919).

Saxer, Victor, *Le Culte de Marie Madeleine en Occident* (Paris:
Librairie Clavreuil, 1959).

*Le Dossier Vézelien de Marie Madeleine: Invention et Translation
des Reliques en 1265–1267* (Bruxelles: Société des
Bollandistes, 1975).

'Les Saintes Marie Madeleine et Marie de Béthanie dans la
Tradition Liturgique et Homilétique Orientale', *Revue des
Sciences Religieuses* 32 (1958), pp. 1–37.

'Philippe Cabassole et son *Libellus Hystorialis Marie Beatissime
Magdalene*', *Publications de l'École Française de Rome* 245
(1998), pp. 193–204.

Schaberg, Jane, *The Resurrection of Mary Magdalene: Legends,
Apocrypha, and the Christian Testament* (New York:
Continuum, 2002).

Scheck, Thomas P. (trans.), *Commentary on Matthew* (Washington,
DC: The Catholic University Press of America, 2010).

Schmidt, Carl (ed.) and Violet MacDermot (trans.), *Pistis Sophia*
(Leiden: Brill, 1978).

Schulenburg, Jane, 'Female Religious Collectors of Relics:
Finding Sacrality and Power in the "Ordinary",' in
Michael Frassetto et al. (eds.), *Where Heaven and Earth
Meet: Essays on Medieval Europe in Honor of Daniel
F. Callahan* (Leiden: Brill, 2014), pp. 152–77.

Schweitzer, Albert, *The Quest of the Historical Jesus: A Critical
Study of Its Progress from Reimarus to Wrede* (London: Adam
& Charles Black, 1954).

Scott, John, and John O. Ward (eds.), *The Vézelay Chronicle*
(Binghamton, NY: Center for Medieval and Early
Renaissance Studies, 1992).

Semler, Johann Salomo, *Commentatio de Daemoniacis Quorum in N. T. Fit Mentio* (Halle: Hendel, 1769).

Sennis, Antonio (ed.), *Cathars in Question* (Rochester, NY: Boydell & Brewer, 2016).

Shaw, Jane, *Miracles in Enlightenment England* (New Haven, CT: Yale University Press, 2006).

Shimmers, John (ed. and trans.), *Medieval Popular Religion 1000–1500: A Reader* (Canada: Broadview Press, 2007).

Shoemaker, Stephen J. *Ancient Traditions of the Virgin Mary's Dormition and Assumption* (Oxford: Oxford University Press, 2003).

Sibley, W. A. and M. D. Sibley, *Peter of Vaux-de-Cernay: The History of the Albigensian Crusade* (Woodbridge, Suffolk: Boydell).

Smith, Yancy, *The Mystery of Anointing: Hippolytus' Commentary on the Song of Songs in Social and Critical Contexts* (Piscataway, NJ: Gorgias Press, 2015).

Southwell, Robert, *Magdalens Funerall Teares* (London, 1592).

Spurgeon, C. H., 'Conversion', in *Spurgeon's Sermons*, vol. 1, no. 45, 1855. Available at www.ccel.org/ccel/spurgeon/sermons01.xlii.html.

Stallings-Taney, C. Mary, 'The Pseudo-Bonaventure "Meditaciones Vite Christi: Opus Integrum"', *Franciscan Studies* 55 (1998), pp. 253–280.

Stanton, Elizabeth Cady, et al., *The Woman's Bible* (New York: European Publishing Company, 1898).

Starbird, Margaret, *The Goddess in the Gospels: Reclaiming the Sacred Feminine* (Rochester, VT: Bear & Company, 1998).

The Woman with the Alabaster Jar: Mary Magdalen and the Holy Grail (Rochester, VT: Bear & Company, 1993), Kindle edition.

Stowe, Harriet Beecher, *Woman in Sacred History: A Series of Sketches Drawn from Scriptural, Historical, and Legendary Sources* (New York: J. B. Ford and Company, 1873).

Strauss, D. F., *The Life of Jesus, Critically Examined* (Cambridge: Cambridge University Press, 2010).

Stretton, Henry, *The Acts of Saint Mary Magdalene Considered, in a Series of Discourses...* (London: Joseph Masters, 1848).

Styler, Rebecca, *Literary Theology by Women Writers of the Nineteenth Century* (Farnham, Surrey: Ashgate, 2010).

Sumption, Jonathan, *Pilgrimage: An Image of Medieval Religion* (London: Faber & Faber, 1975).

Surtees, Virginia, *The Painting and Drawings of Dante Gabriel Rossetti (1828–1882)* (Oxford: Clarendon Press, 1971).

Surtz, Edward, S. J., *The Works and Days of John Fisher...* (Cambridge, MA: Harvard University Press, 1967).

Sykes, Arthur Ashley, *An Enquiry into the Meaning of Demoniacks in the New Testament* (London, 1737).

Talbot (ed.), Alice-Mary, *Holy Women of Byzantium: Ten Saints' Lives in English Translation* (Washington, DC: Dumbarton Oaks, 1996).

Tavuzzi, Michael, *The Life and Works of Silvestro Mazzolini da Prierio, (1456–1527)* (Durham, NC: Duke University Press, 1997).

Taylor, Joan E., 'Missing Magdala and the Name of Mary "Magdalene"', *Palestine Exploration Quarterly* 146 (2014), pp. 205–233.

Temkin, Owsei, *The Falling Sickness: A History of Epilepsy from the Greeks to the Beginnings of Modern Neurology* (Baltimore: Johns Hopkins Press, 1971).

'The Da Vinci Code', Plot Overview. Located at www.sparknotes.com/lit/davincicode/summary/.

The Latin Prologues: The Anti-Marcionite and Monarchian Prologues to the Canonical Gospels. Available at www.textexcavation.com/latinprologues.html.

Thiering, Barbara, *Jesus of the Apocalypse: The Life of Jesus after the Crucifixion* (Sydney: Doubleday, 1995).

Jesus the Man: A New Interpretation from the Dead Sea Scrolls (Sydney: Doubleday, 1992).

'Mary Magdalene.' Available at THE PESHERTECHNIQUE: Dr. Barbara Thiering's Writings (infinitesoulutions.com).

'The Descendants of Jesus...' Available at THE PESHER TECHNIQUE: Dr. Barbara Thiering's Writings (infinitesoulutions.com).

'The Marriage of Jesus'. Available at www.peshertechnique .infinitesoulutions.com/index_Marriage_of_Jesus.html.

Thomas, Islwyn, 'The Cult of Saints' Relics in Medieval England,' PhD thesis, The University of London, 1974.

Thorpe, Benjamin (trans.), 'The Assumption of Saint John the Apostle,' *The Homilies of the Anglo-Saxon Church: The First Part Containing the Sermones Catholici, or Homilies of Ælfric* (London: The Ælfric Society, 1844).

Twain, Mark, *The Innocents Abroad or, The New Pilgrims' Progress* (Leipzig: Bernard Tauchnitz, 1879).

Twells, Leonard, *An Answer to the Enquiry into the Meaning of Demoniacks...* (London, 1737).

van Dam, Raymond (trans.), *Gregory of Tours: Glory of the Martyrs* (Liverpool: Liverpool University Press, 1988).

van Os, Bas, 'A Whore from Bethany? A Note on Mary Magdalene in Early Non-Christian Sources, in Edmondo F. Lupieri (ed.), *Mary Magdalene from the New Testament to the New Age and Beyond* (Leiden: Brill, 2020), pp. 128–132.

Verstegan, Richard, *Odes in Imitation of the Seaven Penitential Psalmes...* (Antwerp, 1601).

Vincent, Nicholas, *The Holy Blood: King Henry III and the Westminster Blood Relic* (Cambridge: Cambridge University Press, 2001).

Viret, Pierre, *De la Vraye et Fausse Religion* (Geneva, 1560). Available at file:///C:/Users/repalmon/AppData/Local/ Temp/De%20la%20vraye%20et%20fausse%20religion %20touchant%20les%20voeus%20et%20les%20sermens %20olicites%20et%20ill-1.pdf.

Wakefield, Walter L. and Austin P. Evans (eds.), *Heresies of the High Middle Ages: Selected Sources Translated and Annotated* (New York: Columbia University Press, 1969).

Walpole, Horace, *The Letters of Horace Walpole* (London, 1759–1769).

Walsham, Alexandra, 'Skeletons in the Cupboard: Relics after the English Reformation', *Past and Present* (2010), Supplement 5, pp. 121–143.

Ward, Benedicta, *Harlots of the Desert: A Study of Repentance in Early Christian Sources* (Kalamazoo, MI: Cistercian Publications, 1987).

Warner, Marina, *Alone of All Her Sex: The Myth and Cult of the Virgin Mary* (London: Quartet, 1978).

Watson, Thomas, *A Body of Practical Divinity: Consisting of above One Hundred Seventy Six Sermons on the Lesser Confession* (London, 1692).

Whitford, David M., 'The Moste Folyshe Fable of the World: Preaching the Maudlin,' in Herman J. Selderhuis and Arnold Huijgen (eds.), *Calvinus Pastor Ecclesiae* (Göttingen: Vandenhoeck und Ruprecht, 2016), pp. 449–464.

Wiedenheft, Elizabeth Anne, 'Circulating Saints: A Study of the Movement of Corporeal Relics in Three Regions of Western Europe, c. 800–1200.' PhD thesis, University of Nottingham, 2018.

Wilkinson, John, *Jerusalem Pilgrims before the Crusades* (Warminster: Aris & Phillips Ltd., 1977).

Williams, Frank (trans.), *The Panarion of Epiphanius of Salamis* (Leiden: Brill, 2009).

Wiśniewski, Robert, *The Beginnings of the Cult of Relics* (Oxford: Oxford University Press, 2018).

Witmer, Amanda, *Jesus the Galilean Exorcist: His Exorcisms in Social and Political Context* (London: T & T Clark International, 2012).

Wood, Juliette, *The Holy Grail: History and Legend* (Cardiff: University of Wales Press, 2012).

Woolston, Thomas, *A Discourse on the Miracles of our Saviour. . .* (London, 1727).

Wordsworth, William, 'Saints', in William Angus Knight (ed.), *The Poetical Works of William Wordsworth* (London: Macmillan & Co., 1896).

Worthington, William, *An Impartial Enquiry into the Case of the Gospel Demoniacks...* (London, 1777),

Wortley, John, *An Introduction to the Desert Fathers* (Cambridge: Cambridge University Press, 2019).

'The Byzantine Component of the Relic-Hoard of Constantinople', *Greek, Roman, and Byzantine Studies* 40 (1999), pp. 353–378.

Wray, George, *A Vindication of the Character of Mary Magdalene* (London: Rivingtons, 1870).

Wright, N. T., *Who Was Jesus?* (Grand Rapids, MI: William B. Eerdmans Publishing Company, 1992).

Wyche, Romy, 'A Provençal Holy Land. Re-Reading the Legend and the Sites of Mary Magdalene in Southern France', *Collegium Medievale* 29 (2016), pp. 111–130.

INDEX